THE ANGER OF ACHILLES

A volume in the series

MYTH AND POETICS

*edited by* Gregory Nagy

A complete list of titles appears at the end of the book.

# THE ANGER OF ACHILLES

*Mênis* in Greek Epic

LEONARD MUELLNER

CORNELL UNIVERSITY PRESS

ITHACA AND LONDON

Copyright © 1996 by Cornell University

All rights reserved. Except for brief quotations in a review, this book, or parts thereof, must not be reproduced in any form without permission in writing from the publisher. For information, address Cornell University Press, Sage House, 512 East State Street, Ithaca, New York 14850.

First published 1996 by Cornell University Press.
First printing, Cornell paperbacks, 2005

Printed in the United States of America

⊖ The paper in this book meets the minimum requirements of the American National Standard for Information Sciences— Permanence of Paper for Printed Library Materials, ANSI Z39.48-1984.

Library of Congress Cataloging-in-Publication Data

Muellner, Leonard Charles.
   The anger of Achilles : mênis in Greek epic / Leonard Muellner.
     p.  cm.
   Includes bibliographical references and index.
   ISBN 0-8014-3230-8 (cloth : alk. paper)
   ISBN 0-8014-8995-4 (pbk.: alk. paper)
   1. Epic poetry, Greek—History and criticism.   2. Anger in literature.
3. Achilles (Greek mythology) in literature.   4. Mênis (The Greek word)
5. Hesiod. Theogony.   6. Homer. Iliad.   I. Title.
PA3015.A58M84   1996
883'.0109—dc20                                                      96-4361
Cloth printing   10 9 8 7 6 5 4 3 2 1
Paperback printing   10 9 8 7 6 5 4 3 2 1

# Contents

| | | |
|---|---|---|
| | Foreword, by Gregory Nagy | vii |
| | Acknowledgments | ix |
| | Introduction: Approaching Anger | 1 |
| 1 | *Mênis* and Cosmic Status in the Hierarchy of Peers | 5 |
| 2 | *Mênis* and the Social Order | 32 |
| 3 | The Narrative Sequence of the Hesiodic *Theogony* | 52 |
| 4 | The *Mênis* of Achilles and the First Book of the *Iliad* | 94 |
| 5 | The *Mênis* of Achilles and Its Iliadic Teleology | 133 |
| | Appendix. The Etymology of *Mênis* | 177 |
| | References | 197 |
| | Index of Sources | 205 |
| | Index of Subjects | 214 |

# Foreword

GREGORY NAGY

*The Anger of Achilles, Mênis in Greek Epic*, by Leonard Muellner, seeks to redefine *mênis*, the first word of the Homeric *Iliad*. When Homer prays to his own Muse to sing the *mênis* of Achilles son of Peleus, he sets in motion the entire story, invoking the driving theme and heading relentlessly toward the inevitable conclusion and self-realization of the story. The subject of the *Iliad* is *mênis*. Conventionally translated as 'anger' or 'wrath', *mênis* means much more. The fulfillment of the word's meaning is the teleology of the story. To understand the meaning of the *Iliad*, Muellner argues, is to follow the sequence of the narration, starting with the word *mênis*: getting the meaning right is getting the sequence right.

The semiotic system reconstructed by Muellner as he traces the meaning of *mênis* through the *Iliad* turns out to be typical of oral traditions. From the experience of fieldwork in living oral traditions it has become clear that meaning is ultimately determined by the rules of performance. The essence of meaning in oral traditions—to restate the formulation of Albert B. Lord—is that the process of composition takes place *in* performance. As Muellner sees it, the actual performing of *mênis* as the first word of the *Iliad* drives the meaning of the entire composition. The interpretive power of Muellner's insight, in all its simplicity, is astonishing. His book rebuilds the ancient listener's cognitive process of understanding a story through its sequence.

Perhaps even more astonishing is Muellner's discovery that the patterning of *mênis* in the Homeric *Iliad* is matched in the Hesiodic *Theogony*. In addition to striking parallels between the contexts of *mênis* in Homer and Hesiod, he even finds an interlocking of narratives, which works both forward and backward, through the themes of *mênis*. The themes of the Hesiodic *Theogony* lead into the themes of the Homeric *Iliad;* a narrative logic connects the *Theogony* with the *Iliad*. Muellner's discovery lays the foundation for a redefinition of intertextuality in oral traditions. It also leads to a powerful new understanding of the main epic theme of the *Iliad;* the baneful anger of its premier hero is authorized, almost authored, by the cosmic sanction of the premier god, who claims to be the plot's ultimate executive—Zeus himself. Muellner's reading of the *Iliad* thus becomes the ultimate exercise in the interpretation of traditional poetry in performance.

# Acknowledgments

During the gestation of this book, I have not lacked for support and material assistance from many people. My sincere thanks go to the following persons who have contributed to, corrected, and encouraged my work: Chris Dadian, Carol Dougherty, Judith Feher-Gurewitch, Allen Grossman, Carolyn Higbie, Stephanie Jamison, Teresa Jesionowski, Claudine Kahan, Leslie Kurke, Françoise Létoublon, Hotze Mulder, Dan Petegorsky, Ian Rutherford, Richard Sacks, Dana Shelley, Rae Silberger, Charles Stewart, Douglas Stewart, Brent Vine, Nick Wallerstein, Calvert Watkins, and Jed Wyrick. I owe special gratitude to Richard Martin and Steven Lowenstam, superb critics who read the manuscript in its final stages with creativity, tact, and understanding. Finally, there are some people without whom there would be no book to begin with: first of all, Greg Nagy, who should have abandoned his faith in me long ago, and whose brilliance and loyalty have been my inspiration; Tim and his friends, whose idealism and companionship have been crucial to my morale; Jacopin, who taught me more about myths and performers than I can ever acknowledge; and Mimie, to whom I dedicate this work, who defended my time with it, and from whom I continue to learn about anger, friendship, and waiting until the end.

L. M.

# THE ANGER OF ACHILLES

INTRODUCTION

# Approaching Anger

The subject of the *Iliad* is the anger of Achilles, not Achilles himself. But what is this anger of his? It is a fair question, since few terms are more complex than those for strong emotions like anger. In fact, the study of emotional terms in modern American English makes it clear that as children acquiring a language we also acquire an elaborate, internally consistent, and widely held set of conventional metaphors to describe emotions.[1] Nor are these metaphors innocent. They embody implicit moral messages from society about the content, differentia, and expression of emotions, and we acquire these embedded messages along with the language itself whether we want to or not. One society may share some of its elaborate metaphors and moral rules with other societies, but there is no reason to assume that the metaphors, the rules, and therefore the emotions that they represent and that we tend to experience as inherent in human nature are actually universal.

Consequently when we read the first book of the *Iliad*, it is possible or even likely that we are "recognizing" manifestations of Achilles' anger, consistently named with the word *mênis*, that in their proper cultural setting have nothing to do with his anger or are at best tangential to it. Correspondingly, features that are central to the epic notion of anger may in fact be invisible to us. Furthermore, the moral rules about the expression of

---

[1] See Lakoff and Kövecses 1987 on anger (thanks to Charles Stewart for this reference). They have contributed an effective way of presenting the systematic, culture-specific metaphorical components of emotional terms, and their work implies an anthropology of emotions. For a study of the complexity and diversity of another emotional term in Greek epic, see Latacz 1966 on Homeric words that we translate as "happy" or the like.

anger that are built into our language may well be inappropriate to the poetic "society" of the *Iliad*, which is more than likely to abide by rules that are probably more conventional and widely held than those embedded in our own conventional social discourse, given the traditional nature of epic poetry and the society in which it arose.

Needless to say, attempting to articulate the precise meaning of the word for Achilles' anger is not a new scholarly pursuit. More than two thousand years ago, Aristarchus, the Hellenistic editor of Homer (second century B.C.), defined *mênis* as "long-lasting rancor (*kótos*)," citing an etymological link between *mênis* and the verb *ménō* 'remain' that is spurious from the standpoint of modern historical linguistics.[2] His definition was transmitted in the twelfth century A.D. by the archbishop of Thessalonica, Eustathius, who reports in his commentary on the *Iliad* that "according to the ancients, *mênis* is the rage that remains, from the verb *ménō*."[3] It was subsequently enshrined in the nineteenth-century German lexicographic tradition, where it appears as the basic definition in the standard reference works of J. H. H. Schmidt (*andauernde Zorn* [persisting anger]) and H. Ebeling (*ira memor, inveterata* [inveterate and unforgetting anger]).[4] Schmidt, however, elaborates a little on the nature of the emotion. For him, *mênis* and its derivatives differ from the epic word *kótos* 'rancor' that Aristarchus used in his definition by virtue of both the persistence of the anger and its righteousness, and he points out a peculiar fact about the distribution of the word: it is generally gods who have *mênis*, except for Achilles. But he does not try to explain why Achilles is an exception or what it signifies that he is one.

Although the content of the discussion has changed considerably, the points on which Schmidt elaborated his definition still constitute the terms of the modern debate on *mênis*.[5] First, in what way does *mênis* differ from other epic words for anger, such as *kótos*? The answers focus on the inner qualities of the emotion and its aspect as a religious or moral concept. Second, why is *mênis* restricted to gods and Achilles?—if it is so restricted. Although the simple noun *mênis* is confined to Achilles among mortals in epic, the verb derived from it, *mēníō*, is also applied to Aeneas, Agamemnon, and Odysseus. Current dictionary definitions still classify the meaning

---

[2] Cited in the first- or second-century A.D. *Homeric Dictionary* of Apollonius Sophistes (Bekker) 112, 24. The A scholia to the first line of the *Iliad* present Aristarchus's etymology in the form of an analogy: as *ménō* 'remain' is to *mênis*, so *énos* 'year' is to *énis* 'yearling'. The ancient lexicographic testimonia are accessible in Ebeling 1885, 1:1095–96 s.v. μῆνις.

[3] Eustathius *Commentary on Homer's "Iliad"* 1.13.10 (Van der Valk).

[4] Schmidt 1879, 3:142, 565, 566; Ebeling 1885, 1:1095 s.v. μῆνις.

[5] For a more detailed discussion of modern scholarship on these issues, see the Appendix.

Introduction: Approaching Anger  3

of *mênis* as either 'of gods' or 'of Achilles/mortals', but there is no common explanation for the distinction. Lastly, what is the etymology of *mênis*, and what does its etymology contribute to our understanding of its meaning in epic? The chief problem has been to provide a convincing account of the form of the word, and the search for solutions has recently added a new facet to the semantic issues with one scholar's suggestion that the word was tabu and therefore deformed, not the object of predictable sound changes. That idea has not met with general agreement.[6]

Rather than enter this debate on the limited terms that have long since defined it, I choose to make a fresh start. The extent of the disagreement among scholars points to a crisis in methodology. The problems are harder than the tools being used to chip away at them. Yet none of those who have taken up the study of *mênis* recently has explicitly invoked and employed the results of the most important research on Homeric language in this century, the contributions of Milman Parry and Albert Lord to our understanding of the compositional technique of Greek epic.[7] The conventional nature of epic diction, in which the tendencies of natural speech have become the constants of a high style, is an especially rich and relatively unexploited resource for the study of the meaning of epic words in general. It is also essential that a semantic analysis take account of the formal features of the verbal behavior it is investigating.[8] My primary goal is to use the insights of Albert Lord on epic themes, compositional units on a higher level than the verse constituents known as formulas, to arrive at a more rigorous and sustainable notion of the word's meaning.[9] To understand the function of a word within a given traditional theme is to discover the contextual consistency (or, it may be, inconsistency) that is built into its use by the poet and its apprehension by the audience. Doing so considerably

---

[6] Calvert Watkins (1977a) suggested that the word was tabu, but all subsequent treatments (Considine 1986; Redfield 1979; Turpin 1988; Snell and Meier-Brügger 1955, s.v. μηνιθμός) known to me except my own (1991) disagree. As an index of the general disagreement on all the issues, the articles by W. Beck on *mênis* and its derivatives published in the 1993 fascicle of the monumental *Lexicon des frühgriechischen Epos* list fourteen works of scholarship on the words since 1932 (even so, the list is incomplete, missing Turpin 1988); those works advance no less than four different etymologies and almost as many views on the meaning and usage of the word as there are authors. Beck himself tries to take a position on the question of the distribution of *mênis* between gods and Achilles, but in the end he cannot decide and simply asks, What other word for anger could be used to begin the *Iliad*? His rhetorical question is a counsel of despair.

[7] The forthcoming work of Thomas Walsh based on his dissertation (1989) on anger words other than *mênis* is exemplary for its concern with the traditional nature of epic diction. The basic works on epic composition are Parry 1971; and Lord 1960, 1991.

[8] For a statement of the principles and issues involved, see Muellner 1976, 12–16.

[9] On the notion of theme, see Lord 1960, 68–98; Nagler 1967, 1974; and Nagy 1990b, 18–35.

broadens the task of semantic analysis, and necessarily so, nor have I shrunk from the need to test the results of my research on the meaning of *mênis* by applying them to an interpretation of the *Iliad* and the *Odyssey*.

In addition, I wish to put to use the perspective that an anthropology of emotions affords, specifically, to view emotional terms not as universal pure feelings but as culture-specific social concepts with no necessary relationship to what we may intend and comprehend by a word like anger. A basic principle of this approach is to try to avoid imposing analytic categories and distinctions from without on terms for emotions and, insofar as possible, to define them from within their cultural context, in terms of each other, as parts of a coherent and articulated set of ideas about the world. Ultimately, a wide-eyed journey into the world of epic and its mightiest feelings stands to benefit both heart and mind.

CHAPTER I

# Mênis and Cosmic Status in the Hierarchy of Peers

A good place to begin reconstructing the meaning of *mênis* is not the beginning of the epic, which may be all too familiar for the perspective I wish to attain, but an extended passage from the middle of it. At the beginning of book 15 Zeus awakes from his seduction by Hera and finds the Trojans being routed by the Achaeans and Hector lying on the plain, spitting blood. Zeus pities him, then vents his anger at Hera and her *dólos* 'tricky plan'. He now understands her to have seduced him and lulled him into a deep postcoital slumber in collusion with Poseidon, so that she could disobey his earlier, explicit prohibition against any god's entering the battle at Troy, under pain of being thunderstruck or hurled to Tartarus (8.5–27). He threatens to lash her with *plēgaí* 'blows', and he recalls the time he strung her up *en aithéri kaì nephéleisi,* "in the bright sky and the clouds," hung two anvils from her feet, and bound her hands with an unbreakable golden chain because of what she did to Herakles. Though the other gods pitied her, they were able to do absolutely nothing, Zeus reminds her, since "whomever I could catch, / I kept grabbing and hurling down from the divine threshold, till each came down to / earth scarcely breathing" (15.22–24).[1] The contrasting treatment of the gods here is worth remembering: Hera bound hand and foot and immobilized on high, and any other gods whom Zeus could catch hurled down one level in the cosmic hierarchy.

In response to this threat, Hera swears to her independence of Poseidon, who, she says, is acting on his own desire to worst the Trojans in defiance of Zeus's order forbidding the gods to interfere in the battle. Zeus smiles

[1] All translations are my own.

knowingly at her oath and then commands her to send for Iris and Apollo: Iris to stop Poseidon, and Apollo to restore Hector and set the Achaeans instead of the Trojans into flight. He then goes on to describe what will happen in the rest of the *Iliad*, including the death of Patroklos and the return of Achilles, as though to reassert his arrested plan on the narrative as well as the political level.[2]

When Hera returns to Olympus, the other gods are dining together. She ignores the greetings of all but one. Only and specifically to Themis does she complain of the excessive and unkind (ὑπερφίαλος καὶ ἀπηνής [15.94]) conduct and the evil deeds (κακὰ ἔργα [97]) of her husband, Zeus. Then she self-righteously predicts the resentment he is about to cause among the other divinities and mortals. In her vexation, the poet tells us, she laughs with her lips but not with her forehead. Zeus doesn't care how we try to stop him, she says, by words or by violence, since he *kartei te sthenei te diakridòn eînai áristos,* "in power and strength is another order of best."[3] The best thing is to act with restraint no matter what evil thing he does.

She then predicts the suffering that will be inflicted upon one of the gods present who is not famous for restraint even under the best of circumstances, namely, Ares, since his son Askalaphos has just been slain. Ares immediately slaps his thighs with downturned hands[4] and speaks of his overwhelming need to avenge the death of his son, even if it is his own destiny, he says, to be struck by the thunderbolt of Zeus (Διὸς πληγέντι κεραυνῷ [15.117]) and to lie with corpses in the blood and dust. He then tells his attendants, Deimos 'Fear' and Phobos 'Rout', to yoke up his horses and puts on his shining armor. This is the point at which the narrator informs us that "*a greater and more grievous anger and mênis*" from Zeus (ἔνθα κ' ἔτι μείζων τε καὶ ἀργαλεώτερος ἄλλος / πὰρ Διὸς ἀθανάτοισι χόλος καὶ μῆνις ἐτύχθη) would have been generated unless Athena had intervened with Ares, out of her fear for all the gods (πᾶσι περιδείσασα θεοῖσιν [123]). Greater and more grievous than what? Than the prior exercise of

---

[2] On the foretelling of the plot at this point and the sequential structure of the whole *Iliad*, see Schadewaldt 1966.

[3] On the meaning of *diakridón*, compare the use of the verb *krínomai* for cosmic disjunctions like the one created between gods and mortals at Mekone (Hesiod *Theogony* 535) or *diakrínomai* for the settling of disputes (*Works and Days* 35) or the disengagement of the armies of the Trojans and the Achaeans (*Iliad* 3.98, 102); Hera means that Zeus's superiority in force is so great that it distances him as a cosmic phenomenon even from the other gods, and that he is therefore invincible. For another expression of this same idea by Zeus himself, see *Iliad* 8.17–27, the boast of the golden chain: τόσσον ἐγὼ περί τ' εἰμὶ θεῶν περί τ' εἴμ' ἀνθρώπων (8.27), "to such an extent am I beyond both the gods and the human beings." See also 86 n. 82.

[4] For this gesture as a sign that lethal danger is at hand, see Lowenstam 1981, 140–43.

Zeus's *mênis* spoken of by Zeus himself at the beginning of the book. In other words, the narrative is making it clear that this is the second example of *mênis* in this context, the first being that inflicted upon Hera and the other gods. What does Athena do now to avert this more terrible disaster? First she acts to restrain Ares physically; she removes the helmet from his head, the shield from his shoulders, and the spear from his hand. She then tells him he has lost his *nóos kaì aidốs*, "intelligence and sense of shame." Didn't you hear what Hera was saying about Zeus? You will go back to Olympus sooner or later in grief and under compulsion, but what will happen to the rest of us? Zeus will leave his place in Troy, and he will grab "one after another whoever is to blame along with whoever is not" (137). Give up your *khólos* 'anger' for your son (138), since someone greater in force has or soon will die in return for his death; the generation of mortals is beyond saving. Saying these things, she sits Ares down, and the danger his intervention would have offered the divine community has passed. The word *khólos* can be used as a substitute for the term whose significance we are trying to rebuild, *mênis*, but at times it contrasts with it. In fact *khólos* is a complex term with its own significance.[5]

The point Athena is making to Ares is that the *mênis* of Zeus will result not just in his own punishment, as Ares had imagined himself thunderstruck in the dust and blood, but in indiscriminate punishment of the whole community of gods, regardless of their complicity. Better to preserve the integrity of the divine community than lose it in a vain attempt to redress a death among mortals. The same point was made earlier in this episode when Zeus spoke of Hera's punishment along with that of any god whom he could catch. Randomly, he threw them down to earth, scarcely breathing. In fact, aside from the language of the thunderbolt and of binding,[6] the most consistent feature of these narratives of Zeus's suppression of other insubordinate gods is the social solidarity they imply. That is why, for instance, Hera appeals only to Themis when she returns to Olympus to report Zeus's behavior. Themis is the guardian of the social order, the one who presides over the feast that ritually binds the divine community together.[7] Hera tells her with some irony that gods and mortals will not all be pleased with what Zeus has done. She has in mind not that Ares will act alone on behalf of his son but that all the gods will be roused to action by what Zeus has done to her and the Achaeans. Before that can happen,

---

[5] On the meaning of *khólos*, see Walsh 1989 and forthcoming; on its use to refer back to previously defined instances of *mênis*, see below, 111 and n. 43.

[6] For the significance of binding in these contexts, see below, 77–78.

[7] For this definition of Themis, see Detienne and Vernant 1974, 105.

however, Athena puts an end to Ares' desire to avenge the death of his own son, and furthermore she quashes any intimation of a wider revolt by speaking overtly of the indiscriminate havoc Zeus will wreak upon the divine community, since his power and force are distinctly greater than anyone else's. Experience has shown that he is willing to use them on the whole social group.

It is important, I repeat, to see this narrative moment in the terms in which it is portrayed: the group's resentment of the random use of supreme physical force on innocent and guilty alike by an authority figure working on the blanket assumption that the group has solidarity with the individual in revolt and that the threat of the random use of violence against disobedience will maintain his status in the hierarchy. The precise word for the random use of Zeus's supreme physical force as a sanction against the social group with an insubordinate member occurs only once in this extended passage, but it is none other than *mênis*. In other words, *mênis* is not a word for a hostile emotion arising in one individual against some other individual, as we may spontaneously understand it. It is the name of a feeling not separate from the actions it entails, of a *cosmic sanction*, of a social force whose activation brings drastic consequences on the whole community.

When *mênis* is invoked, it is not a matter of some minor offense. Here is a list of the other offenses that either incur or threaten to incur it in the *Odyssey*, the *Iliad*, and other Homeric poetry:

disobedience of Ares to Zeus's commands (*Iliad* 5.34)
disobedience of mortal warriors to Apollo's prohibitions (*Iliad* 5.444, 16.711)
defiance by Achilles of Agamemnon's authority (*Iliad* 1.247)
rape of Persephone by Hades (*Hymn to Demeter* 350, 410)
mortals having sex with goddesses (*Odyssey* 5.146; *Hymn to Aphrodite* 290)
leaving the dead unburied (*Iliad* 22.358; *Odyssey* 11.73)
desecrating a sacrifice (*Iliad* 5.178)
violating exchange rules: hospitality (*Iliad* 13.624; *Odyssey* 14.283, 2.66); treatment of beggars (*Odyssey* 17.14); ransom (*Iliad* 1.75); prize distribution (the *mênis* of Achilles, passim)

I conclude two things from this list. First, *mênis* is incurred by the breaking of basic religious and social tabus, though not all the causes given may at first appear to be such; second, there is a variability and consistency in these causes that brings to mind Albert Lord's notion of composition by theme, whereby the traditional singer of tales learns to perform a song by manipulating larger units of composition, constellations of formulas, into associative though not rigidly repeated sequences.[8] Like myths, and unlike musical themes, these themes actually consist of their variations. It has already been suggested that the word *mênis* functions in epic as the *name* of a theme.[9] The loose connection among the offenses in this list raises questions about the unity of the contexts of *mênis*, but it also suggests that the answer to such questions lies in an understanding of the word's function within the context of a compositional theme.

In fact, what any word means in epic diction cannot be discussed without invoking the traditional techniques of epic composition in performance.[10] I offer a brief example that happens to involve this particular word. Some have maintained that the *mênis* of Agamemnon at Achilles in 1.247 is a secondary phenomenon signaled by the use of the secondary verb *mēníō* 'I have *mênis*' as against the historically primary noun (*mênis*).[11] As mentioned in the Introduction, the noun is used only of gods and Achilles, whereas this verb is used of gods, Achilles, and heroes other than Achilles. But in fact thematic analysis of this and related passages will reveal[12] that it has close parallels in context and precise parallels in diction to the passage that features Zeus's *mênis* in book 15. Such parallels argue that, from the standpoint of composer/performer and audience, the use of the verb for Agamemnon and the noun for Zeus are variants of each other. Both are instances of the same theme, and neither can be privileged at the other's expense. My first goal, then, is to begin reconstructing the meaning of *mênis* by considering, in all its specificity and variety, the epic theme it signifies.

---

[8] The notion of themes as deep structures that are articulated in formulas and result in the suppleness and consistency of epic poetic language is essentially the same as the principle of composition in all forms of myth. As Lord's fieldwork taught him, multiformity is the norm in myth, and any single myth consists only of its variants. For a reassertion of Lord's concept of theme in its historical as well as its compositional aspect, see Nagy 1990a, 18–35.

[9] Nagy 1979, 72–73.

[10] As models for semantic analysis based on composition by theme, I have had the following in mind throughout: Nagy 1979; Lowenstam 1981, 1993; Petegorsky 1982; and Martin 1989.

[11] Calvert Watkins (1977a) considers the uses of the denominative verb secondary and not subject to the same semantic restrictions as the noun itself. James Redfield (1979, 97–98 and n. 7) cites pertinent parallels to the distinctive usage of nouns as against the verbs derived from them, but he does not consider the possibility that the difference between the usage of *mênis* and *mēníō* is not significant in terms of context and meaning.

[12] For the details, see the discussion that follows and also Chapter 4, 108–11.

## *Mênis* and the Warrior God

In book 4 of the *Iliad*, shortly before Diomedes' *aristeía* 'deeds-of-valor narrative' begins in book 5,[13] Athena and Ares respectively lead the opposing armies into battle for the first time since Pandaros broke the truce (4.422–39). At the beginning of the fifth book, Athena gives *ménos kai thársos*, "courage and daring," to her favorite, Diomedes, to make him conspicuous among all the Argives and win him glory. Diomedes then proceeds to kill one of the two sons of Dares,[14] a priest of Hephaistos. The other son begins to run away when Hephaistos intervenes and covers him in night, so that the old man, his father, might not be utterly bereft of sons. The Trojans, on the other hand, are aroused by the death of the one son of Dares and the flight of the other, but at this point, somewhat abruptly, Athena takes Ares by the hand and addresses him (5.31): Ἄρες, Ἄρες βροτολοιγέ, μιαιφόνε, τειχεσιπλῆτα! "Ares, Ares, mortal-devastator, defiled-slaughterer, wall-approacher!" She suggests that they allow the Achaeans and Trojans to fight it out on their own, letting Zeus grant glory to whichever side he wishes, and that the two of them withdraw in order to avoid provoking his *mênis*. Ares says nothing, but Athena leads him out of battle and sits him down beside the Scamander (35), where he is still seated when his wounded sister, Aphrodite, begs him to lend her his horses and chariot at line 356. To pinpoint his inactivity, the narrator tells us that Ares' spear and his horses "were leaning in the mist" (356).

According to Bernard Fenik's study of the conventions of battle narratives, the moment at which Athena abruptly stops Ares early in the book, when the son of Dares is killed, is a conventional trigger for a god to intervene in battle on the side of his or her favorites, who are about to be routed.[15] Athena, vigilant of Zeus's prerogatives and her own, wishes to forestall Ares from helping the Trojan side, and an appeal by her to exercise restraint and to fear the *mênis* of Zeus is something Ares cannot decline to heed. It is no weak convention to banish him from the battle. Although other gods intervene in the ensuing struggle (Athena herself, to heal the wounded Diomedes [121–32], Aphrodite, to save Aeneas from death at the

---

[13] On the term *aristeía*, see below, 12 n. 18.

[14] The resemblance of the name Dares to Ares may not be a coincidence in view of the parallel event already discussed, when Athena also prevents Ares from joining the battle to avenge the death of his son, Askalaphos.

[15] Fenik 1968, 14–15; the expression πᾶσιν ὀρίνθη θυμός is an immediate prelude to flight in other battle narratives. Fenik also says that this is the only place in the attested battle books in which the twin brother in such a scene is *not* slain. In other words, Hephaistos's intervention is or should be the start of something extraordinary on the level of divine intervention.

## Mênis and Cosmic Status in the Hierarchy of Peers

hands of Diomedes [311–18], and Apollo, also to protect Aeneas [334–54] when Diomedes wounds Aphrodite and she retires), their role is only to restrain and defend until Apollo finally calls Ares out to fight in a passage that explicitly refers to and contravenes Athena's request that he sit the battle out. That is why his exhortation to Ares to enter the battle begins with exactly the same line as Athena's earlier request that he refrain from fighting: Ἆρες, Ἆρες βροτολοιγέ, μιαιφόνε, τειχεσιπλῆτα! "Ares, Ares, mortal-devastator, defiled-slaughterer, wall-approacher!" (5.455).[16] Ares willingly obliges Apollo, whose authority to request his participation is apparently equal to or greater than Athena's authority to prevent it.

Athena, urged by Hera to enter the battle against Ares, waits until lines 733–39 to arm herself. She must first gain Zeus's permission to do so, since she does not want to provoke his anger (5.757–766, esp. 762). Ares' intervention is the only reason for her own, and once Zeus assents, she immediately accompanies Diomedes into battle against Ares specifically. Aphrodite and Apollo, she says to Zeus, have unleashed him ἄφρονα . . . ὃς οὔ τινα οἶδε θέμιστα "mindless one, who knows no things that are *thémis*" (5.761).[17] In this case, apparently, the gods siding with Ares are perceived to be defending their faction's coherence, not revolting as a group against Zeus; Hera, Athena, and Diomedes, their champion, are acting with Zeus's approval against Ares, who is championing Apollo and Aphrodite. So Athena's original threat to Ares about the *mênis* of Zeus, though it was effective in forestalling his participation in the battle, has lost its force, and the solidarity in whose interest Ares had originally retired is broken. What has taken place to create these factions? On the level of narrative structure, divine *mênis* against Ares has been displaced by a variant kind of heroic *mênis*, and a dramatic change in the cohesion of the divine community is its direct result.

To explain what I mean about a variant kind of heroic *mênis*, I must digress for a moment. An unspoken demand that the god show restraint in battle accounts for the language Apollo uses to rouse Ares to battle. He asks him to join in so as to keep Diomedes from the battle: "Wouldn't you join in and keep this hero from battle?" (5.456). Likewise, Athena, upon entering the fray, asks Zeus's permission to drive Ares from it, "in the hope that after smiting [root *plēg*-] Ares I may chase him from the battle" (αἴ κεν

---

[16] I discuss the meanings of the terms *miaiphóne* 'defiled slaughterer' and *teikhesiplêta* 'wall-approacher' below, 15–18.

[17] Note the language here and its parallelism with the themes and diction of the first example, when Hera appealed to Themis against Zeus, and Ares was characterized as having lost his *nóos* 'intelligence'.

Ἄρηα / λυγρῶς πεπληγυῖα μάχης ἐξ ἀποδίωμαι [5.762–63]). The parallelism in diction and theme between Diomedes and Ares is not an isolated or a chance phenomenon. It is a token of the ritual antagonism between hero and god that is a constitutive principle of Diomedes' *aristeía* if not of *aristeíai* in general.[18] The antagonism cannot exist without a relationship of identity between hero and god on some fundamental level. Antagonism and, paradoxically, heroic glory itself arise when the hero tries to reach and surpass the god with whom he identifies and against whom he struggles. In the case of a warrior in his *aristeía*, the diction and themes of battle narrative make it plain that the god whom the warrior incarnates and competes with is Ares himself. Thus the formula *daímoni îsos*, "equal to the god," which occurs nine times in the *Iliad*, is always and only used of a hero in his *aristeía*, whether it be Diomedes, Patroklos, or Achilles himself. Its metrical alternative, which is all but once applied to heroes in their *aristeíai*, is *îsos Árēï*, "equal to Ares"; the latter expression also occurs in a longer form, *brotoloigôi îsos Árēï*, "equal to Ares the mortal-devastator," with the same contextual restrictions as *daímoni îsos*.[19]

To return from this digression to the variant *mênis* theme of book 5, it, too, is part of the Diomedes-Ares identification/antagonism. Just as Ares is restrained from fighting by Athena's threat that he will incur the *mênis* of Zeus, so Diomedes is restrained from fighting on the grounds that he will incur the *mênis* of Apollo: moreover, the act that threatens to incur Apollo's

---

[18] On *aristeíai*, see Fenik 1968, 9–77, which treats the fifth book of the *Iliad* in its typical aspects; and Krischer 1971, 13–85; see also Nagy 1979, 161–63, on Diomedes as a warrior and on the notion of ritual antagonism between god and hero.

[19] δαίμονι ἶσος 5.438, 459, 884 (Diomedes), 16.705, 786 (Patroklos), 20.447, 493, 21.18, 227 (Achilles); ἶσος Ἄρηϊ 11.295, 13.802 (Hector), 20.46 (Achilles; also in its grandest, most elaborate, and perhaps most archaic variant, encompassing a whole line 22.132: ἶσος Ἐνυαλίῳ κορυθάϊκι πτολεμιστῇ). Line 604 of book 11 (Patroklos) is only an apparent exception to the phrase's restriction to a hero's own *aristeía*. The line occurs during the *aristeía* of Hector, but at the moment that, as the narrator cannot refrain from telling us, was the κακοῦ ἀρχή, "start of woe," for Patroklos. He comes out of Achilles' hut and sees the Achaeans perishing under Hector's onslaught, a scene that motivates him to ask Achilles if he can return to battle. This makes it the true beginning of his *aristeía* and the use of the formula elegantly marks it so. On the other hand, the use of ἶσος Ἄρηϊ for a Trojan named Leonteus at 12.130 is a real exception, but the only one. For more on Leonteus, see Nagy 1979, 295 n. 8; Nagy points out that Leonteus is also called ὄζος Ἄρηος, which is a synonym of θεράπων Ἄρηος. The terms imply a greater significance for this figure than Homeric epic attests. Also relevant is the existence of yet another pair of formulaic alternates occurring in these same contexts: ἶσος ἀέλλῃ, "equal to a wind blast" (11.297, 12.40), vs. λαίλαπι ἶσος, "equal to a gale" (11.746, 20.50). This last citation actually equates Ares himself in battle to the *laîlaps* 'gale'. For the traditional association of Ares with the wind, compare the Indic war god with functions parallel to Ares', Vāyu, whose name actually means "storm wind," and see Nagy 1979, 323–47. Another formula in this semantic class, θοῷ ἀτάλαντος Ἄρηϊ, "equal in weight to swift Ares," is less contextually constrained than the others.

*mênis* is precisely the one in which Diomedes is said to be *daímoni ísos* (431ff.). That act is his quadruple assault upon Aeneas, who is being protected by Apollo himself. Three times he attacks Aeneas, and Apollo violently repels him each time; but when Diomedes stubbornly rushes at Aeneas a fourth time, the narrator qualifies him as *daímoni ísos*, and only at this point does Apollo explicitly threaten him, shouting:

"φράζεο Τυδεΐδη καὶ χάζεο, μηδὲ θεοῖσιν
ἶσ' ἔθελε φρονέειν, ἐπεὶ οὔ ποτε φῦλον ὁμοῖον
ἀθανάτων τε θεῶν χαμαὶ ἐρχομένων τ' ἀνθρώπων."
ὣς φάτο, Τυδεΐδης δ' ἀνεχάζετο τυτθὸν ὀπίσσω,
μῆνιν ἀλευάμενος ἑκατηβόλου Ἀπόλλωνος.

"Think, son of Tydeus, and yield, and don't be
wanting to think like the gods, since the class of the
immortal gods and the class of mortals who go on the
earth is never the same." So he spoke, and the son
of Tydeus did hold up a little, shunning the wrath [*mênis*] of
Apollo who shoots from afar.

(440–44)

Diomedes, to whom Athena has given the magical ability to distinguish gods from mortals (5.127–28), so that he can literally see the cosmic difference that he is being told here to respect, finally retreats so as to shun[20] the *mênis* of Apollo. A few lines later the incident motivates Apollo to invite Ares to return to battle and confront Diomedes. "He would fight even Zeus himself" (ὃς νῦν γε καὶ ἂν Διὶ πατρὶ μάχοιτο [457, cf. 362]), Apollo says, and he attacked me *daímoni ísos* (459), repeating the formula used at the climactic moment of the incident. The statement that Diomedes would fight even Zeus brings right to the surface of the narrative the thematic linkage I am arguing for between the *mênis* of Apollo against Diomedes and the *mênis* of Zeus against Ares for rebellion against him.

So Diomedes is actually behaving in a way that closely parallels Ares' behavior in this book and in book 15. Not long before he took on Apollo himself, Diomedes had even been warned by Athena to fight with no other god than Aphrodite (5.130–32).[21] Apollo's insistence on the difference

---

[20] The verb ἀλεύω is also used of avoiding spears on the field of battle, as in *Iliad* 3.360, 7.254, 20.281, 22.285. See also 30 n. 50 below.
[21] For the view that even Diomedes' encounter with Aphrodite is transgressive, see Clay 1983, 82–83 n. 56.

between gods and mortals makes it clear that the boundary is dangerous to cross. What could incur the *mênis* of Apollo is Diomedes' attempt to compete with him as an equal. On the other hand, the diction implies that Diomedes, in his stubborn fourth assault on Aeneas, actually does transcend the limits of human nature and become the god's equal. Yet he stops there and retreats a little; he does not kill Aeneas, nor is he punished. This conclusion saves Diomedes while it keeps the cosmic categories intact.

In that regard it contrasts dramatically with the only other attested example of *mênis* in such a context. I am referring to the use of these same motifs and diction in the *aristeía* of Patroklos in the sixteenth book of the *Iliad*. After Patroklos slays Sarpedon, the narrator tells us that he made a big mistake (μέγ' ἀάσθη [16.685]); he *would have* escaped death if he had kept to the word of Achilles. When Achilles sent him into battle, he had told him (16.84–96; repeated in Achilles' prayer to Zeus, 16.240–48) to drive the Trojans from the ships and then return, not to press on toward Troy itself, lest some god ἐμβήῃ 'step in, intervene', for Apollo really loves them. But at lines 698–704 we are told that the Achaeans with Patroklos *would have* captured Troy but for Apollo's intervention, since Patroklos three times went at the angle of the wall, and three times Apollo shoved him away:

ἀλλ' ὅτε δὴ τὸ τέταρτον ἐπέσσυτο δαίμονι ἶσος
δεινὰ δ' ὁμοκλήσας ἔπεα πτερόεντα προσηύδα·
"χάζεο, διογενὲς Πατροκλέες· οὔ νύ τοι αἶσα
σῷ ὑπὸ δουρὶ πόλιν πέρθαι Τρώων ἀγερώχων,
οὐδ' ὑπ' Ἀχιλλῆος, ὅς περ σέο πολλὸν ἀμείνων."
ὣς φάτο, Πάτροκλος δ' ἀνεχάζετο πολλὸν ὀπίσσω,
<u>μῆνιν ἀλευάμενος</u> ἑκατηβόλου Ἀπόλλωνος.

But when he was rushing in <u>like the god [*daímoni îsos*]</u>,
he threatened him terribly, speaking winged words:
"Give way, Zeus-born Patroklos; it is not your destiny
that the city of the proud/prize-winning Trojans be sacked beneath your spear,
or even that of Achilles, who is really much better than you."
So he spoke, and Patroklos withdrew far behind,
<u>shunning the *mênis*</u> of Apollo who shoots from afar.

(16.705–11)

Apollo draws two distinctions for Patroklos in this passage, as opposed to the single one between gods and mortals that he articulated to Diomedes in

*Mênis* and Cosmic Status in the Hierarchy of Peers   15

book 5. The first is between Patroklos and the eventual sacker of Troy; the second is between Patroklos and Achilles; by implication, there is a third distinction being drawn, between Patroklos and a god, since, like Diomedes, he is said to be equal to a *daímōn* 'divinity' (in this context, Ares) when he charges the wall a fourth time. In answer to Apollo's threat he retreats an ironically great distance[22] in order to avoid his *mênis*. It is not that Apollo's *mênis* might be provoked because of Patroklos's misguided attempt to sack Troy or his disregard of the difference between himself and Achilles. The point is that his disregard of those distinctions parallels and reinforces his disregard for the here-unspoken distinction between gods and mortals, and that Patroklos is impersonating Ares just as he is impersonating Achilles.[23] To justify supplying this inexplicit rationale, I invoke a simple principle of interpretation: that a given traditional theme can carry with it ideas that poet and audience have learned to associate with it elsewhere. It is also my hope that the remainder of my discussion will make it clear that the word *mênis* consistently implies the prohibited transgression of fundamental cosmic rules.

Nor is it a coincidence that all this takes place as Patroklos in his *aristeía* is assaulting the wall of Troy: τειχεσιπλῆτα 'wall-approacher' is one of two fixed epithets of Ares, and approaching a wall is an appropriate metaphor for that god's tendency to reach the limits of behavior as well as the great heroes' similar and dangerous tendency to reach the limits between mortality and divinity.[24]

The tension of this moment is lessened when Patroklos retreats, but Apollo in disguise incites Hector against him. Patroklos, aiming at Hector, succeeds in slaying only his charioteer, Kebriones, with a rock to the forehead. A protracted battle ensues between the two heroes and then the

---

[22] Compare Diomedes' shorter retreat in the parallel passage (τυτθόν 'a little way' [5.441]), which in fact reflects an ultimately *greater* respect on his part for the boundary in question. Patroklos's distance (πολλόν 'far') appears to be a spatial equivalent to the πολλόν in the preceding line that Apollo places between him and Achilles, from whom Patroklos differs all too little. Achilles himself perishes at the hands of Paris and Apollo while attempting to enter the city, as we know from the summary of the *Aethiopis* in Proclus (*Chrestomathia* 2) τρεψάμενος δ' Ἀχιλλεὺς τοὺς Τρῶας καὶ εἰς τὴν πόλιν συνεισπεσών, "Achilles routing the Trojans and attacking the city"; the deaths of Patroklos and of Achilles take place in the Scaean gates, *Iliad* 18.453 and *Aethiopis* (Allen 126). In other words, the distance that the hero retreats is in inverse proportion to the distance between god and mortal to which he admits.

[23] For Patroklos's impersonation, see Sinos 1980 on *therápōn*.

[24] *Iliad* 5.31 and 455; on the significance of τειχεσιπλῆτα, see Lowenstam 1981, 76; Lowenstam points out that both Patroklos's and Achilles' deaths take place around a charge against the wall. See *Iliad* 23.80–81.

two armies over the body of Kebriones, and as the day wanes the Achaeans begin to get the upper hand. Then, suddenly, the following happens:

> Πάτροκλος δὲ Τρωσὶ κακὰ φρονέων ἐνόρουσε,
> τρὶς μὲν ἔπειτ' ἐπόρουσε <u>θοῷ ἀτάλαντος Ἄρηϊ</u>,
> σμερδαλέα ἰάχων, τρὶς δ' ἐννέα φῶτας ἔπεφνεν.
> ἀλλ' ὅτε δὴ τὸ τέταρτον ἐπέσσυτο <u>δαίμονι ἶσος</u>,
> ἔνθ' ἄρα τοι, Πάτροκλε, φάνη βιότοιο τελευτή·

> Patroklos sprang upon the Trojans with evil intent,
> three times then he sprang upon them, <u>equal to rushing Ares</u>,
> shrieking terribly, and three times he slew nine men.
> But when he was rushing forward that fourth time <u>equal to the *daímōn*</u>,
> then the end of life rose up before you, Patroklos.
>
> (16.784–87)

The killing of nine (= three, three times) men three times is a remarkable intensification of the notion of "threeness" in this theme. In this regard it parallels the culminant grouping mathematics of a war that ends in its tenth year (= the year *after* three groups of three years, like the fatal assault *after* three murderous others), which is by no means irrelevant to Patroklos's attempt to storm Troy. The functional equivalence of *thoǐ atálantos Árēï*, "equal to rushing Ares," to *daímoni ísos*, "equal to the *daímōn*" is flagrant in this text, and the absence of any mention here of Patroklos's attempt to sack Troy or to surpass Achilles is eloquent: his final transgression is across the line that Apollo guards between mortals and Ares. Moreover, the other fixed epithet of Ares (occurring in the two passages cited from book 5—lines 31 and 455—as well as at 5.844 and 21.402), μιαιφόνος 'who defiles himself by murder', as Pierre Chantraine understands it, seems profoundly relevant to the transgressive, murderous behavior of Patroklos in this context, just as τειχεσιπλῆτα was relevant to the prior instance of the three assaults theme.[25]

This time the fourth, tabu assault does not elicit verbal warnings or threats from Apollo; there is no way Patroklos can ward off what is about to happen to him, since Apollo stalks him silently, from behind, and as though to make his imperceptibility triply plain, in a mist. Even were Patroklos to turn around, he would not know he was being attacked. Apollo smites (the root *\*plēg-*: πλῆξεν [791]; again, θεοῦ πληγῇ [816]) the mortal from behind

---

[25] Chantraine 1968–79, s.v. μιαίνω.

with downturned hand on the back and shoulders, making Patroklos's eyes twirl and the helmet fall off his head. Its plumes are defiled (the verb μιαίνεσθαι 'defile' is used twice) with dust and blood, which was not *thémis* before (796–99). Then his spear shatters, his shield falls to the ground, his breastplate comes undone, ἄτη 'derangement' takes his wits, and his limbs are loosed. Violence to the eyes and loosed limbs, the first and last two consequences of the blow to the back, are usually sufficient to describe a hero's death, but they and all the details between are only a prelude to death in Patroklos's elaborate, operatic demise. Steven Lowenstam has suggested that Apollo's invisible *plēgḗ* is one of several elements that lend a sacrificial cast to the death of Patroklos, who is the ultimate *therápōn*, a word whose original but now latent meaning was, precisely, 'ritual substitute'. The *plēgḗ* corresponds to the oblique, stunning blow dealt a sacrificial animal before its throat is cut.[26] At the same time it is a reflex of the *mênis* motif, in which the root *\*plēg-* regularly specifies smiting, usually, as we shall see, by a thunderbolt.

Here Patroklos has reached the climax of his life as a warrior, performing inhuman feats of strength and violence which intrinsically demand that his mortality be asserted and his life ended. The blow of the god with *mênis* marks at one and the same time the sacrifice of the hero's beloved companion, the punishment of a human who has transgressed too far and too often the limits of his condition, and the glorification of a literally extraordinary achievement. Patroklos has become the incarnation of Ares and a dead man at the same moment. To us, this expression of Apollo's *mênis* upon an individual may seem very different from the communal devastation we have seen to be the result of *mênis* in previous cases, but the death of Patroklos is a devastating blow not just to Achilles but by definition to the whole host of fighting men and, beyond that, as we will see, to the whole human estate.

All four invocations of *mênis* we have been considering have the same purpose: to enforce the sovereign cosmic order. In the case of Ares, it is the social and political coherence of the divine community that Athena invokes to suppress his lust to avenge the death of his son or to intervene on behalf of the Trojans, whom he favors. Should Ares incur the *mênis* of Zeus by failing to defer to his sovereignty, the divine community would be destroyed by Zeus's violent assertion of his rule. In the case of Diomedes and Patroklos, it is the hierarchical distinction between gods and mortals that is

[26] On the etymology and underlying meaning of *therápōn*, see Van Brock 1959; and Lowenstam 1981.

tested by the heroes. More could be said about the especially rich context of Diomedes' *aristeía;* by no coincidence, it also contains a long digression on the mythology of divine "mortality," on moments when gods such as Ares were close to death, and it concludes with a literal duel between Ares and Diomedes in which Athena serves as the mortal hero's charioteer. In short, the ritual antagonism between warrior and war god and its dangerous and empowering consequences are the fundamental structuring principle of Diomedes' whole *aristeía.*

## Mênis and Divine Sex

On three occasions *mênis* is aroused in divinities by sexual transgressions. The first occurs when Hermes visits Kalypso in the fifth book of the *Odyssey* to relay Zeus's request that she 'send back' ἀποπέμπειν Odysseus; she reacts with anger at the gods as a group οἵ τε θεαῖς ἀγάασθε παρ' ἀνδράσιν εὐνάζεσθαι / ἀμφαδίην, "who are jealous of goddesses' blatantly bedding down with mortal men" (5.119–20). She then goes on to give specifics. Eos, who snatched Orion, whom Artemis then "smote, attacking with her jealous arrows" (οἷς ἀγανοῖς βελέεσσιν ἐποιχομένη κατέπεφνεν [124]);[27] Demeter, who made love to Iasion in the thrice-plowed furrow, but Zeus "smote him, hitting him with a blazing thunderbolt" (μιν κατέπεφνε βαλὼν ἀργῆτι κεραυνῷ [128]); and now there is Kalypso herself, who rescued Odysseus after Zeus had struck his ship with a thunderbolt and destroyed his companions, and whom she offered to make ageless and immortal forever. Even so, she is willing to let him go over the resistless sea, since Zeus's *nóos* 'mind' is inescapable. To which Hermes responds with a stern warning:

οὕτω νῦν ἀπόπεμπε, Διὸς δ' ἐποπίζεο μῆνιν,
μή πώς τοι μετόπισθε κοτεσσάμενος χαλεπήνῃ.

So now send him back, and <u>watch out for the *mênis*</u> of Zeus,
so that he won't hold a grudge and be harsh on you somehow afterwards.

(5.145–46)

In the context of the other uses of *mênis* we have been considering, the

---

[27] Meier-Brügger (1993, 267–68) shows that the usual translation of the word ἀγανός as 'gentle' is inappropriate here as elsewhere. He derives the adjective from the verb ἄγαμαι 'be jealous', which is actually attested just above (line 119, ἀγάασθε; again, line 122, ἠγάασθε) in exactly this semantic context.

punishments in the list of Kalypso imply that in such instances the actual object of Zeus's wrath at her ("hold a grudge and be harsh on you" τοι... κοτεσσάμενος χαλεπήνῃ [146]) would be Odysseus rather than the goddess herself. So in the case of Ares or his stand-in Diomedes, it was the male god or the hero who was smitten by the thunderbolt. Is this case a hybrid of the previous ones, in which both god and mortal, not just one or the other, are incurring the wrath of Zeus?

The picture is not very clear until we look at another example that features a similar triangle. It occurs in the *Hymn to Aphrodite,* which tells how Zeus finally managed to subjugate Aphrodite to a male mortal in return for the way she had beguiled gods, including himself, to have sex with mortal women and other goddesses to have sex with mortal men (*Hymn to Aphrodite* 45–52). In order to humble her as well, Zeus makes her fall in love with the shepherd Anchises, before whom she appears as a virginal girl. Sexual desire takes hold of him as soon as he sees her, and he greets her as a goddess. But she totally denies any resemblance to divinity, and explains that Hermes has brought her to him to be called his wife and to bear his children (126–27); she asks him please to wait and carry out the formalities of marriage. If you are mortal, he replies, and a woman bore you and a mortal is your father, and you have been brought here by a god, then no god or mortal will keep me from making love to you right now,

> οὐδ' εἴ κεν ἑκήβολος αὐτὸς Ἀπόλλων
> τόξου ἀπ' ἀργυρέου προΐῃ βέλεα στονόεντα.
> βουλοίμην κεν ἔπειτα, γύναι εἰκυῖα θεῇσι,
> σῆς εὐνῆς ἐπιβὰς δῦναι δόμον Ἄϊδος εἴσω.

> not even if far-shooter Apollo himself should
> shoot woeful arrows from his silver bow.
> Woman like the goddesses, at that point, after
> mounting your bed, I would be content to enter the house of Hades.
> (151–54)

Once they make love, Aphrodite reveals herself to him and describes the birth and rearing of Aeneas, whose name expresses her αἰνὸν ἄχος, "awful grief [*ákhos*]" at having gone to bed with a mortal man; but their descendants will be ἀγχίθεοι 'near-gods', she says, and Aeneas himself will be θεοείκελος 'like a god'.[28] Nevertheless, she warns Anchises that if he is

---

[28] Compare the initial description of Anchises himself in the *Hymn* (55): δέμας ἀθανάτοισιν ἐοικώς, "like the immortals in build." See also Segal 1974.

asked who is the mother of their child, he is to name one of the nymphs who will actually rear him once he is born.

> εἰ δέ κεν ἐξείπῃς καὶ ἐπεύξεαι ἄφρονι θυμῷ
> ἐν φιλότητι μιγῆναι ἐϋστεφάνῳ Κυθερείῃ,
> Ζεύς σε χολωσάμενος βαλέει ψολόεντι κεραυνῷ.
> εἴρηταί τοι πάντα· σὺ δὲ φρεσὶ σῇσι νοήσας
> ἴσχεο μηδ' ὀνόμαινε, θεῶν δ' ἐποπίζεο μῆνιν.

but if you speak out and declare mindlessly
that you had sex with well-garlanded Cythereia,
Zeus in his anger will smite you with his smoky thunderbolt.
That is all I have to say; but you think
and keep it in your mind and do not mention
my name, and watch out for the *mênis* of the gods.

(286–90)

The explicit use of the word *mênis* in this admonitory passage is completely consistent with its use in regard to Kalypso and Odysseus. The triangle in both cases consists of Zeus (representing the gods as a group),[29] a goddess, and a mortal. Zeus will exercise his wrath by striking the mortal lover with a thunderbolt, but in the case of Anchises, strangely, an explicit condition is added: he will be punished only if he reveals who is the true mother of his child. Actually this condition recalls Kalypso's complaint that what the gods begrudge goddesses is their going to bed 'openly' ἀμφαδίην (5.119) with a mortal man. From the contexts in the *Odyssey* and the *Hymn,* it becomes clear that by "openly" Kalypso means "with the knowledge of Zeus." Thus Hermes in his initial remarks to her stressed the distance of her island from everyone, but he added:

> ἀλλὰ μάλ' οὔ πως ἔστι Διὸς νόον αἰγιόχοιο
> οὔτε παρεξελθεῖν ἄλλον θεὸν οὔθ' ἁλιῶσαι.

---

[29] In regard to Kalypso, compare Hermes' ascription to Zeus of the order to send back Odysseus (5.99), and Kalypso's answering reference (5.118) to the gods' jealousy of goddesses who sleep with mortal men; and in the passage just cited, compare the reference to the thunderbolt "of Zeus" (*Hymn to Aphrodite* 288) but the *mênis* of "the gods" (290). *The notion of social solidarity is never far from mind when it comes to mênis.* There is another parallel between the two triangles in the variation between Zeus's thunderbolt and Artemis's arrows (Kalypso), as against that between Apollo's arrows and Zeus's thunderbolt (*Hymn to Aphrodite*). For more on the relation between arrows and thunderbolts, see below, 101–2.

> But there is just no way for another god either to
> outstrip or to nullify the mind of aegis-bearing Zeus.
>
> (*Odyssey* 5.104–5)

Hermes immediately went on to explain that φησί 'he [Zeus] says' that Odysseus is there. Kalypso responded by remarking on the gods' intolerance of goddesses' openly going to bed with men, and when she told the stories of Orion and Iasion, she said of the latter:

> οὐδὲ δὴν ἦεν ἄπυστος
> Ζεύς, ὅς μιν κατέπεφνε . . .
>
> nor was Zeus ignorant for long, and he smote
> him . . .
>
> (5.127–28)

Finally, when Kalypso acceded to Zeus's will, she repeated what Hermes had said about the impossibility of hiding her relationship from Zeus. "I kept telling him I would make him immortal and ageless all the days," she says,

> ἀλλ' ἐπεὶ οὔ πως ἔστι Διὸς νόον αἰγιόχοιο
> οὔτε παρεξελθεῖν ἄλλον θεὸν οὔθ' ἁλιῶσαι,
> ἐρρέτω, εἴ μιν κεῖνος ἐποτρύνει καὶ ἀνώγει.
>
> but since there is no way for another god either
> to outstrip or to nullify the mind of Zeus, let
> him go, if he urges and demands him.
>
> (5.137–39)

The implication of this repeated language is that as long as Zeus *had not found out about* her sleeping with Odysseus she did not have to give him up.

This situation is precisely relevant to the context of the *Hymn to Aphrodite*. Aphrodite's concluding admonition to Anchises that he not announce his having gone to bed with her (ἐξείπῃς καὶ ἐπεύξεαι [286]) is intended to keep Zeus and the other gods from finding out that she had made love to a mortal man, whereas it had been Zeus's goal from the start of the hymn to put an end to her status as the only nonvirginal goddess not to sleep with a mortal while announcing and declaring (ἐπευξαμένη εἴπῃ [48]) among all the gods her power to cause male gods to sleep with mortal women and goddesses with mortal men (48–52). The irony of the warning about the wrath of Zeus at the conclusion of the hymn is exquisite. Aphrodite does not yet know that Zeus made her fall in love with Anchises in the first place, and she thinks that by invoking his wrath she will retain her powerful status in the divine community despite the way she has degraded herself with Anchises. Moreover, as the last lines of a poem to which we are privy, Aphrodite's warning itself makes it clear that Anchises did announce and declare the identity of his son's mother. In this case he should have been thunderbolted. The tradition in fact exists that he was and that his subsequent inability to walk (as from the ruins of Troy) was the consequence of that punishment.[30]

But why should Zeus be so threatened as to strike the mortal lovers of goddesses once he learns of them? One part of the problem is that for a divinity to keep a secret lover is in itself a challenge to Zeus's *nóos* 'mind'. Compare, for example, the language in the passages I have cited: οὔ πως ἔστι Διὸς νόον αἰγιόχοιο / οὔτε παρεξελθεῖν ἄλλον θέον, "there is no way for another god to outstrip the *nóos* of aegis-bearing Zeus."[31] Actually, this is a variation on the pattern of power consolidation in the *Theogony*, in which Zeus uses his thunderbolt against Gaia's youngest son, Typhoeus (lines 820–68) and prevents Metis from having a child stronger than himself by swallowing not the child, as Kronos had done unsuccessfully (453–506), but her mother (886–900).[32] It is as though making love to a goddess raises a mortal man toward the level of Zeus just as much as it degrades the goddess. The mortal is exactly like the warrior hero who becomes *daímoni îsos*, in a powerful and dangerous but not inevitably fatal place, though his sexual prowess is disturbing indeed to Zeus and Apollo or Artemis in their pride of rank. His divine equivalence explains why Anchises does not perish from the blow of the thunderbolt. Like Hephaistos, whose thunderbolting by Zeus will be discussed, Anchises is only lame, not dead, the lameness being at once a paradoxical talisman of his transgression and his sexual conquest. Given the strong masculine bias of this culture, the mortal male who makes love to a divine female is taking a much more threatening

---

[30] Sophocles fr. 373; Hyginus *Fab.* 94; he was either blinded (Servius on *Aeneid* 1.617) by the thunderstroke or paralyzed (Servius on *Aeneid* 2.649) by it. See below, 125–28: the thunderbolt has a similar effect on Hephaistos's ability to walk. The parallel carries with it an implication about Anchises' near-god status that is consistent with the evidence given here (above, 10–18 with n. 19, and below, 23).

[31] See Nagy 1974b, 265–78, on the relation among *médea*, *nóos*, and sexual activity for Zeus, Kronos, and Ouranos.

[32] For a detailed analysis of these episodes in the context of the *Theogony* as a whole, see below, Chapter 3.

step up in the cosmic hierarchy than a female mortal who makes love to a god. We are also in a better position now to understand why Hermes speaks of the *mênis* of Zeus against Kalypso, when it is not she but her lover who will be thunderbolted. The goddess is instrumental in enabling the mortal to transgress the cosmic boundaries, but the direct threat to Zeus comes from the male who threatens to displace him, not from the female.[33] The sanction, however, is clearly against the pair. In this context, the destruction of a bonded pair's mortal partner is precisely analogous to the indiscriminate, solidarity-breaking devastation that marks divine *mênis* in its other attestations.

The basic issue in these episodes involving mortals behaving like gods is that gods and mortals are not, as Apollo said to Diomedes, φῦλον ὅμοιον, "the same class [*phûlon*]."[34] The traditional role of Apollo in making just this distinction and reinforcing it with an appeal to the destructiveness of *mênis* is what lies behind the remarks of Anchises. "No god or mortal will keep me from making love to you right now," he said to the disguised Aphrodite, not even if Apollo were to shoot his arrows. "After mounting your bed, I would be content to enter the house of Hades" (*Hymn to Aphrodite* 151ff.). His bravado is somewhat undermined by the fact that the girl has just assured him that she is no goddess, but that is only one of several ironies.

In attested Greek epic there remains one more instance of *mênis* in the context of a sexual offense, when Demeter is angered at Zeus and the other Olympians by the rape of Persephone. Once the Eleusinians have built Demeter a temple to propitiate her for Metaneira's interruption of baby Demophon's immortalization process, Demeter sits within it to distance herself from the divine community (*Hymn to Demeter* 303–4), grieving for her daughter who has been lost to the land of the dead. Instead of fasting, as she had before,[35] she keeps the seed from sprouting by hiding it (κρύπτει) and thereby creates a universal famine that threatens to destroy the race of

---

[33] Again, Zeus can and does thunderbolt or bind divinities in such circumstances.

[34] For the special use of the term *phûlon* 'class [as in classify, not social class], group, kind' and its derivative *phulokrineîn* to single out the marked category from a distinctive, diverse, but complementary set of alternatives, see Loraux 1978, 77 n. 78; and Nagy 1990a, 290–91.

[35] The conventional sign of grief, *Hymn to Demeter* 49–50; cf. her refusal to eat as the raped woman in the "Cretan lie" she tells the daughters of Keleos. *Hymn to Demeter* 129. For more on her specific refusal to eat honey-sweet food, see Muellner, "μελιηδής," forthcoming, and compare the sexual symbolism of the one thing that Persephone eats in the underworld, the pomegranate pip that Hades pops into her mouth, with the hidden seed (σπέρμα [307]) of the famine. Demeter's action is as much a threatening demonstration of her power as a sympathetic attempt to prevent Persephone from being impregnated by Hades.

mortals as it deprives the gods of the *timé* 'honor' of sacrifice (310–13). Zeus responds not by thunderbolting Demeter for threatening his world order but by sending Iris to ask her to return to the "class [*phûla*] of the gods" (φῦλα θεῶν [322]).[36] The one explains the other. Zeus's world order depends on Demeter's solidarity with the Olympians. But she simply refuses, whereupon he sends out *all* the gods (326) to give her gifts and whatever *timaí* 'honors' she might choose among the immortals. Again she firmly refuses (330), but this time she stipulates the condition for her return. She will not set foot on Olympus or let the fruit sprout until she sets eyes on her fair-eyed daughter. That is when Zeus sends Hermes to Hades to retrieve Persephone:

> Ζεύς με πατὴρ ἤνωγεν ἀγαυὴν Περσεφόνειαν
> ἐξαγαγεῖν Ἐρέβευσφι μετὰ σφέας, ὄφρα ἑ μήτηρ
> ὀφθαλμοῖσιν ἰδοῦσα χόλου καὶ μήνιος αἰνῆς
> ἀθανάτοις παύσειεν· ἐπεὶ μέγα μήδεται ἔργον
> φθῖσαι φῦλ' ἀμενηνὰ χαμαιγενέων ἀνθρώπων
> σπέρμ' ὑπὸ γῆς κρύπτουσα, καταφθινύθουσα δὲ τιμὰς
> ἀθανάτων. ἡ δ' αἰνὸν ἔχει χόλον, οὐδὲ θεοῖσιν
> μίσγεται.

> Father Zeus ordered me to bring proud Persephone
> out of Erebos to them, so that her mother might see
> her with her eyes and cease from her anger [*khólos*] and
> terrible *mênis* at the immortals; since she is
> devising a great deed, to destroy the feeble class [*phûlon*] of
> earth-born humans by hiding the seed beneath the
> earth, also destroying the privileges [*timaí*] of the immortals.
> She has terrible anger [*khólos*], nor does she mingle with the
> gods.

(348–55)

Almost every aspect of Demeter's alienation is similar to the aggrieved alienation of Achilles caused by the loss of an unwilling girl (ἀέκουσα 'unwilling' [*Iliad* 1.348]; κούρη 'girl' [1.98, 275, 337, etc.]), the indiscriminate devastation it causes his own social group, his initial rejection of the offer of gifts and 'honor' *timé* by his colleagues if he will return to society, then the softening and stipulation of a single condition for return: when the

---

[36] For the meaning of the plural *phûla*, see Loraux 1978, 54.

fire reaches the ships.³⁷ More pertinently, there is also a clear similarity to the theme of *mênis* as a sanction for transgression against the structure of the cosmic hierarchy. What has aroused Demeter's *mênis* is the forceful (βίη), unwilling (ἀέκουσα), and inescapable (ἀνάγκη) removal of her divine daughter (κούρη) from the surface of the earth to the world below.³⁸ In contrast to the passionate upward thrust of the mortal warrior or the insubordinate Ares, and in contrast to the uplifting, willing seduction of mortal men by goddesses, the offensive, dangerous act here is unwilled and downward in the cosmic hierarchy: not a man's seduction but a maiden's rape, not the immortalization of a mortal but the relegation of an immortal to the land of the dead. Demeter's grief-stricken *mênis*, the consequence of these retrograde transgressions, literally threatens to undo the structure of both the divine and the human worlds. Zeus has no choice but to accede to her uncompromising demand, since the solidarity and integrity of his whole domain has been breached by the rape of Persephone and is being threatened by the *mênis* of her mother. It is worth stressing here and for the purposes of subsequent discussion that *theogonic* principles of Zeus's rule are at issue in the instance of Demeter's anger, where Zeus is not the subject but an object of the goddess's cosmically destructive intentions. Zeus's explicit goal in response to her act is to achieve the reintegration of Demeter into Olympian society (321–68), as though the most disturbing aspect of her *mênis* is her removal to a temple and her refusal to "mingle with the gods" (355).³⁹

## Disobedient Warriors and Sexual Politics

Internally, the consistency within each of these two sets of attestations of *mênis* is beginning to become clear, but what do disobedient warriors and sexual transgressors really have to do with each other? If we think of *mênis* as merely denoting a familiar emotional state, there is a low-level link

---

[37] On the wrath of Demeter and Achilles and their psychological connection with mourning, see Loraux 1986, 253–57; on the thematic parallels, see Lord 1967, 241–48.

[38] *Hymn to Demeter* 72, 124, 413, 8 (cf. 66, 333, etc.).

[39] Consider also the way Persephone's return is described as Hades' willing acceptance of the wishes of Zeus βασιλεύς (*Hymn to Demeter* 367–68). As Richardson 1974 remarks, βασιλεύς 'king' is the *theogonic*, not the Homeric title of Zeus. The threat to Zeus constituted by mortal males in connection with the *Hymn to Aphrodite* is also a theogonic theme, as is the issue of the *nóos* 'mind' of Zeus (*Hymn to Aphrodite* 36, etc.), since Zeus's power consists in his superiority in force and in *nóos*, and Zeus's stated goal in the myth of the hymn is to assert his power vis-à-vis Aphrodite.

between them that does not account for the intimate and detailed relationships between the passages in which they occur. But *mênis* is not just a term for an emotional state. *It is a sanction meant to guarantee and maintain the integrity of the world order;* every time it is invoked, the hierarchy of the cosmos is at stake. So in all these examples, it is a question either of maintaining Zeus's sovereignty over other gods or of enforcing the limit that keeps mortals from becoming gods, a limit that heroic figures, to their credit and at their risk, must test.

In fact, we are witnessing the establishment and maintenance of tabus within the epic world. In her classic comparative study of such concepts in small-scale societies, *Purity and Danger,* Mary Douglas shows how prohibitions are one way that societies cope with the combination of danger and power that arises when their classification schemes are subject to stress. Disorder in the classification scheme is destructive to existing patterns of experience but also potentially creative of new patterns. Thus, it can receive various treatments. It can be ignored or denied or violently suppressed or constituted as a new category or incorporated in such a way as to "ambiguate" and thus enhance the richness and meaning of existing patterns. In small-scale societies the power to enforce prohibitions regularly resides in no person but inheres in the structure of the world.[40] In the world of Greek epic, by contrast, the Olympian gods who represent and maintain the structure of the world wield this power, which has been formalized as *mênis* and made specific and generalizable for a set of prohibitions. Within the mythological tradition of Greek epic, *mênis* is, as I hope to show in detail, a continuing expression of the reign of Zeus which emerges in the traditions that culminate in the *Theogony* of Hesiod.[41] From a more archaic perspective, the enforcement of prohibitions I have been discussing supports the inherited tripartite ideology of social structure reflected in Indo-European languages, as described by Georges Dumézil.[42] According to him, the ideal structure of Indo-European society as represented in the mythological tradition comprises three domains: sovereignty, warfare, and fertility. In fact, we have observed offenses in the realms of warfare (Ares,

[40] Douglas 1969, 38–40, 104. Parker 1983 is concerned with a specifically legal, institutional form of μίασμα 'defilement (from tabu violation)' and is not relevant to the subject at hand.

[41] On the consistent presentation of an interconnected series of theogonic myths as a paradigmatic backdrop to the events in the *Iliad,* see Lang 1983, 140–64; and Nagy 1992. The backdrop of myths noted by Lang center on the theme of Zeus's *mênis,* but Lang does not bring out this feature. On the whole question of the relation of the *mênis* theme to the theogonic tradition, see below, Chapters 3 and 4.

[42] For an overview of this hypothesis, see Dumézil 1958; for a more detailed presentation of evidence from epic texts in the Indo-European languages, see Dumézil 1968.

Diomedes, Patroklos) and fertility (Kalypso, Aphrodite, Demeter) that were arrested or punished in the interest of maintaining the sovereignty of Zeus. Later we will see an offense in the realm of sovereignty itself.[43]

Yet, it is also a fundamental goal of epic heroes to create disorder within the defining categories of the Olympian order and thus to "enrich and ambiguate them," to apply Douglas's formulation. Her anthropological discussion of the danger and power arising from a challenge to the fundamental categories of nature precisely suits the position of such heroes as Patroklos or Anchises at their acme. It is also worth noting that the divine enforcement of prohibitions is not necessarily to be thought of as the attribution of moral and ethical functions to epic gods. At issue is world maintenance, asserting and preserving the prevailing order of the cosmos, not an individual's right or wrong behavior. As Walter Burkert puts it in another context, "More important than individual morality is continuity, which depends on solidarity."[44] So we can understand the logic, however repugnant it may seem, in Zeus's threat to punish a whole social group for an offense committed by just one of its members.[45] The idea of *mênis* is utterly bound up with principles of solidarity and continuity, which it exists to maintain and by virtue of which it maintains itself. Burkert's distinction between individual morality and social continuity is a provocative one for Greek epic, but his statement that one is more important than the other is not borne out in Greek epic or in small-scale societies either. According to Mary Douglas, rules of right and wrong (that is, rules of morality) coexist and randomly conflict with prohibition rules (tabus) in small-scale societies as they do in more complex ones. She offers a set of principles describing the ways in which the two can interrelate, such as this one: "When the sense of [moral] outrage is adequately equipped with practical sanctions in the social order, pollution is not likely to arise. Where, humanly speaking, the outrage is likely to go unpunished, pollution beliefs tend to be called in to supplement the lack of other sanctions."[46] After all,

---

[43] I am referring to the regulation of sovereignty issues between Zeus and Poseidon and Zeus and Demeter and to the episode alluded to in *Iliad* 1.396–406 discussed in Chapter 4, below, 118–23.

[44] Burkert 1985, 248.

[45] For a society in which such a rule of solidarity actually applies in daily life, the standard anthropological example is the Nuer; see Evans-Pritchard 1940. Other societies with so-called corporate kin structure have similar rules about blood vendetta. My thanks for this information to P.-Y. Jacopin.

[46] Douglas 1966, 132. For a comparative discussion of the relation between moral rules and prohibitions and the conflicts that can arise between them in small-scale societies, see Douglas 1966, 129–58, including chap. 9, "The System at War with Itself," 140–58.

a code of morality exists to serve and preserve the existing social structure in the same way as a set of prohibitions does. The intersection and divergence of principles of world maintenance and principles of morality will occupy us again later. Within the Homeric epic, however, it is not yet clear whether any meaningful distinction can be drawn between the two; I will assert that they are in fact continuous with one another.[47]

## Mênis and the Hierarchy of Peers

Zeus's concession to Demeter's *mênis* is ultimately consistent with the patterns of transgression and the issues of world maintenance raised in other instances of the *mênis* theme, but it is not without its surprising aspects. In particular, Demeter wields against Zeus the cosmic sanction that is elsewhere appropriated by him or by his delegate. But the problem in her myth is a structural one in the Olympian order, and there is another allusion to it in the passage with which this analysis began, the beginning of book 15 of the *Iliad*. A difficulty arises from the potential contradiction between Zeus's dominance over the world of gods and mortals as against his cooperative relationship with his two brothers, Poseidon and Hades, who are his peers: Demeter, also Zeus's sibling, in fact has the same power relationship to Zeus as his two brothers. Though she lacks the thunderbolt, her cosmic powers—in epic terms, her *tîmê*—when applied negatively, are adequate to menace the very structure of the world.[48] So rather than menace her and her peers with random violence—in this regard, it is significant that she has physically isolated herself from Olympus, having withdrawn to her temple at Eleusis—it behooves Zeus to restore the solidarity of the gods by granting her request and importuning her to return to the divine community. For Zeus, domination does not rule out undoing his own mistakes.

By contrast, in the sequel to the opening scene of book 15, Hera knuckles under to Zeus's threats despite her misgivings about his actions, and she reluctantly tells Iris and Apollo to go to Mount Ida and receive Zeus's

---

[47] See Chapter 4.

[48] For the meaning of *tîmê* in epic and in cult, see Nagy 1979, 118, sec. 1 n. 2. The local hero's everlasting *tîmê* is his cult; for the epic hero, the imperishable prize that compensates for his death is *kléos*; in the domain of the Olympian gods, a particular divinity's *tîmê* or cult includes a definition of that god's ritual domain or sphere. This is the sense of the word in the *Theogony*, for instance, in which Zeus caps his victory over Prometheus, the Titans, and Typhoeus by distributing to the gods their *timaí* (*Theogony* 73–74, 111, and esp. 885: ὁ δὲ τοῖσιν [sc. θεοῖς] εὖ διεδάσσατο τιμάς, "and he divided well their *timaí* among them"). See also Nagy 1990b, 216, on *timaí* vs. *tékhnai*.

commission. There Zeus tells Iris to descend to the Trojan plain and get Poseidon off the battlefield: he should return either to his own domain, the bright sea, or to the *phûla theôn,* "class of the gods" (*Iliad* 15.161, 177). But if Poseidon does not heed the words of Zeus, strong as he is, let him carefully consider, awaiting the onset of Zeus, who is his superior (φέρτερος) in violence as well as his elder in birth (15.163–66 γενεῇ πρότερος). The threat of physical force is even more explicit when Iris actually delivers the message (179–84). Others should dread even to appear as Zeus's equal (τόν τε στυγέουσι καὶ ἄλλοι [167, 183]), she tells Poseidon.

Again in contrast to Demeter's case, Poseidon's isolated disobedience is met with a request for compliance to the will of Zeus. Either reintegration into the divine community or retirement to his own separate but equal domain is what is required of him—alternatives that are familiar from Demeter's myth. Nor is Zeus hesitant to threaten violence and pull rank. The assertion of prior birth is as significant as the threat, for it is an attempt to legitimate his superiority over his brother in terms other than just force. Neither, however, seems to have the least effect on Poseidon, who claims he has equal *timê* to Zeus (ὁμότιμος [186]), along with the other of the three sons of Kronos and Rhea, Hades. In the cosmic division (τριχθὰ δὲ πάντα δέδασται, "everything was divided into three shares" [189]), each was awarded a domain (as it was for Demeter, the domain is designated by the word *timê*), sky, sea, or underworld, with earth and Olympus common to all three, says Poseidon (186–93). Zeus should respect that division, save his threats of violence for those who are really base (196), and keep his harsh words (ἐκπάγλοις [from the root *plēg-*] ἐπέεσσιν) for his own sons and daughters, who are obligated to heed them (197–99).

In other words, Poseidon, who is not Zeus's child, is neither intimidated by Zeus's violence nor respectful of his claim to outrank him in birth. Here again the distinction is being drawn between ranking behavior among members of the same generation (such as Zeus, Hades, and Poseidon) as against that between a younger generation and its elders (as between Zeus and his children—Athena, Apollo, and other junior Olympians). Poseidon's overt point is that Zeus is inappropriately asserting his status over him, his peer, as an elder would over a younger. The underlying point is that Poseidon is just as powerful as Zeus and just as capable as Demeter was of menacing the cosmic order. It is no coincidence—and I shall return to this point in some detail later on—that precisely the same relationship obtains between Agamemnon and Achilles, and that their conflict is couched in precisely the same terms. Agamemnon claims to be superior (φέρτερος [1.186]) to Achilles, as well as his elder (γενεῇ προγενέστερος [9.161]) in birth, and he also claims that he is taking away Briseis from him so that others may dread to appear as his equal (τόν τε στυγέουσι καὶ ἄλλοι [1.186–87]). Moreover, Achilles and Poseidon share an analogous 'grief' *ákhos* (15.218, Poseidon = 16.52, Achilles) at the disregard of their equal status in the community and at authoritarian abuse of the communal division that guarantees it (Achilles: τὸν ὁμοῖον 'peer' [16.53] vs. Poseidon ἰσόμορον 'having an equal share' [15.209]; Poseidon: δέδασται 'has been shared' [15.189] vs. Achilles δέδασται 'has been shared' [1.125], δασμός 'process of dividing into shares' [1.166]). Ultimately, Poseidon, exactly like Achilles, chooses to come to terms with Zeus and save face by redrawing the uncrossable line a little farther back: he will not confront Zeus this time, but should he try to keep Troy from destruction, Poseidon says, then there will be incurable anger between them.[49] But what accounts for the deep and patent parallelism between him and Achilles?

Lurking behind both characters' reactions is the dark theme that crystallizes the tradition's words and thoughts, the theme of *mênis*. In the case of Achilles and Agamemnon, the word (or rather, the verb derived from it) is used of both heroes (ἐμήνιε of Agamemnon [1.247], μήνιε of Achilles [1.488]). In the case of Demeter and Zeus, the goddess explicitly uses *mênis* as the ultimate sanction (μήνιος *Hymn to Demeter* [350], μήνιος [410]). By doing so, she puts Zeus in an untenable position between the conflicting demands of two peers, herself and Hades. The intermittent return of her daughter is the perfect and only solution. Lastly, in the case of Poseidon and Zeus, the word itself remains unspoken but is referenced for both gods by its near synonym *khólos* (Zeus: ἀλευάμενος χόλον αἰπύν, "shunning sheer anger" [223], χολωτοῖσιν ἐπέεσσι, "with angered words"; Poseidon and Zeus: ἀνήκεστος χόλος, "incurable anger" [217]) and the other diction that is elsewhere consistently associated with the *mênis* theme.[50] In fact, the

---

[49] Compare Achilles' speech at 1.293–303, in which he agrees to give up Briseis ἐπεί μ' ἀφέλεσθέ [you, plural] γε δόντες, "since you (the group) are depriving me of my prize that you (the group) gave me," but if you Agamemnon (at 301 the text switches back to "you, singular") come and try to take anything else against my will, then your blood will spurt around my spearshaft." For an analysis of this scene that complements mine and anticipates some of its conclusions, see Lowenstam 1993, 73–77.

[50] To which can be added the expression just cited, ἀλευάμενος χόλον αἰπύν, "shunning sheer anger [*khólos*]." The object of the verb ἀλεύω 'shun' is the word *mênis* in three other places: 16.711, 5.34, and 5.444, passages I have already discussed. This is its only occurrence with *khólos* as its object. Otherwise, its object is a spear or death. This is one among several examples in which a speaker referring to the *mênis* theme uses the word *khólos* instead. For more on *mênis* and *khólos*, see above, 7 n. 5, and below, 111 with n. 43. For reticence about uttering the word *mênis*, see the Appendix.

*absence* of the word *mênis* can be as much an aspect of its meaning as is its presence, given that the acts incurring it are in principle unspeakable.

Such a pattern of variation in dramatis personae but consistency in diction is typical of the way themes function in traditional poetry. In fact the opening of book 15 comprises three successive, interwoven variations on the theme of *mênis*, around Hera, Ares, and Poseidon. From this perspective, we can also see how *mênis* suits its diverse thematic contexts. In each instance, it is the irrevocable cosmic sanction that prohibits some characters from taking their superiors for equals and others from taking their equals for inferiors.

CHAPTER 2

# *Mênis* and the Social Order

An irrevocable cosmic sanction that prohibits some from taking their superiors for equals and others from taking their equals for inferiors—this abstracted definition implies a rigid hierarchical structure and a predictable punitive response to violations of it that belie the richness and flexibility of Greek epic. There are indeed examples of such rigidity. For instance, there is no uncertainty whatever about maltreating the body of a dead person. As soon as Odysseus can, he responds appropriately to Elpenor's statement from the underworld that unless he is mourned and buried, Elpenor will become a *mênima* 'cause of *mênis*' to someone's disadvantage in the gods' eyes (*Odyssey* 11.73). At issue is the cosmic status of the dead man's *psukhḗ*, whose transition to Hades is ensured by the funeral ritual that the living are obliged to enact (*Iliad* 23.71ff.); the *psukhḗ* belongs with its like in the lower world.[1]

As much power and danger, however, accrue to the epic character who wields the ultimate sanction as to the one who crosses the uncrossed line and incurs it.[2] That is why Achilles responds the way he does to the dying Hector's similar warning not to make him a *mênima* 'cause of *mênis*' among

---

[1] The implied analogy between death, a passage to the lower world, and loss of status is not inappropriate. Compare Achilles' statement (*Odyssey* 11.489ff.) that he would rather serve a man without land in the upper world than rule all the dead corpses. Achilles may mean that the difference between life and death is incommensurate with social status, but he positively characterizes death as an extreme loss of social prestige, such that the lowest serf among the living is superior to the highest king among the dead; see also the remarks in Chapter 1 regarding the rape of Persephone, 23–25, 28–29.

[2] See again the discussion in Douglas 1966, 38–40, of the power and danger that goes with impurity.

the gods on the day when Apollo and Paris destroy Achilles at the Scaean gates (*Iliad* 22.355ff.). Achilles had just told Hector that dogs and birds will share out his flesh and that if he could Achilles would cut up and eat his dead body raw. Hector's intent is to save his body from desecration by alerting Achilles to his own impending death and to the destructive consequences for all the Achaeans if he carries out those threats.[3] Achilles' retort is a competitive assertion of fearlessness, power, and identity that is in kind, if not in degree, not unlike those found in other speeches over a vanquished enemy. He pointedly ignores the warning, and as he orders Hector to die, he also asserts his readiness to accept his own death whenever it will come. In fact, Achilles intends to be the instrument of his own death as well as others'—as Cedric Whitman put it, he has now become the "angel of death," an all-powerful figure—and so there is no limit that he will not at least threaten to cross.[4]

Aside from the paradoxical and dangerous power that accrues to even the potential breaker of tabus, another factor that complicates the epic order is the uncertainty of the world hierarchy itself, which is a matter of blood, social status, cosmic function, competitive achievement, error, and dispute. In the human domain, as in the divine, the hierarchy that *mênis* enforces is defined in a process of division—cohesive in principle but divisive in fact.[5] For the Achaean heroes at Troy, as Gregory Nagy points out, the division of spoils (*dasmós* [1.166], from the verbal root in *datomai* 'divide'), which distributes to each hero a *géras* 'prize' according to his *timê* 'prestige', inherits the metaphors and also the diction of a sacrificial feast (*daís*, derived from the same verbal root as *dasmós*), which is also described and conceived as a division. Even the word for the feast itself is also used for a share of the meat. The Iliadic treatment of this theme of division has distanced it from sacrificial ritual. The quarrel between Achilles and Agamemnon, like the one between Poseidon and Zeus, is over the division of booty and social prestige, not slices of meat.[6] Yet the links between the

---

[3] *Pace* Ameis and Hentze 1906, 2:427 (on line 358), who suppose that Hector is threatening maltreatment of Achilles' body; such maltreatment would only bring down *mênis* on the Trojans themselves.

[4] Whitman 1958, 207. On the conventions of such killing speeches, see Muellner 1976, 92–97. It is also true that Achilles does not carry out this threat. In fact, no one's body is actually left as prey for dogs and birds in the *Iliad*, Achilles' and the poet's statements to the contrary notwithstanding. The tabu against the desecration of the dead body stands, but so does the power that arises from the bravado to defy it. For more on the *mênis* attached to unburied corpses and to Achilles' identity, see below, 168–72.

[5] Loraux 1987; see also Detienne and Svenbro 1969; Nagy 1990b, 143 n. 40.

[6] For the identity of the "morceau du héros" in the division of spoils and the division of the

apportionment of food and the distribution of booty and honor are persistent and powerful. The blood sacrifice redefines and reasserts the hierarchical structure of the divine, human, and animal worlds, but that hierarchy is not limited to the relationship between basic cosmic categories. Within the society of humans, there are ritual distinctions to be made in the sacrifice. Different pieces of the sacrificial meat are assigned to different persons as a function of their social status.[7] As there is an overt social aspect to the ritual sacrifice, so there is an implicit cosmic aspect to the distribution of booty in the human domain, to which I shall return.[8] For the moment, I note that here again there is no sharp distinction between the maintenance of the cosmos and the moral equilibrium of human society.[9] The human social hierarchy is simply continuous with the hierarchy of the world as a whole.

The social/cosmic hierarchy is ceaselessly reestablished and redefined by communal divisions, sacrificial or otherwise, because in the society represented in epic there is no notion of value other than relative value and no notion of relative value other than publicly witnessed and approved exchange value such as that defined in a communal division. For instance, when Achilles wishes to express the idea of the absolute value attaching to his life's breath (*psukhḗ*), he says that other objects of value, such as horses' heads or sheep or tripods, can be plundered or won, but that once your life's breath has crossed the barrier of your teeth, you cannot plunder or capture it (9.406–9). If there is no way to plunder a lost *psukhḗ*, then nothing is worth as much as it. In Achilles' words, prizes like Agamemnon's are not ἐμοὶ ψυχῆς ἀντάξιον, "exchange-worthy for my life's breath" (9.401). The point is that in such a value system a hero can only approximate our idea of absolute value as a special case of relative value, the case when something or someone lacks any exchange-worthy equivalent.

---

sacrificial animal, see Nagy, 1979, 126–41, esp. 132, sec. 19 n. 3, on the use of the words *géras* and *timḗ* for "honorific portion (of a sacrifice)" and "cult," respectively. In sec. 18 n. 1, Nagy alludes to a brief summary in the *Cypria* of the *daís* 'sacrificial meal' at Tenedos to which Achilles was not invited in time, resulting in his dishonor (*atimazómenos*) and his *mênis* (Aristotle *Rhetoric* 1401b18–19; Proclus 104.21–24 Allen). Note also that the quarrel of Odysseus and Achilles in the first song of Demodokos takes place at a *daís* (*Odyssey* 8.76), and see Nagy's analysis of all these recurrent elements in a series of quarrels involving Agamemnon, Achilles, Odysseus, and Achilles' son Pyrrhus/Neoptolemos. Pyrrhus's quarrel is actually attested in the context of Panhellenic cult, the Delphic Theoxenia.

[7] So the phrase *daís eísē*, "equal share," used in epic of a share of sacrificial meat actually means "proper share in terms of one's relative status in the community" or "equitable share," not the same share for all. Nagy 1979, 128 and sec. 14 n. 4, citing Motto and Clark 1969.

[8] At the conclusion of this chapter, 50–51.

[9] For the nature of this distinction, so apparent to us, see above, 27–28.

The function of *mênis* is anterior even to the hierarchy established by the division of value-laden objects or subjects. It actually protects the rules that define exchange value as well as the hierarchy that those rules establish. The epic word for such a rule is *thémis* (θέμις), which is an inherent aspect of the *mênis* theme in several of the scenes discussed in the previous chapter.[10] Ares' desire to fight despite the prohibition of Zeus proves that he does not know what is and is not *thémis* (5.761); in book 15, Hera appeals specifically to the goddess Themis herself in her desire to protest Zeus's assertion of his dominion over her and his management of the war. Hera orders her to govern the *daís* 'feast, division' in the Olympian halls, but Themis is silent before Hera's indignation (15.87–103), supporting, by implication, Zeus's place in the hierarchy, not Hera's. There is even a passage in which *thémis* prevents mortals from engaging in battle with immortals (the sword in question is Poseidon's): ἄορ . . . εἴκελον ἀστεροπῇ· τῷ δ' οὐ θέμις ἐστὶ μιγῆναι / ἐν δαῒ λευγαλέῃ, ἀλλὰ δέος ἰσχάνει ἄνδρας (15.385–87), "a sword . . . like lightning; it is not *thémis* to mix with it in woeful battle, but fear keeps men away from it."[11]

*Thémistes*, the concrete plural of *thémis*,[12] are not just rules that enforce the cosmic hierarchy, however. They are also rules for social behavior, including rules that govern the division and reciprocal exchange of goods.[13] As Emile Benveniste has shown, the *thémistes* are not "arbitrary rules invented by those who apply them: they are of divine origin."[14] In fact, they

---

[10] See above, 6–7, 11.

[11] Poseidon's weapon is here associated with Zeus's thunderbolt, the instrument of his *mênis* as has been noted above, 6–7.

[12] For the semantic typology of abstract singular noun > concrete plural noun, compare English parallels such as liberty > liberties, art > arts, etc., and see Wackernagel 1950, 92–93.

[13] On reciprocal exchange in social institutions, the monograph of Marcel Mauss (1925) is fundamental. It has been translated into English twice, Mauss (1967) and Mauss (1990). For the vocabulary of exchange in Ancient Greek, see Benveniste 1966a. There are important clarifications of Mauss in Sahlins 1972 and an application of Mauss's theory to Homeric epic in Finley 1977.

[14] The meaning of the Indo-European root of *thémis*, \**dhē-*, is "create and define, establish in existence," Benveniste 1969, 2:104. I disagree, however, with Benveniste's statement that *thémis* concerns the *génos* 'family' and *díkē* 'justice' is inter-familial. Though supported by comparative evidence and perhaps vestigial in epic, the distinction is belied by examples he himself provides (*Iliad* 9.97) as well as by passages such as 1.237–39 and 16.387–88 (cited just hereafter). If the *thémistes* belong to the king, he uses them to adjudicate disputes εἰν ἀγορῇ, "in the assembly" (16.387), not just within the family. The goddess Themis, we learn, "dissolves and seats assemblies of men" (*Odyssey* 2.68–69) as well as "ruling the equal feast in the divine household" (*Iliad* 14.95). J.-P. Vernant and Marcel Detienne's definition of the function of *thémis* is pertinent: "Her role is to indicate what is forbidden, what frontiers must not be crossed, and the hierarchy that must be respected for each individual to be kept forever within the limits of his own domain and status." See also Detienne 1973, 43; and for bibliography on this word, Lloyd-Jones 1983, 186–87, with addendum on 249 (wherein read "P. 186" for "P. 166").

come from Zeus himself, who provides them to the king along with the scepter (*Iliad* 1.238–39, 9.97–99).¹⁵ The violation of such rules provokes *mênis* from Zeus against the whole community. The point is explicit in the following passage, a generic image from a simile in which the word *ópis*, as elsewhere, functions as a synonym of *mênis*.¹⁶

> ὅτε λαβρότατον χέει ὕδωρ
> Ζεύς, ὅτε δή ῥ' ἄνδρεσσι κοτεσσάμενος χαλεπήνῃ
> οἳ βίῃ εἰν ἀγορῇ <u>σκολιὰς κρίνωσι θέμιστας</u>
> ἐκ δὲ δίκην ἐλάσωσι, <u>θεῶν ὄπιν οὐκ ἀλέγοντες</u>·
> τῶν δέ τε πάντες μὲν ποταμοὶ πλήθουσι ῥέοντες,
> πολλὰς δὲ κλιτῦς τότ' ἀποτμήγουσι χαράδραι,
> ἐς δ' ἅλα πορφυρέην μεγάλα στενάχουσι ῥέουσαι
> ἐξ ὀρέων ἐπικάρ, μινύθει δέ τε ἔργ' ἀνθρώπων.

> when Zeus pours down torrential rain, when he acts harshly out of anger at men whose judgments violently <u>twist the *thémistes*</u> in the assembly and who <u>drive out justice [*díkē*] without a care for the *ópis* of the gods</u>; all of their flowing rivers are filled, and then torrents chop off hunks of slope and they flow down head first to the purple sea from the mountains, and the fields of men decrease.
>
> (16.385–92)

Here the storm from Zeus destroys by water rather than fire, but the language of this offense and the broad swath of destruction it results in are by now familiar aspects of the *mênis* theme. From the comparative perspective of Marcel Mauss, it is clear why the violation of social rules like those that govern the exchange and distribution of goods should have direct cosmic consequences. In his terms, reciprocal exchange is a "total social phenomenon." Exchange rules govern economic, political, legal, religious, and moral institutions, and in archaic societies, "social phenomena are not discrete: each phenomenon contains all the threads of which the social fabric is composed."¹⁷ Under such circumstances, the violation of a rule

---

¹⁵ On the *díkē* and *thémistes* of the king in Hesiod and Theognis, see also Nagy 1990a, 63–79.
¹⁶ Watkins 1977, 201–3. For the expression here, θεῶν ὄπιν οὐκ ἀλέγοντες, "not heeding the *ópis* of the gods," compare the functionally related phrase in *Hymn to Aphrodite* 290: θεῶν δ' ἐποπίζεο μῆνιν, "watch [root \**op*-] out for the *mênis* of the gods." The same association of verbal derivative of *ópis* with *mênis* occurs in the *Odyssey* (14.283). For the connection between seeing (\**op*-) and *mênis*, see Watkins 1986, 298 n. 26. A derivative of the likely Indo-European root of *mênis* (the root \**men*- 'mente agitare') is attested in Luvian with the meaning "see" (Starke 1980, 142–44.). For more on the etymology of *mênis*, see the Appendix.
¹⁷ Mauss 1967, 1.

about exchange directly jeopardizes the whole social fabric. It is easy to understand, then, why exchange rules have the same status as rules that enforce the basic structure of the world, since they actually do enforce the basic structure of the world, however much they may appear to us to govern discrete aspects of individuals' social lives.

Like *mênis*, which stands behind such rules, *thémis* governs the treatment of guests, who are accordingly under the protection of Zeus himself. In book 13 (624ff.) Menelaos, in high dudgeon, tells the Trojans of the *mênis* of Zeus Xenios, "Zeus having to do with *xénoi* (guests, hosts, and strangers)," which the Trojans failed to heed when they (plural, not singular) made off with his wife and her possessions, ἐπεὶ φιλέεσθε παρ' αὐτῇ, "since you [plural] were hosted by her." But Zeus will one day utterly destroy their city. To us, the insistent use of the plural in this passage is disconcerting, for we would blame the *individual* concerned for the abduction of Helen. Menelaos looks to us like an angry man willfully expanding his target. He is not: offenses that incur *mênis* are by nature group offenses. The logic of the social system represented in the epic requires the annihilation of Troy for the offenses of Paris; the literal notion that the Trojans as Menelaos's guests were favored by their hosts and stole Helen and her dowry is utterly consistent with the bloc concept of solidarity at work in all the contexts of *mênis*.[18]

## The *Mênis* Theme and Exchange Rules in the *Odyssey*

Violations of the proper treatment of beggars—for beggars are just a particular type of guest[19]—are as much a matter of *thémis* as violations of cosmic status boundaries. The *thémistes* about exchange apply irrespective of differences in social status. When Odysseus, the beggar in disguise, is

---

[18] Pierre Chantraine (1954) says that the passage about the storm sent by Zeus against the world of men who twist the *thémistes* and drive out *díkē* (Iliad 16.385–92) is consistent with Hesiodic religious ideas and not, therefore, genuinely Homeric. He cites *Works and Days* 240–47, where the "whole *pólis* together" (ξύμπασα πόλις) suffers for the offenses of one bad man (κακοῦ ἀνδρός), their *basileús* 'king'. M. L. West (1978, 216–17) on *Works and Days* 240 pertinently cites Iliad 1.408–10 on King Agamemnon's offense and its consequences for the people—they are the result of Apollo's *mênis*, discussed in detail below, Chapter 4—as well as Hesiod fr. 30 MW, which describes the way the people (λαοί) of the hubristic King Salmoneus were thunderbolted on account of his offenses (he acted as and claimed to be the thunderer himself). I agree with Chantraine about the consistency of these epic passages with the Hesiodic tradition, but I contend that they are not therefore incompatible with the Homeric world view. On the contrary, I present the sequential relation between Homeric *mênis* and the Hesiodic tradition in Chapter 3.

[19] Just as giving alms is merely a particular case of obligatory, reciprocal gift. See Mauss 1967, 10–12.

hospitably received at the hut of his swineherd, he prays aloud that Zeus grant his host, Eumaios, whatever he most desires—in this instance, that is surely what is happening at that very moment, the return of his master, Odysseus—for receiving him so well. In response the swineherd both deprecates and justifies his generosity:

ξεῖν', οὔ μοι θέμις ἔστ', οὐδ' εἰ κακίων σέθεν ἔλθοι,
ξεῖνον ἀτιμῆσαι· πρὸς γὰρ Διός εἰσιν ἅπαντες
ξεῖνοί τε πτωχοί τε· δόσις δ' ὀλίγη τε φίλη τε
γίγνεται ἡμετέρη·

Guest [*xénos*], it is not *thémis* for me, not even if a man worse off than you
    should arrive,
to dishonor [*atimêsai*] a guest [*xénos*]: for all are protected by Zeus,
guests [*xénoi*] and beggars both; our giving is meager but cherished.
(14.56–58)

With their anaphoric repetition of the word *xénos* 'guest, host, stranger', these lines are a vigorous, heartfelt statement of traditional notions about hospitality and even the inherent prestige (thus the word *atimêsai* 'dishonor') that a beggar gets because of *thémis*. The *Odyssey* massively confirms these notions in both positive and negative outcomes, in the reinstatement of Odysseus, the beggar who becomes king, and in the unavenged massacre of the suitors, those great abusers of the privileges and obligations of guest-friendship. It is not a joke or a secularization of a sacred notion, as some have suggested,[20] when Telemachus subsequently instructs Eumaios to do as follows to the selfsame beggar:

τὸν ξεῖνον δύστηνον ἄγ' ἐς πόλιν, ὄφρ' ἂν ἐκεῖθι
δαῖτα πτωχεύῃ· δώσει δέ οἱ ὅς κ' ἐθέλῃσι
πύρνον καὶ κοτύλην· ἐμὲ δ' οὔ πως ἔστιν ἅπαντας
ἀνθρώπους ἀνέχεσθαι, ἔχοντά περ ἄλγεα θυμῷ.
ὁ ξεῖνος δ' εἴ περ μάλα μηνίει, ἄλγιον αὐτῷ
ἔσσεται· ἦ γὰρ ἐμοὶ φίλ' ἀληθέα μυθήσασθαι.

Bring this poor guest [*xénos*] to town, so that he can
beg his portion there. Whoever wants to will give him
a scrap of bread and a drink. There is no way that I
with the troubles I have on my mind can support every single human being.

---

[20] Turpin 1988, 257 n. 40; Watkins 1977.

And if this guest [*xénos*] really has *mênis*, it will be that much harder for him:
it is just near and dear to me to tell the truth.

(17.10–15)

Turning a *xénos* 'guest' out of one's house against his will is a violation of *thémis* that can bring down *mênis*. Telemachus's remark that his *mênis* will only make things worse for the beggar himself is not trivial or inconsistent with other examples. A person aggrieved with *mênis*, like Demeter or Zeus in passages already discussed, is by definition alienated from the solidary group subject to sanction, and that person is often portrayed as suffering.[21] Such alienation would be literally painful to a beggar, who is so intimately dependent on the social group for his survival. Nor is the lowly status of a beggar incompatible with an offense worthy of *mênis*. To think so would be to fall prey to the gross error in which Odysseus's disguise later entraps the suitors (18.346–404, etc.), in other words, to make a crucial mistake about the status of beggars as individuals in the cosmic hierarchy.

But there is another dimension to this passage. The beggar in question is, after all, Odysseus, and Telemachus is setting him up to deny a claim to *mênis* against his own household, which is for the moment headed by his son. In fact, the *Odyssey*, as it does here, withdraws from attaching this theme to the actions of its hero. Odysseus's release from Kalypso's island, which starts the tale of his return, is predicated on the cancellation of a threat of *mênis*.[22] It is also possible that Athena, in requesting that Odysseus return, has implicitly relinquished her *mênis* against the Achaeans, incurred for unspecified events during the capture of Troy.[23] When Telemachus assembles the Ithacans in book 2 to complain of his plight and enlist their help in his struggle against the suitors, he tells them this:

οἶκος ἐμὸς διόλωλε· νεμεσσήθητε καὶ αὐτοί,
ἄλλους τ' αἰδέσθητε περικτίονας ἀνθρώπους,
οἳ περιναιετάουσι· θεῶν δ' ὑποδείσατε μῆνιν,
μή τι μεταστρέψωσιν ἀγασσάμενοι κακὰ ἔργα.
λίσσομαι ἠμὲν Ζηνὸς Ὀλυμπίου ἠδὲ Θέμιστος,
ἥ τ' ἀνδρῶν ἀγορὰς ἠμὲν λύει ἠδὲ καθίζει·

---

[21] See above, Chapter 1, for the distance between Zeus and the other gods and his attempts to make Demeter return to the *phûla theôn* 'class of the gods'. For the social alienation of Achilles in his *mênis*, see below, Chapter 5.

[22] See above, 18–23.

[23] Jenny Strauss Clay 1983, 51, 186–212, who has brought attention to the reference to Athena's *mênis* in the *Odyssey* (3.135), believes that Odysseus by himself was responsible for Athena's wrath. See below, 46–47 and n. 44.

> My household has perished; you yourselves should be
> outraged, and you should be ashamed before others,
> neighboring people who live around us; <u>fear the *mênis* of the gods</u>,
> lest in anger at evil deeds they indeed turn things
> upside down. I implore both Olympian Zeus and Themis,
> who dissolves and seats assemblies of men.
>
> (2.64–69)

The unspeakable abuse of hospitality by the suitors is not only shameful for others to witness but a violation of the rules of exchange that merits divine *mênis*. Telemachus invokes the relevant gods: Olympian Zeus, who stands for the divine community as a whole, and Themis herself, the guardian of the social order. He warns his fellow Ithacans that for an offense of this type, members of the offending party's solidarity group are liable to be caught up in the resulting retribution, whether or not they are blameworthy. So the Ithacans should be afraid.

Now this passage actually implies that a basic component of the story of Odysseus's return, the massacre of the suitors, is a variant of the *mênis* theme. Even though Telemachus is a youth and this is his first attempt to convene and address an assembly, there is no reason to doubt the legitimacy of that contention. Indeed, there is evidence to confirm it. In a supposition that appears to depend on this speech of Telemachus, Antinoos uses the verb *apomēniō* 'invoke *mênis*' of Telemachus in predicting his willingness to provoke resentment against the suitors for their plot to kill him (16.378), and Eumaios and Philoitios, Odysseus's trusty servants, both ascribe to the suitors a disregard for *ópis*, which is, as mentioned, a virtual synonym of *mênis* (14.82, 20.215).[24] Lastly in his first Cretan lie, the disguised Odysseus pointedly refers to the way a scrupulous Egyptian captor, suppressing his just anger at the offenses of the Cretan's men, had not slain him but received him as a suppliant and "watched out for the *mênis* of Zeus protector of *xénoi* [guests, hosts, strangers], who is especially outraged at evil deeds" (Διὸς δ' ὠπίζετο μῆνιν / ξεινίου, ὅς τε μάλιστα νεμεσσᾶται κακὰ ἔργα [14.283–84]).[25] A few lines earlier (14.156–64), after hearing from Eumaios of the suitors' abuses, the beggar Odysseus had sworn a powerful oath on the name of Zeus and the table of hospitality that Odysseus would soon return and pay the suitors back for the dishonor they were doing his wife and

---

[24] See Watkins 1977, 201–3.
[25] For the equivalence of suppliants and guests, see Muellner 1976, 87–88.

son.²⁶ The two passages do not seem unrelated. In addition, there may be a final, ritualized reflex of the *mênis* theme in the use of sulfur and fire on the great hall by Odysseus as a κακῶν ἄκος, "cure of evils" (22.481), once the massacre of the suitors is over.²⁷ A sulfurous smell follows the thunderstroke, which is the primary expression of *mênis*.

Ultimately, however, the poem mutes the idea that Odysseus's revenge is an expression of *mênis*. What eventually happens, for example, to the Ithacans whom Telemachus addressed, the innocent bystanders who have not acted in any way upon their moral outrage? In view of the intense social bonds in this world and the solidarity rules associated with *mênis*, this question demands an answer. As if that answer were the teleology of the whole poem, it is provided at the very end of book 24, where there is an assembly of the men of Ithaca in which more than half decide that their brothers and their children who were slain in the massacre actually deserved it, for μέγα ἔργον ἔρεξαν ἀτασθαλίῃσι κακῇσι, "they did a big thing in their evil wantonness" (24.458), using language that recalls the very beginning of the *Odyssey*, the seventh line of the proem.²⁸ So this first group of relatives goes home. They are not refusing to acknowledge any bond between themselves and their own children or brothers just because of the moral circumstances of their violent death; they are also excluding themselves from the fatal social consequences of any *mênis*.

The other Ithacans, led by Eupeithes, the father of Antinoos, do not share their view. They now set out to avenge their kin (24.470–71). Before they actually confront Odysseus and his family in battle dress, a brief conversation takes place between Athena and Zeus. The goddess asks Zeus whether he will make war between them or *philótēs* 'friendship'.²⁹ He answers:

τέκνον ἐμόν, τί με ταῦτα διείρεαι ἠδὲ μεταλλᾷς;
οὐ γὰρ δὴ τοῦτον μὲν ἐβούλευσας νόον αὐτή,
ὡς ἦ τοι κείνους Ὀδυσεὺς ἀποτίσεται ἐλθών;

---

²⁶ This oath deserves comparison, in both diction and theme, with the oath of Achilles on the scepter in *Iliad* 1.233–44.

²⁷ Compare the use of the same stem for Agamemnon's attempt to appease the *mênis* of Athena, *Odyssey* 3.145, ὡς τὸν Ἀθηναίης δεινὸν χόλον ἐξακέσαιτο, "so that he might completely cure the dreaded anger [*khólos*] of Athena," where the word *khólos* is functioning as a synonym of *mênis*. *Mênis* is the explicit term for her anger at 3.135. This is an instance of the use of *khólos* to cross-refer to *mênis*: see below, 111 n. 43.

²⁸ On the problems of the proem, see Nagler 1990. I shall return to the overarching significance of the *télos* 'outcome, end result' in mythological narrative in Chapter 3.

²⁹ For the connection between *mênis* and *philótēs*, see below, Chapter 5.

> My child, why are you asking and begging these
> things of me? In fact, didn't you yourself devise this plot,
> so that Odysseus would come and pay those people [*keînoi*] back?
> (24.478–80)

In the context of book 2 and Telemachus's invocation of the word *mênis* against the suitors there, one would expect that the pronoun *keînoi* 'those people' in a sentence answering Athena's question refers to the suitors *and also the Ithacans*, who are marked for *mênis* by virtue of their passive solidarity with the vicious suitors. In fact that expectation is dashed. Zeus does not pronounce himself in favor of their destruction. Instead he goes on to say that "since Odysseus has already paid back the suitors" (ἐπεὶ δὴ μνηστῆρας ἐτίσατο [482]), he and Athena should let Odysseus rule and make the Ithacans forget about their children and brothers (ἔκλησιν θέωμεν, "let us make a complete forgetting" [485]).[30]

What happens next makes it doubly clear that the *Odyssey* is subtly shedding the *mênis* theme in favor of something else. Odysseus and his father and son along with Dolios and his six sons arm themselves to meet the approach of the suitors' kinsmen. The scene begins to unfold as a battle, with Athena in the guise of Mentes urging Laertes to pray to Athena and hurl the first spear. He does so, kills one person, Eupeithes, and the battle is joined. Not until this moment, when, as the narrator tells us, Odysseus and his son would have killed them all (528), does Athena intervene as a disembodied voice telling the Ithacans to disengage and end the bloodshed. They retreat in fear, whereupon Odysseus swoops down upon them like an eagle. At this point, Zeus sends down a thunderbolt not to destroy the Ithacans but to threaten Odysseus with *khólos* from Zeus if he does not cease from battle (μή πως τοι Κρονίδης κεχολώσεται Ζεύς, "lest Zeus the son of Kronos will somehow become angered at you" [544]). Telemachus's implicit threat of mass destruction against this group with solidarity to the suitors has become a threat of divine anger aginst a transgressive Odysseus in the interest of social reintegration. Unlike Diomedes or Patroklos, who resist

---

[30] For the notion of numbing the powerful emotions associated with collective loss and death by the instillation of forgetfulness, compare the Hesiodic description of Memory, the mother of the Muses (λησμοσύνη τε κακῶν ἄμπαυμά τε μερμηράων, "forgetfulness of evils and ceasing of woes" [*Theogony* 55]) and Helen's "antigrief medicine," φάρμακον νηπενθές, which would keep people from shedding a tear even if they witnessed with their own eyes the death of "a brother or son by bronze" (*Odyssey* 4.225–26). For the relation between Helen's medicine and the Muses', see Clader 1976. The parallels imply that something approaching enchantment is required for the suitors' kin to relinquish a sense of solidarity with their slain relatives. There is perhaps a reflexive reference here to the function of the *Odyssey* itself.

## Mênis and the Social Order 43

the divine imposition of such limits and surpass themselves in the face of such a challenge from above,[31] Odysseus immediately and gladly obliges ("he was rejoicing in his heart" [545]).

How can we account for this turn of events? Not by suspecting the genuineness of the conclusion of our *Odyssey* or by impugning Telemachus's moral stance at the beginning of it. What happens in book 24 is consistent with the way in which the whole *Odyssey* treats questions of solidarity in blame. The *Odyssey* implicitly acknowledges the *Iliad*'s bloc solidarity rule for the consequences of *mênis*, but it consistently refuses to confuse offending parties with the groups to which they belong. From the very beginning, this poem is concerned to differentiate blame. Using language that echoes that of the Ithacans who decide not to join battle against Odysseus, the proem tells us that Odysseus's companions "perished by their own acts of wantonness" (αὐτῶν γὰρ σφετέρῃσιν ἀτασθαλίῃσιν ὄλοντο [1.7]) although Odysseus strove to win their *nóstos* 'return to light and life'.[32] Actually Odysseus is asleep when his men make the fatal error of eating the Cattle of the Sun. They all perish by the thunderbolt of Zeus, but Odysseus, albeit barely, manages to survive. Likewise, in the massacre of the suitors, Odysseus is at pains to kill with special brutality such persons as Melanthios (22.171–77, 474–77) or Leodes (22.310–29) but to spare the lives of those such as the herald Medon or the singer Phemius (22.330–60) who were forced to take part in the suitors' activities. He also learns from Eurykleia which serving women actually slept with the suitors, so he can slaughter them (22.441–73) but not those who remained loyal to their master.[33]

I submit that such differentiations of blame are impossible in the *Iliad* but that the *Odyssey* is at pains to legitimate them. The distinction is even a matter of formular usage, of semantic distinctions between formulas held in common by the two traditions.[34] In the *Iliad* formulaic references to *atasthalíai* 'acts of wantonness' consistently point to the responsibility of a whole group, including its leaders, for what it suffers, but in the *Odyssey*, the term is used to differentiate blame. For instance, in the *Iliad*, book 4, Agamemnon taunts Diomedes and Sthenelos as epigones whose second

---

[31] See above, 10–18.
[32] For this translation of *nóstos*, see Frame 1978.
[33] For another non-Iliadic feature of the massacre of the suitors, see Muellner 1976, 96.
[34] The observation of the existence of such contrastive semantics for the same words in the *Iliad* as against the *Odyssey* goes back at least as far as Aristarchus's view that the word δαΐφρων means one thing in the *Iliad* and another in the *Odyssey*. For more on the use of ἀτασθαλίῃσιν, see Clay 1983, 36–37. For more on contextual differentiation of diction in the *Iliad* as against the *Odyssey*, see Nagy 1974b, 138–39, on the word θεοείκελος; the restricted meaning it has in the *Iliad*, which is reflected in Sappho 44 (L-P), is not reflected in the *Odyssey*.

expedition against Thebes was inferior to that of the original Seven, which included their fathers, Tydeus and Kapaneus. Diomedes refuses to respond, but Sthenelos cannot keep from pointing out that "those men [the Seven] perished by their own *atasthalíai*" (κεῖνοι δὲ σφετέρῃσιν ἀτασθαλίῃσιν ὄλοντο [409]). He does not mean that the death of the Seven was not his fault, but that they all perished together and deserved it. Or again, when Hector addresses his own *thumós* 'heart' before doing battle with Achilles in book 22 and tells himself "but now since I have destroyed the host of fighting men by my own *atasthalíai*" (νῦν δ' ἐπεὶ ὤλεσα λαὸν ἀτασθαλίῃσιν ἐμῇσιν [104]) he is girding himself to go down, as we would say, like a captain with his ship, to take the responsibility that is his and share the destiny to which his actions have consigned his host. His resoluteness soon fades, but it remains a heroic ideal to which he aspires and ultimately returns. By contrast, the craven and distrustful Eurylokhos uses the same traditional expression to ascribe blame to Odysseus for the companions lost in the Cyclops's cave: "for those men [*keînoi*] also perished for the *atasthalíai* of this one [Odysseus]" (τούτου γάρ καὶ κεῖνοι ἀτασθαλίῃσιν ὄλοντο [10.437]). His "also" implies that Odysseus's blameworthy mistakes are now about to cost the remaining blameless companions their lives in the cave of Circe, with the further implication that, as before, Odysseus himself will survive.

So it appears that our *Odyssey* places a moral distance between the massacre of the suitors and the theme of *mênis*. Indeed, it is as though the Odyssean tradition constrains the social dimensions implicit in Iliadic *mênis* and domesticates its cosmic scope: the target is not the blameless and blameworthy alike but only the blameworthy, and the cosmic dimensions have been scaled down to ritual proportions, such as Odysseus's purification of his home by fire and sulfur. It may appear that there is a progressive evolution in social thought from the *Iliad* to the *Odyssey*, that a moral code distinct from a system of world maintenance is being generated. As I have noted, however, societies that are much less complex than those of ancient Greece maintain side-by-side both a moral code and a set of world-maintaining prohibitions.[35] This particular difference between the *Iliad* and the *Odyssey* is analogous to the difference between the *Theogony* and the *Works and Days*. The mythological narrative of the *Theogony* describes the emergence of the structure of the world and the principles of its maintenance; while in the *Works and Days*, the world that has emerged becomes more and more narrowly developed and described, and moral rules and

---

[35] Again, see Douglas 1966, 129–39; see above, 26–28.

prohibitions about more and more minute aspects of daily life are specified.[36] The second narrative in the sequence subsumes the prior one: the moral differentiation in the *Odyssey* knows of, can incorporate, and would be impossible without the demiurgic bloc solidarity rule in the *Iliad* narrative. The point is not that the *Odyssey* is more evolved and sophisticated than the *Iliad* but that within the Homeric tradition, morality is "invented" by the differentiation of the bloc solidarity rule which applies to the violation of world-maintaining prohibitions.[37] The contrast is more likely to be a matter of completeness in world description than progress.

The episode of the suitors' massacre is not a minor aspect of the poem's content but a central feature of Odysseus's homecoming, although certainly not its only one. It begins to make sense, then, that no one in the *Odyssey*, neither the narrator nor any character in the text, ever explicitly ascribes *mênis* to Odysseus in connection with the suitors. But this lack also makes sense from another point of view that cannot be separated from the moral one: the explicit central theme of the *Iliad* is the *mênis* of Achilles, and the Homeric tradition will not validate the *mênis* of any other hero. This phenomenon has already been noted within the *Iliad* itself.[38] In other words, the muting and transmuting of the Iliadic *mênis* theme into its Odyssean counterpart is an aspect of the traditional mutual differentiation process that lies behind the formation of our particular versions of the *Iliad* and the *Odyssey*.[39] From this standpoint, the concluding scene of the *Odyssey*, which effectively puts a seal on a morally selective, socially integrating revision of the *mênis* theme, seems to belong where it is as a statement of the identity of the *Odyssey* as against the *Iliad*.

This perspective on the *Odyssey* as a whole also helps us to understand why the cause of the *mênis* of Athena (3.135) is so unclear. Nestor is answering Telemachus's inquiry about the circumstances of his father's supposed death (3.89–91). He tells the tale of the Achaeans' departure from Troy and the parting of the ways between himself and Odysseus after the sack of the city, which was the result of the second of two internecine quarrels (ἔριν [3.136], then ἔριν . . . δεύτερον αὖτις [3.161]). The first quarrel arose between Agamemnon and Menelaos in a late assembly called

---

[36] On the structural distinctions between the *Theogony* and the *Works and Days*, see Slatkin 1987. In Chapter 4, I explore the relation of the *Iliad* to the principles of world maintenance set forth in the *Theogony*.
[37] On the sequence rules of mythical narrative, see below, Chapter 3.
[38] Nagy 1979, 78 and sec. 8 n. 2.
[39] On this process, see Nagy 1979, 15–25. See also the forthcoming work of Walsh (based on his 1989 dissertation) and its portrayal of Odysseus as the man of *kótos*, as against the *mênis* of Achilles.

to decide how to respond to the *mênis* of Athena (on the reason for the assembly, see 3.137–45):

καὶ τότε δὴ Ζεὺς λυγρὸν ἐνὶ φρεσὶ μήδετο νόστον
Ἀργείοις, ἐπεὶ οὔ τι νοήμονες οὐδὲ δίκαιοι
πάντες ἔσαν· τῶ σφεων πολέες κακὸν οἶτον ἐπέσπον
μήνιος ἐξ ὀλοῆς γλαυκώπιδος ὀβριμοπάτρης,
ἥ τ' ἔριν Ἀτρεΐδῃσι μετ' ἀμφοτέροισιν ἔθηκε.

and then Zeus devised a grievous homecoming in his mind
for the Argives, since not all of them were at all intelligent[40] or just,[41]
and for that many of them took a bad path
because of the destructive *mênis* of the grey-eyed daughter of a mighty father,
who made strife between the two sons of Atreus.

(3.132–36)

In an assembly called to decide how to respond to a god's *mênis*, one hero recommends appeasement through sacrifice, and the other is in favor of returning home. The dispute ends in a parting of the ways.[42] All these

---

[40] For the relationship between the words *noḗmōn* 'intelligent' and *nóstos* 'homecoming' in passages such as this one, see Frame 1978. Frame finds that a special sort of initiatory insight is required to achieve the "return to light and life" in a series of mythological contexts; these myths support and flesh out the notion that these two Greek words were derivatives of the same Indo-European root *nes- 'return to light and life'. On two other occasions, persons incurring *mênis* are said to lack *nóos* 'intelligence' (*Iliad* 1.343, 15.129; cf. 5.761).

[41] Although some hesitate to translate the word δίκαιος as 'just' in Homeric epic, there is no doubt that the traditional language is referring here to the kind of action that incurs *mênis*, which is not only foolish but also against what is *thémis* (for instance, compare the words used to characterize the behavior of Ares [5.761]: ἄφρονα τοῦτον ... ὃς οὔ τινα οἶδε θέμιστα, "this mindless one ... who does not know any cosmic rule [= *thémis*]"). Thus, Homeric diction is consistent with the terminology in Hesiod for just and unjust behavior, where there is no hesitation to translate δίκαιος as 'just' (see above, notes 15 and 18).

[42] For a series of parallels to the way in which the *Odyssey* presents variants of the quarrel that is the starting point of our *Iliad*, see Nagy 1979. The way in which Zeus seconds Athena in her wrath is typical of the special intimacy between the two that is built into the epithet she receives here (ὀβριμοπάτρη 'daughter of a mighty father') and reflected in the behavior of the two in the assemblies of the first and the fifth book of the *Odyssey*. The basis of Athena's intimacy with Zeus is her relationship to him as son to mother—in which Zeus is the ersatz mother and Athena the ersatz son (to be discussed in detail in Chapter 3). The gender skewing makes the relationship between them noncompetitive; in other words, they can be close because Athena does not threaten Zeus's sovereignty as a male son would have. The same issue lies in the background for Achilles, who might have replaced Zeus if his mother, Thetis, had not wed Peleus. See below, Chapter 5; Slatkin 1986; and Holway 1989. The close relationship between Zeus and Achilles depends on the relationship between Zeus and Thetis, as book 1 of the *Iliad* makes clear; in other words, Achilles is an ersatz son of Zeus, like Athena.

details sound familiar, but Nestor becomes imprecise just when he could describe what the heroes actually did to arouse the *mênis* of Athena in the first place: "Not all of them were at all intelligent or just and . . . many of them took a bad path." There are so many ways to account for the suppression of these particular details, however, that in the end their absence seems overdetermined. Acts that impose *mênis* are, as I have argued, violations of basic prohibitions, and a reluctance to speak of unspeakable acts needs no justification (which is not to deny that in appropriate circumstances, full disclosure of such acts can have admonitory value). Furthermore, Nestor may be inhibited by the desire or the need to suppress details that a young man like Telemachus should not hear. Athena/Mentes bowdlerizes when she tells the boy that "cruel men are holding his father" (1.197); cruel men are in fact holding Telemachus, not his father, who is being held by a sexy goddess, Kalypso. Athena's lie replaces the truth with a false notion that puts the boy in the same spot as his father and so serves her larger purpose.[43] Nestor may well have similar intentions. In the matter of his evasion, Jenny Clay even suspects, and not without reason, that Odysseus himself was the one responsible for incurring the *mênis* of Athena.[44] Yet it is also true that the formulation in lines 132–36 is consistent with the diction and thought of other instances of the *mênis* theme. The offense is social ("not all of them"), whether or not an individual is responsible from our standpoint, and the response is broad and indiscriminate ("many of them"). Finally, this whole episode is another potentially Iliadic *mênis* tale that the *Odyssey* will broach, encapsulate, and veer away from.

## Exchange Rules and the *Mênis* Theme in the *Iliad*

As I have said, in book 13 of the *Iliad* (624ff.) Menelaos effectively characterizes the Achaean expedition against Troy to retrieve Helen as an expression of the *mênis* of Zeus Xenios. Not only is the offense a group offense—Menelaos maintains that the Trojans were Helen's guests and then stole her—but so also is the response a group effort to achieve either the return of Helen and her possessions or the devastation of the Trojans' city. Two other passages appear directly related to this one. There is a moment

[43] She behaves like a father to him, but also she has contrived things so that Telemachus reminds himself of his father and vice versa. As explained in Nagy 1974b, 266–69, *Men*-tes' purpose is formulated as putting *ménos* 'mental energy' and *thársos* 'courage' inside Telemachus and Athena/Mentes "reminded [*hupémnēsen*] him of his father more than before" (*Odyssey* 1.320–22).

[44] Clay 1983. Odysseus's long-delayed return may also correlate with a failure of intelligence and with divine *mênis*. See note 23, above.

in Achilles' *aristeía* in which he himself is likened to divine *mênis*—that is, not to a divinity with *mênis* but to the *mênis* itself—unleashed upon a blazing city:

> Τρῶας ὁμῶς αὐτούς τ' ὄλεκεν καὶ μώνυχας ἵππους.
> ὡς δ' ὅτε καπνὸς ἰὼν εἰς οὐρανὸν εὐρὺν ἵκηται
> ἄστεος αἰθομένοιο, θεῶν δέ ἑ <u>μῆνις</u> ἀνῆκε,
> πᾶσι δ' ἔθηκε πόνον, πολλοῖσι δὲ κήδε' ἐφῆκεν,
> ὣς Ἀχιλεὺς Τρώεσσι πόνον καὶ κήδε' ἔθηκεν.

> He kept on destroying Trojans and their horses as well,
> as when smoke going up reaches the wide heaven
> when a city is ablaze, and the <u>mênis</u> of the gods sent it up,
> and made toil for all and attached woes to many,
> so Achilles made toil and woes for the Trojans.

(21.521-25)

The language and syntax of the simile echo the description of Achilles' *mênis* in the prologue to the *Iliad*. In both contexts, the noun *mênis* is the subject of three active verbs: ἀνῆκε, ἔθηκε, ἐφῆκεν; versus ἔθηκε, προΐαψεν, τεῦχε (1.2, 3, 4). In both places, two of the sentences have complements stressing the social scope of the destruction wrought by *mênis*: μυρί' ... <u>ἄλγεα</u> [countless woes] ἔθηκε (1.2) and <u>πολλὰς</u> ... <u>ψυχὰς</u> προΐαψεν [many *psūkhaí*] (1.3), versus πᾶσι δ' ἔθηκε πόνον [woe on all] and πολλοῖσι δὲ κήδεα [many woes] ἐφῆκεν (21.524). So Achilles has come to *resemble* the sanction against the Trojans that Menelaos had spoken of as something real. As *mênis* has now become a metaphor for Achilles rather than his attribute, so also the social target of this now metaphorical *mênis* has been transferred from Achaeans to Trojans.[45] Both changes bespeak the distance the hero has by now put between himself and *mênis*.[46]

It may appear that the following lines also refer to the *mênis* of Zeus Xenios against the Trojans:

> ἀλλ' ἄγε τῷδ' ἔφες ἀνδρὶ βέλος, Διὶ χεῖρας ἀνασχών,
> ὅς τις ὅδε κρατέει, καὶ δὴ κακὰ πολλὰ ἔοργε
> Τρῶας, ἐπεὶ πολλῶν τε καὶ ἐσθλῶν γούνατ' ἔλυσεν·
> εἰ μή τις θεός ἐστι κοτεσσάμενος Τρώεσσιν
> ἱρῶν <u>μηνίσας</u>· χαλεπὴ δὲ θεοῦ ἔπι <u>μῆνις</u>.

---

[45] On the theme of the *transfert du mal*, see Nagy 1976.
[46] For more on this passage and the overall trajectory of Achilles' *mênis*, see below, Chapter 5.

*Mênis* and the Social Order   49

> up and raise your hands to Zeus and let loose an arrow at this man
> whoever he is in his power, who has wrought much havoc already
> upon the Trojans, since he has unstrung the knees of many brave men;
> unless he is some god angered at the Trojans,
> one with *mênis* on account of a sacrifice;[47] the *mênis* of a god is hard to bear.
>
> (5.174–78)

This passage occurs during the *aristeía* of Diomedes, when Aeneas tells Pandaros to shoot the man and end the massive slaughter he is causing—unless, that is, he is a god with *mênis*. In response, Pandaros says that he recognizes the hero's shield, helmet, and horses as Diomedes', but he also allows that he does not know for certain if Diomedes is really a god; at the very least, he decides, there is an angry god beside Diomedes protecting him from Pandaros's arrows, which are useless even though they hit their mark. So here is a third reference to divine *mênis* against the Trojans in the context of an Achaean warrior's efforts.

However, the generic nature of the descriptions in these last two examples argues against a specific reference in either of them to Menelaos's claim of divine *mênis* against the Trojans for the abduction of Helen (13.624). From the standpoint of traditional poetics, it is likely that the reverse is true, that Menelaos's citation of the *mênis* of Zeus Xenios at the Trojans is a specific reflex of a conventional association of the devastation of *mênis* with a victor's speech over his fallen enemy, which is the context of both his and Achilles' invocation of the word; Aeneas's use of the term in anticipation of a losing confrontation in battle can be understood as an extension from such a context. In other words, it is not possible to claim with confidence that the last two passages cited are examples of *mênis* as a sanction for the violation of the rules of reciprocal exchange in connection with the abduction of Helen. They may also be "generic" examples of the *mênis* theme that are vague or inexplicit in regard to cause since in those particular contexts it is the consequences of *mênis* that are significant, not its cause; there may well be other factors that come into play, such as a general reticence about acts that provoke *mênis*.[48] Whatever the reasons for this

---

[47] "Sacrificial offering" is the consistent meaning of the substantive ἱρά in epic; Aeneas offers the violation of a ritual tabu as a typical provocation of divine *mênis*. Even so, the language and the context in which it lies cannot be said to rule out a reference to the abduction of Helen. Aeneas may be willfully vague: there is an exact parallel that features the same willful vagueness ("a prayer" or "a sacrifice") concerning the well-known cause of a god's *mênis* in *Iliad* 1.64–65. On the other hand, the parallel itself suggests that desecrated prayers or sacrifices are in fact generic causes of *mênis*.

[48] See above, 30–31, 47; for more on *mênis* as a tabu word in itself, see below, 124 n. 65, and the Appendix.

particular silence, it is worth recognizing that these passages do voice other recurrent aspects of the *mênis* theme: group offenses incur *mênis* (as in *Iliad* 5.177, κοτεσσάμενος Τρώεσσιν "angered at the Trojans"), which is a sanction characterized by implacable, usually fiery devastation on a massive scale.

My survey of the uses of *mênis* is almost at an end, but I have postponed discussing three instances: the *mênis* of Apollo (*Iliad* 1.75), Agamemnon (1.247), and Achilles (1.1, etc.). Before I consider them, I wish to investigate the mythical backdrop of the *mênis* theme, a backdrop that I believe they presuppose. For the moment, I note that in all three cases, *mênis* is incurred by violations of the value system based on group distribution and reciprocal exchange. Apollo's is incurred by Agamemnon's refusal to accept an exchange with the priest Chryses for a woman awarded to Agamemnon even though the same community that awarded the woman approves the exchange (1.22–23). Agamemnon's is incurred by Achilles' unwillingness to honor his superior authority (1.185–86), as established in the communal division of plunder (1.119–20, 166–67). Achilles' is incurred by Agamemnon's depriving him of the symbol of prestige provided him in the communal division (1.391–92). In each instance, someone's social prestige (*timê*) is at issue. The priest is dishonored (1.11); Achilles is dishonored (1.171); Agamemnon is dishonored by the loss of his prize and by Achilles' disrespect (1.118–20, 175). In a hierarchy established by a communal division based on the rules of exchange, a person's social value is in view and at stake in every exchange in which he or she takes part. Moreover, a slight to a person's authority or rank is the same thing as an offense against the rules of reciprocal exchange, which support and define that rank. The connection between social status and exchange rules explains why in book 15 (185–99) Poseidon immediately refers to the story of the distribution of the cosmos when Zeus does not treat him as an equal, and why a botched prayer or sacrifice—prayers and sacrifices are transactions based on the rules of reciprocal exchange—can be experienced as an offense to a person's or a god's status (the word is the same for both: *timê*). If you do not accept or provide my gift, that is because you do not consider me worthy of exchange with you or because what you are offering or being offered is an inappropriate return; likewise, if you do not accept my authority over you, you reject the system of distribution and exchange that justifies my rank relative to yours. Since the rules of exchange are *thémistes* whose violation threatens the structure of the world, the world's coherence is menaced by an offense to them. From this perspective, the unity of all the examples of the *mênis* theme discussed thus far as well as those in the first book of the *Iliad* can emerge: when a person dies, or a hero surpasses himself, or a god ignores the rank of another god, or a goddess sleeps with a mortal, or a king rejects an offer of exchange, the value of a person and the continuity of the world are at stake because the hierarchy of persons based on the *thémistes* of exchange is being breached. Such permeability of the social fabric is characteristic of a "total social phenomenon."[49] The stability of such a system depends on several conditions: the means at its disposal to calibrate and recalibrate the hierarchy so that all understand and agree to it; a clear and common notion of the equivalences or commensurabilities of goods[50] that are subject to exchange or, to put it more simply, a shared system of value (not "values" in our sense); and a hearty adherence to the reciprocal rules of exchange and distribution that establish and match the shared, perceived, and acceptably recalibrated value of goods. In the world of Greek epic, these conditions are rarely met. Instead of saying that they constitute the system's stability, it would be more accurate to say that perennial difficulty in achieving these conditions is responsible for the system's frailty. What that has to do with the "real world" or the social context of epic for which this system is a metaphor is another question, but it is worth emphasizing that there is no reason to suppose that this system and the problems inherent in it mirror an external "reality." They are just as likely to be excursions from that "reality."[51]

[49] For Marcel Mauss's definition of this term, see 36 with note 17.

[50] Goods in the archaic societies reflected in the Indo-European languages comprise movable and immovable property, in other words, animals and people, on the one hand, and what we call objects, on the other. On this distinction and its survival in Greek epic, see, for example, Benveniste 1969, 1:37–45.

[51] For an attempt to link such features as the end of the *Odyssey* to a politically evolving reality, see Seaford 1994, 30–73. From my standpoint, the *télos* of the *Odyssey* is not an appendage but a goal inherent in its beginning (on the teleological nature of mythical thought, see Chapter 3). Moreover, I am skeptical of term-to-term (as opposed to system-to-system) correspondences between an epic text and external reality, since the myth is as much a coherent system as the society without. Social behavior in epic has the epic itself as its frame of reference, not the external reality (see also 61 n. 20). But I am in hearty sympathy with Seaford's assumptions about multiformity and his effort to bring to light the relationship between an evolving version of the epic and its social context.

CHAPTER 3

# The Narrative Sequence of the Hesiodic *Theogony*

The purpose of this chapter is to articulate the relationship between the Hesiodic *Theogony* and *mênis*, the starting point of the Homeric *Iliad*. The existence of a global relationship between these poetic traditions has already been postulated by Laura Slatkin, who has described its essential content.[1] Formal criteria also give us reasons to suspect the existence of links between the Hesiodic *Theogony* and the Homeric epics. Hermann Koller has shown that the *Theogony* has the structure of an expanded, even an overdeveloped *prooímion* 'prelude, song to precede another song'.[2] So the question suggests itself: *prooímion* to what? This chapter is an attempt to explore the possibility that an expanded *prooímion* like our *Theogony* had an outsized epic, an *Iliad*, as its sequel in potential performance and that in understanding both poetic traditions in themselves and in their relationship to each other the notion of *sequence in performance* is key.[3]

---

[1] Slatkin 1987, 259–68.
[2] Koller 1956; and Nagy 1982; revised in Nagy 1990a, 36–82.
[3] For the perspective of performance on the study of epic in general and Homeric epic in particular, see Martin 1989. I speak of "potential performance" because my concern is with the systematic and internal relationship between the *Theogony* and the *Iliad*, a relationship which may or may not have been actualized in performance. Note however, that Socrates asks Ion the rhapsode (Plato, *Ion* 531a) if he is *deinós* 'clever' in Hesiod and Archilochus as well as Homer; the answer is no, but the question implies that a performer's competence in all three is a possibility. Even more pertinent are the following lines, the starting point of a song by Pindar (*Nemean* 2.1–3): ὅθεν περ καὶ Ὁμηρίδαι ῥαπτῶν ἐπέων τὰ πόλλ' ἀοιδοὶ ἄρχονται, Διὸς ἐκ προοιμίου 'starting from the very point where the Homeridai, singers of sewn-together utterances, most often take their start, from the prelude [*prooímion*] of Zeus' (translation from Nagy 1996, 62). The Homeridai were performers of epic (here referred to as 'sewn-together utterances'), and from the perspective of Koller's analysis of the expandable structure of a *prooímion* 'prelude', the *Theogony*

Sequence in performance is not the usual approach to such a subject. For instance, an especially fruitful anthropological theory for the analysis of mythological narratives, that of Claude Lévi-Strauss, is based on a repudiation of the cognitive value of the sequential (or syntagmatic) dimension of mythical narrative.[4] He asserted that meaning arose in myth not in the horizontal dimension, not in the relation between the components of myth over the course of narrative time, but in the vertical dimension, in the persistent structure of their relation to one another at any given moment in time. In other words, the myth must be read the way an orchestral score is, vertically, not horizontally, to apprehend the harmonic relation between the notes that the instruments are playing at each moment. The formulation and the analogy are both strange, since people apprehend and derive pleasure from the sequence in a musical performance. Indeed, the sequence of notes is a critical aspect of musical form even for the most elaborate polyphony. In a different sequence, the music is either another piece or noise. Counterpoint demands the chronological dimension in order to be apprehended in the first place, on the principle that the apprehension of harmonies, like that of notes or colors, is fundamentally a matter of differentiation in context. The order of events has similar constitutive and identifying functions in narrative, mythological or not. Yet the rules for such sequences have been a nonsubject, as though they were inaccessible to analysis, trivial, or self-evident.

At issue is the whole "logic" of the movement from one event, one episode, to the next. For the analysis of this logic we now have a complementary anthropological model in the work of Pierre-Yves Jacopin, whose syntactic analysis of a single myth from one small-scale society in the Colombian Amazon is in marked contrast to the theoretically endless, constantly ramifying study of mythical variants that typifies the work of Lévi-Strauss.[5] I refer the reader to Jacopin's exemplary study for a fully developed instance of the theory and practice of syntactic analysis. At the risk of oversimplifying his work, my point of departure for an application of its results will be the formal rules for the relation between episodes. According

---

could be considered a prelude to Zeus. A highly reduced (four lines) *prooímion* to Zeus is attested in the surviving collection of Homeric Hymns as Hymn XXIII (Allen). Its way of encapsulating Zeus is to describe him in intimate conversation with his wife Themis. For the sewing and weaving metaphor applied to poetic performers and the traditional background of the Pindaric passage, see Nagy 1996, 63–86; on the relationship between Zeus and Themis, his second wife after Metis in the *Theogony*, see above, Chapter 2.

[4] Lévi-Strauss 1970, 14–16, and 1976.
[5] Jacopin 1987; for a more concise example, see Jacopin 1988.

to Jacopin, the myth has both a syntagmatic and a paradigmatic axis, and the "logic" of episodic transition along the syntagmatic axis is a fundamental aspect of mythical performance. That logic is *metonymic:* the relation of one episode to the next is like that of one stanza to the next in a nursery rhyme such as "The House that Jack Built."[6] With a kind of perfect economy, each element generated in one episode of the myth is preserved, assumed, and subsumed in the next episode, which then bases all its elements on the existence in sequence of the elements generated in the previous ones, such that the last episode, logically if not explicitly, incorporates the whole sequence. Each episode of a myth is something like a hollow wooden doll that can be taken apart to reveal a smaller doll within; that smaller doll, in turn, contains another even smaller doll, and so forth. In the same way each episode in a myth can reveal its metonymic relationship to previous ones by recapitulating them, and such recapitulation is a narrative tendency, if not a constant, of mythical performance. Nor is it important to decide once and for all what constitutes an episode. As disturbing as it may seem, what is needed is just a reasonable, functional demarcation of units that can be subject to analysis, for it must be admitted that the analysis of a myth is heuristic, not an exact science that arrives at some definitive and unitary truth.

Concrete examples of these abstract formulations are forthcoming. After a sample analysis of the beginning of the *Theogony*, I propose to apply this model to the myth of Zeus's succession in the hope of clarifying its unfolding meaning, its sequential relationship to the *Iliad* tradition, and ultimately, the relation of both the *Theogony* and the *Iliad* to the social context of their performance.

From a syntactic standpoint, mythical thought is above all teleological. The narrative is intended to justify the situation that obtains at its conclusion. So while the trajectory of the performed mythical narrative is linear, its goal is always uppermost in mind. That it is explains, at least in conceptual terms, why the *prooímion* to the *Theogony* can summarize its retelling by the Muses either forward, in performance sequence (45–51, etc.), or backward, in thought sequence (11–21).[7] Likewise, my metaphorical hollow

---

[6] John Miles Foley (1991, 7–8, 14) also uses the term *metonymic* in connection with the interpretation of traditional performance, but his usage and application of the term differs significantly from Jacopin's.

[7] For insight into the significance of the contrastive context of these two summarizing strategies in the *Theogony*, see Nagy 1990a, 57–58. Richard Hamilton's objection (1989, 11) that the Muses are called Olympian in the Heliconian part (line 25), is answerable; the prelude to the *Theogony* is globally a prelude to the Olympian Muses, and *they* visit the poet on Mount Helicon before being described as singing to Zeus on Olympus. The Heliconian Muses are a local

doll can be conceived either as the largest one that contains all the others in decreasing order of size or as the sequence of dolls in increasing size that constitutes it. The Theogonic myth has as its goal the creation of the world and the establishment of the kingship of Zeus over gods and men; in turn, it actually represents an emergent, not a permanent or rigid, solution to a set of problems that do not thereby disappear forever. As we shall see, the teleology of this particular myth can in turn become metonymized—it should be clear that I am calling metonymic an incorporating relation between elements over time, not within the same time frame in the accustomed sense of the term—into the starting point of another myth that is its conceptual sequel.

From the standpoint of a syntactic analysis, the teleological aspect of the myth exists on a smaller scale as well. Although it may at first seem vacuous to say so, each episode provides what is necessary for the next episode to occur. As Jacopin puts it, "Any sequence is the consequence of the one that precedes and the cause of the one that follows."[8] It is also clear that such a system of thought cannot have a starting point for the origin of the world that *we* might consider a logical point of departure. To put it more concretely, since a myth cannot begin with a logical "zero," it must begin with a logical "one." In the *Theogony*, which recounts the beginnings of the world, the starting point is the birth of a featureless being. Unlike the other primordial beings, the primordial Chaos, meaning "Gap" or "Chasm," has no epithets or descriptive phrases applied to it, and it is born from no parent (*Theogony* 116). Although this Gap may appear to us to be an empty space that the subsequent cosmogony will fill and so replace, at line 814 Chaos turns out to be located in the depths of Tartaros, with the hideous Titans situated *on the far side* of it. So Chaos is still there, now as part of an emerged cosmos. Instead of being filled and so *replaced*, it has only been *displaced* and bounded by the things and creatures generated since the beginning.[9] Chaos

---

manifestation of the Olympian Muses, not a different set of divinities. Hamilton (12) also considers the backward summary of the *Theogony* (11–20) "chaotic," but it is so only if one ignores the teleological in favor of the linear aspect of mythical narrative: its ordering principle is not that of an actual unfolding narrative but of its goal.

[8] Jacopin 1988, 151.

[9] This difference between the earlier and the later Chaos within Hesiod was well understood by J. Bussanich (1983, 216), cited by Robert Mondi (1989, 10). See also Mondi's own statement (32): "not the replacement of the original χάος by the structured world, but its *dis*-placement to the outer fringe of the world, in mythic space beyond the reach of normal human experience." I came upon Mondi's formulation only after writing this passage. His comparative and historical approach differs from mine, but our results often converge. I am not convinced, however, as he is, of the lexical independence, from the standpoint of Indo-European linguistics, of the roots of the words χαίνω, χάσκω, χάσμα as against χά(ϝ)ος and χαῦνος. Compare φαίνω and φάσμα with

is not at all a zero or a name for nothingness. Yet from another, contrasting standpoint, that of cosmogonic myths in small-scale societies, the parentless birth of featureless Gap as a starting point for the emergence of the phenomenal world strangely resembles a conceptual zero, though it assuredly falls short of being one.[10] In fact the *Theogony* otherwise betrays concern about its starting point: It begins with its own *prooímion*, a hymn to the Muses, even though it is apparently itself a *prooímion*, and this *prooímion* to a *prooímion* keeps on stopping, starting again (not less than three times [35, 53, 104]), and retelling three times in summary the myth it is about to perform before it actually begins to do so. At one of these stopping points, after going back to the story of his initiation (*sic*) as a poet, the poet says: ἀλλὰ τίη μοι ταῦτα περὶ δρῦν ἢ περὶ πέτρην; "But why do I have these things about the oak and the rock?" Gregory Nagy has convincingly interpreted this question as a reference to inherited myths about the birth of humankind from oaks or rocks struck by a thunderbolt; in his formulation, the poet is "asking why he has lingered at the beginning of beginnings."[11] This is not yet the place to try to account in detail for these postponements of the beginning of the myth; for the moment, I merely point out that a metonymic, syntactic way of thinking, in which a given state of affairs is always justified by a previous one and which lacks our concept of zero, might have trouble initiating a tale that is actually about "the beginning of beginnings."

Once the cosmogonic myth begins, it takes the form of a genealogical catalog with narrative digressions. Actually, these digressions occur only when the procreative processes that generate the world are disturbed or interrupted, and they explain how those processes are restored so that the genealogical format and the procreative processes it recounts can resume. In fact, there are two kinds of narrative: genealogical and nongenealogical on the way to becoming genealogical again. We may not be in the habit of thinking of genealogy as narrative, but it certainly is that, and it contains mythical thought just as nongenealogical narrative does.[12]

---

φά(ϝ)ος and πι-φαύ-σκω; the latter also has a strong semantic association with φάσκω, from φημί, to which we may compare χάσκω. See Muellner 1976, 104–5.

[10] *Pace* M. L. West (1966, 192), who asserts that the birth of Chaos without explanation of how or from whom betrays Hesiod's lack of interest "in cosmogony for its own sake," citing parallels from Anaxagoras, *Genesis*, and the *Rig Veda* in which there is a prior state of the world "on which creation supervened." I note that West offers no parallels from less complex societies. His come from archaic and classical Greece, ancient India, Phoenicia, and the Hebrew Bible.

[11] Nagy 1974a, 113–31, newly revised as chap. 7, "Thunder and the Birth of Humankind," in Nagy 1990a, 181–201, esp. 199.

[12] On mythical genealogy as an artifact of systematic thought, see Vernant 1985a, 22: "Pour la

In fact, the sequence in a genealogy carries meaning in the same way as the sequence in a narrative. For instance, the cosmogony in the *Theogony* begins with the parentless birth of a featureless Chaos; it is immediately followed by a list of three other beings whose birth or parents are also not spoken of, though they are endowed with features and attributes that make sense only in terms of their ultimate place in the created world—in other words, in terms of their teleology in the myth: broad-breasted Earth, safe home of all the Olympian gods, misty Tartarus, beneath the ground, and Eros, most beautiful of gods, limb-loosing dominator of the minds of all gods and all men (117–22). So the myth is once again looking forward and backward at once.

Chaos is clearly first (*prótista* 'first of all', not just *próton* 'first') and distinct from these others, who constitute a group among themselves. If Chaos is a kind of tangible nullity that is a precondition for creation, the other three are unparented initial entities that existed along with it. The first of them is Gaia 'Earth', followed by Tartarus 'Underground'. In traditional poetic diction, Earth is an adjectival genitive of Tartarus,[13] "Tartarus of Earth," as though it were not inside it but part of it or at least next to it; here, in the primordial state before such a metonymic relationship to Earth has come about, Tartarus is presented as a separate entity, no more "a part of" Earth than Eros; so in the next generation, each has its own distinctive offspring. Nevertheless it belongs here and comes after Earth precisely because of its subsequent adjectival relationship to it, in order both to explain or justify that relationship and to express a categorical distinction between it and Earth. Tartarus does not and cannot belong to Earth, cannot be "a child of Earth" like Mountains or like Sky. Instead, it is Earth's secondary and contrastive peer, another primordial place associated with it but having a distinctive identity from it—*not its child, not its parent, not its sibling*. Ultimately, what is being articulated here in precise and concrete terms is the conceptual disjunction between what will eventually become the land of the living and what will eventually become the land of the dead. Finally, the last primordial principle is Eros. In a cosmogonic system in which, aside from these initial beings, there is no creation distinct from

---

pensée mythique, toute généalogie est en même temps et aussi bien explication d'une structure." Despite this powerful insight, Vernant does not decode the syntagmatic aspect of the genealogies, as I am attempting to do.

[13] See *Theogony* 807 and West on *Theogony* 119 and 841 concerning the expression τάρταρα γαίης, "*tártara* of earth," a collocation that recurs in tragedy (Euripides *Hippolytus* 1290) and the Orphic fragments. The expression survives into modern Greek as well, as τὰ Τάρταρα τῆς γῆς, Lawson 1910, 98.

procreation, the sexual principle is a sine qua non, and therefore it is last in the first series of created beings. Not a spatial entity like the others, it is what has to preexist so that the process of procreation, which has not yet begun and is about to begin, actually can begin. In other words, since the previous entities (including Eros) were not produced by procreation, and since all subsequent entities will be produced by it, Eros could not be situated anywhere else in the genealogy.

This explanation for the place of Eros in the sequence is not contradicted by the fact that both Chaos's and Earth's first procreative act is without a partner. Until each of them generates at least one match (Chaos: Night and Darkness; Earth: Sky and itself), there can be no heterosexual procreation. So the underlying metonymic sequence is: birth (Chaos, Earth, Tartarus, Eros), birth-from-one (Night, Darkness, Sky), birth-from-pair.[14] The Hesiodic notion of sexual reproduction does not exclude procreation by a female entity without a male, only (and radically) its opposite, procreation by a male without a female; but that is not what is at issue here, in this primordial state of the world. Until there are matched pairs, it is not even proper to speak of male and female: both Chaos and Earth are as yet of indeterminate sex. That Eros is prior in sequence to birth-from-one and not intermediate between birth-from-one and birth-from-pair, as we might expect it to be, signifies that sex is a precondition for and a part of procreation, whether the birth is from one or two. To put it another way, since they procreate, Chaos and Earth are of indeterminate (or still undifferentiated) sex, not lacking in sex.[15]

We are witnessing, then, in these initial genealogies not just the birth of primordial beings, but the creation of procreation itself. If this metonymic creation of procreation had not been a goal, the first two creatures born

---

[14] Compare the remarks of Nagy 1990a, 76–77 on Hekate and the theme of the *mounogenēs* 'born-alone', which is undifferentiated into positive and negative valence; the principle Nagy articulates for that context is a metonym of this primordial sequence of differentiations.

[15] So it is misleading to equate Eros with *philótēs*. *Philótēs* demands the participation of two partners (*phíloi*) in sex; Eros, cosmologically prior, does not (*pace* West on *Theogony* 120; see *Theogony* 132 and 927, where sexual reproduction by a female without a partner is said to be "without *philótēs*"). Note that the steps in the creation of procreation are another example of the difference between a metonymic way of thinking and our own. The movement is not from zero to one but from one (γένετο [116]) to pair, from pair to (group of) three, etc. It is significant that *two* in this sequence is *pair*, which is probably based on the absence of interspecies reproduction in nature. It is also a factor that in arithmetic systems that lack a zero, counting is indistinguishable from grouping, as attested in *Iliad* 2.123–28. In order to express the idea that there are many more Achaeans than Trojans, Agamemnon says that if the Achaeans were divided up into groups of ten, and a Trojan was placed beside each group of ten, there would be many groups of ten Achaeans without any Trojans beside them.

might have been, for instance, a sexually contrasting pair like Sky and Earth, who could then begin procreating immediately. I also note that this metonymic process is similar to but by no means identical with a progressive, evolutionary process. As in the psychoanalytic concept of human psychological development or in the image of the smaller dolls inside the larger ones, the earlier manifestations are not eradicated or rendered obsolete by the later ones; on the contrary, later ones incorporate the former, which remain accessible constituents of reality and experience.

The foregoing discussion is a small example of a syntactic analysis of a short mythical discourse. It respects the coherence and integrity of the narrative and attempts to discover the consistent "logic" and significant thought processes behind its sequencing rather than impose a concept or a metaphor on it from our perspective.[16] The sense of the narrative would be destroyed or drastically altered if the sequence were changed, just as the sense of any story would be if the episodes were told out of order.[17] In contrast to a structural analysis of myth, the survival of a myth's variants over time and space is not obligatory to recover meaning in a syntactic analysis. The unfolding of the discourse itself provides at least an initial context in which the sense of the myth can arise. It is only an initial context, however, since the analysis of a myth should answer to the myth's functions in ever broader contexts. Such a method of analysis also requires that the myth's individual episodes be defined within the context of the whole myth; that the whole myth be defined in its performance context, perhaps necessitating explication of its relationship to other myths; and finally, that the performance itself be defined within the social setting in which it functions.

---

[16] Compare West's loose formulation (192): "The universe is, naturally [sic], built from the bottom upward, starting with the foundations (Chaos: see on 116). Then come the floor and the walls (Earth, with her subsidiary parts Tartarus, mountains, and sea), and the roof (Uranos)." West's house-building metaphor is interesting as an intimation of the metonymic structure of the myth (cf. the metaphor of "The House that Jack Built"). West's reference to his discussion of Chaos at line 116 is puzzling, since he describes it there as "the space between Earth and Tartarus," which does not square well with the notion that Chaos is "the foundations." Nor is the notion that Tartarus is a "subsidiary part" of Earth justifiable from the text, in my opinion, whereas mountains and sea, Earth's offspring, are indeed conceived as such.

[17] In Homeric epic, the desire to tell the story in the correct sequence is reflected by the word *katalégō* 'tell in order, catalog' often accompanied by the adverb *atrekéōs* 'not twisted'. The existence of the formula should in itself dispel lingering doubts that a Hesiodic genealogical *catalog* is a narrative form. Interestingly, the word is attested only once in the Hesiodic corpus (fr. 280.11 M–W), in the speech of Theseus to the shade of Meleagros telling why he has come down to the underworld with his trusted companion; as attested, the speech of thirteen lines contains at least three genealogies.

## The First Narrative Episode of the *Theogony*

It should be possible to undertake an analysis of the entire genealogical content of the *Theogony* along these lines, but that is not my goal. Instead, I propose to discuss the episodes in which the process of procreation here initiated and defined is transformed, disturbed, or interrupted, since those episodes relate directly to my overall theme. Without prejudice to any general theory of the structure of the poem, I consider the first episode to occupy lines 154–210, on the simple grounds that the narrative immediately before and after these lines has the form of a genealogical catalog, but lines 154–210 do not.[18] Moreover, form echoes function: the genealogical catalog is suspended in these lines because the procreative process itself is first arrested and then restored in them.[19] The narrative begins by expanding upon a descriptive detail in the foregoing genealogical catalog about Kronos, the youngest (*hoplótatos*) of the first group of children born to Earth (Gaia) and Sky (Ouranos), namely, that he was "the most dreadful (*deinótatos*) of children, and he hated his swelling [θαλερόν] sire" (138). At lines 154–55 it turns out that all of the children of Earth and Sky are most dreadful (*deinótatoi*), and the hatred that Kronos felt for Sky is reciprocated by him for all his children. In other words, the hatred and dread between Kronos and Sky are only a metonym of the reciprocal hatred and dread

---

[18] I take no position here on the overall structure of the *Theogony*, a subject best discussed in relation to an interpretation of its content. The issues have been treated by Hamilton (1989, 3–43), who offers a critique of previous accounts and claims (14–15) that the poem's structure is the one given in the third summary of the Muses' song in the *prooímion* (*Theogony* 106–13, setting aside as controversial lines 108–10; this is a minimal account—5 hexameters—of the overall structure of a poem of more than a thousand lines). Hamilton offers a severely limited analysis of the content of the form that he wishes to describe; moreover, he tries to describe that form without reference to formal features or compositional style. As a result, his description of the poem's form and his critiques of others' descriptions of it are too reductive, however commonsensical they may appear to be. Of previous attempts to account for the poem's structure, only Hans Schwabl's (1966, 1970) takes into account the formal features of the text, but his penchant for arithmetic symmetry has been severely criticized at the expense of his overall contribution. His formal analysis is based on the principle that formulas can consistently be understood as structural elements (Schwabl 1966, 6), but he says that his concept of "formula" must not be confused with Milman Parry's, since its value as a structural element is a matter of its function in context, not its traditionality. In view of Schwabl's own work and that of others (such as Nagler 1967; and Lowenstam 1981), I would suggest that there is no contrast and never was one between a structural and a traditional formula. The underlying notion of theme accounts for the structural phenomena with which Schwabl is concerned.

[19] Along the lines of Schwabl's formal analysis, I point out that the nongenealogical narrative begins with a relative clause—ὅσσοι γὰρ (154)—and the resumption of genealogy within the episode is marked by an echoing relative clause that begins ὅσσαι γὰρ (183); the standard-form genealogies (of the type "X begot Y," etc.) resume after the conclusion of the episode, 211.

between this, the first father, and all his children. No prior cause is provided for this hatred and dread (ἤχθηρε of Kronos [138]; ἤχθοντο of the children to Sky [155]), and none is needed; they are a given aspect of the primordial family (ἐξ ἀρχῆς, "right from the start" [156]), the point of departure of this myth, like the birth of Chaos in the cosmogonic myth. The hatred also stands in fundamental contrast to the *philótēs* 'sexual desire' but also 'love' (177) that Sky evinces for Gaia.[20] Whenever one of his children is born (γένοιτο [156]), Sky hides it away (ἀποκρύπτασκε) and does not allow it "into the light" (ἐς φάος [157]). Being let forth into the light is elsewhere a metaphorical expression for birth, as the absence of persons from the light is equivalent to their death.[21] The apparent contradiction between the children's birth and their not being let into the light is explained by the place in which Sky puts his children, "a hiding-place of Earth," Γαίης ἐν κευθμῶνι (158). In other words, once they are born, he returns them to a physical feature of their mother that has the symbolic value of a womb or a tomb. Their confinement within their mother causes her pain and sorrow (159–60). The language suggests both the pain of pressure and confinement associated with childbirth and grief at death (στοναχίζω, στείνομαι). Sky has put Earth in a continuous, deadly state of childbirth, with maximum pain and without issue or end. The children's death is impossible, but Sky's acts are an attempt to invent death for his immortal children.

This bad deed devised by Sky is a source of pleasure to him (158), in stark contrast to the horrible suffering it causes Earth.[22] She reciprocates by contriving a bad and crafty device of her own, first generating the "family of adamant"[23] and then fashioning a great sickle from it. The devising of

---

[20] It is certainly significant from the standpoint of the external social context of the myth that the first family in the world is characterized by ἔχθρη 'hatred' between father and children rather than the φιλότης 'friendship' that ideally governs family relations in the epic world and in daily life, but until we understand the logic of the myth in syntagmatic terms the significance of this provocative inversion cannot be determined. In other words, the myth is to be understood as a consistent system in itself, which must ultimately be set against the society's system as a whole to determine its meaning. Any attempt to find the correspondence between pieces of the mythical world taken out of context and pieces of the external reality can only mislead us about the goals of the text.

For more on hostility between generations as opposed to solidarity within them in this myth, see n. 47 below and the discussion in Chapter 4, 118–20.

[21] For the parallels to birth in epic diction, see West on line 157. The death symbolism is concrete in the name of the goddess Kalypso (from καλύπτω 'conceal') and in the consequences of Odysseus's stay *in a cave* on her godforsaken island: he is ἄϊστος 'unseen, dead' (*Odyssey* 1.235, 242).

[22] Bad deed: κακῷ ἔργῳ (158); ἀεικέα ... ἔργα (166). Devising: μήσατο (166), a term from the language of craft and cunning. See Detienne and Vernant 1974, 220, 229.

[23] This language is consistent with the concrete notion that metals are born from Earth, since

adamant is already a metonymic antidote to Sky's reversal of procreation, since it is a kind of generation from within Earth; moreover, Earth then fabricates something from it, the sickle (in fact, both of her actions here are the first instances of an important principle later in the myth, namely, the symbolic equation of the cunning creation of crafted things with the procreation of children). She then presents the sickle to her children and exhorts them to pay back their father for his prior outrageous acts (164–66).

Her speech offers no instructions on the use of this dangerous tool, but her children are all seized by dread[24]—all except Kronos, whose standard epithet, ἀγκυλομήτης 'curved- [or crooked-]plotter', is given here.[25] It refers to his devious cunning, which is in evidence in what follows and is analogous to the cleverly devised curved tool invented by his creative and procreative mother.[26] He promises her to carry out the deed, and she hides (κρύψασα [174]) him in ambush (in itself a cunning strategy that repays Sky's hiding of his children, 157) with the sickle. She also provides him with the tricky tutoring proper to an adolescent being initiated into adulthood (δόλον ὑπεθήκατο πάντα [175]).[27] It is no coincidence, then, that such a transition to adulthood is often symbolized as a rebirth, since the act

---

they come out from inside her; the same metaphors occur later in the passage concerning Zeus's thunder, thunderbolt, and lightning, which are always conceived of as crafted weapons like the sickle of adamant. We are told explicitly that before they were given to Zeus, great Earth had kept them hidden, κεκεύθει (505). Compare the κευθμῶν in which the children are hidden here (158). For another Hesiodic instance of a metal born from Earth, see fr. 287 M–W, the scholion to the reference to the "silver race" in *Works and Days* 128: τὸ δ' ἀργύρεον ἔνιοι τῆι γῆι οἰκειοῦσι λέγοντες ὅτι ἐν τοῖς μεγάλοις Ἔργοις τὸ ἀργύριον τῆς Γῆς γενεαλογεῖ.

[24] Δέος, referring in another way to their being δεινότατοι, 'most dreadful' but also 'most full of dread'!

[25] West on *Theogony* 18 claims that the ending -μητις rather than -μήτης is required for the word to be related to *mêtis* 'cunning'. This assertion is disputable (see Frisk 1970 and Chantraine 1968–79, s.v. μῆτις), and it leads him to the also disputable notion that Κρόνος ἀγκυλομήτης originally meant "Kronos of the curved sickle." *Mêtis* is consistently characterized as devious, crooked, or curved (see Detienne and Vernant 1974, 55). The point is that there is a symbolic analogy between *mêtis*, the sickle, and Kronos himself, not that Kronos's epithet literally derives from the story of the sickle (which is not to deny that there is a folk-etymological link between the two).

[26] It is also implicit in the word applied to him previously, δεινότατος 'most dreadful' as well as 'most dreadfully clever'. Earlier (137) Kronos was called ὁπλότατος, an expressive word for youngest (vs. the unmarked term νεώτατος, as in *Iliad* 7.153), with etymological and punning connections here to the epic word for tool (especially of a blacksmith: see LSJ⁹ s.v. and for further examples, see below) and weapon, ὅπλον. For the etymology, see Frisk 1970 s.v. ὁπλότερος and Chantraine 1968–79, s.v. ὅπλον. The meaning "young" seems to have developed from "capable of bearing arms" (therefore not "old").

[27] On ambush as an aspect of *mêtis*, see Detienne and Vernant 1974, 69–70; ὑποτίθεμαι is the proper term for instructions by an adult to an adolescent initiate; see Friedländer 1913. For the role of cunning in adolescent initiation, see Vidal-Naquet 1981.

Kronos is about to perform is a counteraction to his own and his siblings' "un-birth."[28]

Once Kronos is instructed, Sky comes.[29] In his desire for sex, he embraces Earth and extends himself everywhere (ἐτανύσθη πάντη [177–78]). At this point, Kronos seizes him from ambush with his left hand and with the huge, toothed sickle in his right hand he "hurriedly harvested [sic] the genitals [μήδεα] from his dear [φίλου] father" (180–81).[30] He throws them away behind him, and not without issue: here the first part of the episode ends and procreation is about to resume in dramatic fashion.

Let me recapitulate the metonymic logic of the myth so far. The point of departure for this episode is the reciprocal, primordial (ἐξ ἀρχῆς) hatred and dread between Sky and the children born from Earth and himself. As each of these children is born, he hides it from the light in a hiding place within their mother, causing her pain and grief: it is a womb to which he returns them as if to a tomb. This action on Sky's part is described by Earth as a bad, unseemly trick that must be paid for. It also arrests the procreative process that is the business of this poem; thus, it is not surprising if her repayment takes the form of much more tricky actions that are at the same time fertile. She generates adamant from within herself, as though it were a child hidden within her, and craftily makes it into a sickle, a tool for harvesting. She then gives it to her youngest and most devious son, along with tricky instructions, and hides him, in turn, in ambush. When Sky, hankering for sex in the evening, stretches himself around Earth, Kronos stretches out his arms from ambush and literally 'harvests', ἤμησε, with the sickle, his father's μήδεα, a word that means 'genitals' and at the same time 'cunning plans'.[31] Its root verb, μήδομαι, was the verb Earth used to describe Sky's devious, provocative actions in the first place (166). Compare:

πρότερος γὰρ ἀεικέα μήσατο ἔργα

he [Ouranos] was the first to devise unseemly deeds

(166)

---

[28] For adolescent initiation and rebirth, see van Gennep 1909.
[29] For the sexual connotations of ἦλθε 'came' (176), see Detienne and Vernant 1974, 67 n. 27.
[30] After the text's earlier insistence on the reciprocal hatred (ἔχθρη) obtaining between this father and his children, and given what the son is doing to him in this context, the occurrence of the formula "dear father" seems jarring, but one can compare the way that phílos is regularly used of parts of one's body, and see Slatkin 1988, 130–31. In fact, as Slatkin points out, only a phílos can be ekhthrós, since the word ekhthrós 'enemy' applies only to members of one's own group. The Trojans do not use it of the Greeks, nor do the Greeks use it of the Trojans; only Helen can be ekhthrós to both Greeks and Trojans since she has been phílos to both.
[31] On the double meaning of μήδεα, see Nagy 1974b, 265–78.

φίλου δ' ἀπὸ μήδεα πατρός/ἐσσυμένως ἤμησε

he [Kronos] <u>harvested</u> his father's genitals/devisings

(180)

So Kronos is also providing his father with the verbal fruits of his own trickery; the metonymic relationship between the words *mḗsato* and *ḗmēse* is not coincidental. It is even emblematic of the relationship between father and son.[32]

The castration of the father by his youngest son is a tricky act by a devious child with the help of a crafty tool devised by his cunning mother. Once he has acted, procreation resumes, first metonymically, from just the drops of the blood of Ouranos's harvested genitals falling upon Earth like semen or seeds; after a gestation period, Earth produces the Erinyes, spirits of vengeance, then the fully armed warriors with far-shadowing spears called Giants (their mythical variants are the Spartoi, the "sown" warriors who spring up full-grown from the Earth), and then the Meliai, ash-tree nymphs, ash being the hard and heavy wood used for warriors' spears. Giants are nothing more or less than walking spears, and the Meliai are their female counterparts; the paradox in the generation of anything at all from the blood of a castration is heightened and also explained and even compensated for by the spear's symbolic value as a warrior male's projectile cut from a female tree that springs from the Earth. But the ultimate paradox is the climax of the episode: the birth and maturing from the severed male genitals themselves, in combination with the sea, an element that is otherwise characterized as sterile and fruitless (in contrast to the Earth),[33] of none other than Aphrodite, the cunning goddess of sex and desire. The embodiment of female sexuality and fertility is born in an overt paradox from a violent act that should epitomize the vulnerability of male sexuality but is actually represented as a reciprocal, fruitful act undertaken by the mother and her youngest son consorting in trickery to restore fertility.

---

[32] I am suggesting that the metonymic relationship between Ouranos and Kronos is symbolized by the sound of the semantically unrelated stems *mēs-* and *ēmēs-*. The endings of the words, in one case middle voice and in the other active (-ατο vs. -ε), of the third person, are not part of the symbolic effect. Richard Martin brilliantly points out to me that an additional interpretation of the two forms is possible: *ḗmēse* could also be understood as the negation of *mḗsato*, 'undevised' as against 'devised'.

[33] See the use of the feminine adjective τραφερή 'ripening' to designate land in the formula ἐπὶ τραφερήν τε καὶ ὑγρήν, "over ripening and wet" (*Iliad* 14.308; *Odyssey* 20.98), as against the sea foam (ἀφρός) in which Aphrodite 'was ripened' ἐθρέφθη (190–91), from the same root as τραφερή).

To prove the efficacy of the myth's solution to Sky's trick, the mythological poem returns at line 211 to the form of a genealogical catalog. Nothing direct is said at the end of the episode about the liberation of Kronos's siblings from their hiding place; nor is anything mentioned about the physical separation of Earth from Sky that some consider the goal of the castration myth.[34] This is because the myth is not (or is no longer) concerned with either; its focus is on undoing Sky's strategy of exercising his male sexual prerogative at the expense of female procreation. It concludes with Sky's naming of his children as a group, in implicit acknowledgment of their birth, but he calls them Titans because of their overreaching (*ti-taínontas* [209]) and their bad deed (μέγα ῥέξαι / ἔργον [209–10]) and because of the payment (*tí-sis*) that will eventually result. We need not be surprised that the big reach of Kronos (ὠρέξατο [178]) is here extended to his peers. This instance of social solidarity is nothing more than the principle of metonymy (Kronos = the Titans) applying in a way that is no longer intuitive either socially or cognitively speaking.[35] It is worth emphasizing that instead of arresting the birth of his and Earth's children, Sky's strategy costs him his sexual prerogative altogether. At the moment, he is the one who pays by having his genitals cut off, harvested, and reborn into Aphrodite, the principle of procreative sex herself. Sky's attempt to suppress female sexuality in favor of male sexuality is a turn in a game of all or nothing, in which the only result of Sky's action can be its complete reversal. Female sexuality displaces male sexuality, as male had displaced female. That is the impeccable and extreme logic of the transformation of Sky's severed genitals into the feminine sexual principle herself (his mere castration would not have been enough!). But the story is not over, as Sky implies. The transactions, the metonymic sequences of payment and repayment, have only begun.

In discussing the *prooímion* to the *Theogony*, which qua prelude to a prelude as well as in its repeated stops and starts betrays concern about the difficulty of beginning, I mentioned the inherent difficulty of finding a starting point in a metonymic system of thought. Each step in the sequence

---

[34] For instance, West, commenting on lines 154–210, explains that "primitive man wonders why the sky stays so high and does not rather fall down upon the earth." It is also worth noting that Aither 'Bright Upper Air' is the first child of Night, born back in line 124. It is difficult to miss the resemblance between Chicken Little and West's "primitive man." On the contention of Marcel Detienne and J.-P. Vernant (1974) that the episode involving Ouranos is purely cosmogonic and to be disjoined from the following episodes, see below, 68–69 with n. 41.

[35] West (on line 209) is puzzled by the ascription of the reaching to the Titans, not Kronos, but he explains it by citing a summary of this episode in Apollodorus 1.1.4 in which the solidarity of Kronos with the other Titans is even more overt than in Hesiod.

is built upon a previous one, but the absolutely first step has nothing prior to build upon. The same difficulty is reflected in the conception and representation of the ultimate beginnings of the world; likewise here, in this first episode of the poem, the first extended generation of created beings undergoes a similar start and stop before it is finally "brought to light" (the light for them to be brought into having been created in the prior generation [124]). We have also seen a formal analogy between the cosmological and the poetic process present in it as well: the beginning of the episode is marked by the suspension of the genealogical catalog, and the end by its resumption, so that the actual form of the poem, whether genealogical or narrative, is implicitly at issue in the myth's first episode. Nor is it a coincidence that Ouranos closes off the story by naming and then etymologizing the name of his children (καλέεσκε ... φάσκε [207–11]). In an irrevocable acknowledgment of their birth and a last expression of his hostility to them (παῖδας νεικείων, "insulting his children" [208]), Ouranos is here putting the seal on this episode by assuming and resuming the genealogical poet's conventional name-listing and name-justifying function.[36] Ouranos's castration has in fact liberated the teleological nominalism of the genealogical poet, who had also been stuck at the beginning of beginnings. There now exists a starting point in terms of form (a nongenealogical style) and in terms of content (a nonprocreative father) to build upon and against. In other words, the cosmogonic poem has, among other things, actually provided us with a genealogy of narrative itself, in the specific context of the initiation of genealogy itself.

## Learning Metonymically, Part 1

When procreation resumes at line 211, it returns to the offspring of Night, as though her solitary generative processes, begun at 125, had been interrupted by the coupling of the primordial procreative pair, Earth and Sky. Actually, as noted, just enough of her children were born to enable the story of the first family's disturbed procreation to take place. Right after that story is over, important creatures for the next episode of the myth, which does not take place for several hundred lines, are born into the world: first among them (211–12) are Moros 'Fate', Ker 'Doom', and

---

[36] Functions of the poet that have been to the fore in the lines just preceding this passage on the birth of Aphrodite (190–200). For naming and etymologizing as distinguishing marks of Hesiodic style even in the context of Homeric epic, see the remarks of Slatkin 1991, 60–77 on *Iliad* 1.403–5.

Thanatos 'Death', who are soon followed (217) by the Moirai 'Fates' and the Keres 'Dooms'. Again, the logic of the sequence is metonymic. First the concrete entities are generated, then the divinities who preside over them. We have already seen how Sky's actions toward his children are a prefiguring of death, in which created beings are relegated to the space below the earth and cannot emerge; the issues raised in the episode as a whole about the limits on behavior seem to justify the generation of all these creatures. Their birth prompts the narrative to look ahead, with the teleological perspective I have remarked, to their ultimate function:

αἵ τ' ἀνδρῶν τε θεῶν τε παραιβασίας ἐφέπουσιν
οὐδέ ποτε λήγουσιν θεαὶ δεινοῖο χόλοιο,
πρίν γ' ἀπὸ τῷ δώωσι κακὴν ὄπιν, ὅστις ἁμάρτῃ.

goddesses who track the missteps of mortals and gods
and never cease their terrible anger,
until they pay evil vengeance[37] in return to anyone who misses the mark.
(220–22)

Mortals have not yet come into the world, and we have no explicit instance as yet of a god's misstep (παραιβασία [220]), but this brief excursus on the function of the Moirai and Keres is suggestive by virtue of its context and content: it immediately follows Sky's statement (210) about the ultimate (μετόπισθεν) repayment that awaits the Titans for their ἀτασθαλία 'recklessness, folly'.[38]

When the next episode of the succession myth does begin, at line 459, the language of this passage is in fact instantiated for a second time. The first instance was when Earth told her children to pay (τεισαίμεθα) back the outrage of their reckless (ἀτασθάλου) father (164–65). In general, naming is a metonymic process in which key actions or concepts are not namable (as in 220–22) until they occur concretely. It is as though a definition in action must precede an appropriate naming. For instance, immediately

---

[37] On the meaning of *ópis*, see above, Chapter 2, 36. The translation here is that of LSJ⁹, s.v.

[38] For the possibility of a popular etymological link between *ópis* and *ópisthen*, see Chantraine 1968–79, s.v. ὄπις. Moreover, Detienne and Vernant (1974, 73 n. 55) have noted a thematic kinship between these and other children of Night born here (Nemesis, Apate, Philotes, Pseudeis Logoi) and the creatures born from the castration of Ouranos, namely, the Erinyes (185) and the seductive and deceitful Aphrodite herself, with whom *apátē* 'deceit' and *philótēs* 'friendliness' are explicitly associated (205–6). It is as if the creatures born of Ouranos's castration are relatively positive, and those born of Night immediately thereafter are their relatively negative counterparts. Note also the metonymic relation between the two, not unlike that between action and naming discussed just below; see also below, 71.

after the genealogical catalog of the children of Kronos and Rhea, the narrative of the second episode begins with the information that Kronos gulped down (κατέπινε [459]) his children as each of them emerged from its mother's womb to her knees; and we are told that Kronos did so in order that he might not lose the "king's privilege" (βασιληίδα τιμήν [462]).[39] J.-P. Vernant and Marcel Detienne understand this to mean that Kronos was the first king in the history of the world, and they can point to mythical and cultic evidence in Hesiod and elsewhere that strongly associates Kronos with kingship.[40] Ouranos, they claim, is nowhere a king in Hesiod, although Apollodorus's summary of the *Theogony* makes him the first in a series of three (Ouranos, Kronos, then Zeus). Yet it is clear that Ouranos is a paterfamilias like Kronos, and that Kronos in several ways emulates him in the assertion of his power.[41] I suggest that Ouranos is a kind of king who is both a zero and a one, a proto-king and a non-king at once, just as Chaos is a primordial entity who is positively nothing. Ouranos is a father whose children are not actually born until he loses his gonads and a patriarch with no family to preside over until the very moment when he is displaced by his successor. When the concept of king concretely recurs, as it does in the case of Kronos in the second episode—and it is no coincidence that the word is not used of Kronos until then, when it is a question of his *losing* the title to the next generation—then the word "king" can be uttered, but not before. Perhaps this contention will be more convincing if I can point to more instances of the same conceptual movement from action to name. Clearly,

---

[39] The word *timé* 'privilege' is a complex one. Within human society, it seems to indicate the relative social prestige in an individual as recognized by his peers, but in the divine world, it denotes the particular sphere over which a given divinity presides and which is the focus of his or her cult in the society of humans. It is as though the mutually exclusive and perfect "division of labor" in the divine world precludes the social competitiveness of the human one.

[40] On Ouranos's not being king, see Detienne and Vernant 1974, 66–103; on the kingship of Kronos, see Vernant 1985, 27.

[41] It seems to me that Detienne and Vernant go too far in asserting (1974, 66–103) discontinuity between the Ouranos-Gaia episode and the subsequent episodes of the myth. For them, the story of Sky's castration is purely cosmogonic and has nothing to do with the struggle for sovereignty. Kronos's swallowing of his children looks forward to Zeus's swallowing of Metis and is unrelated to Sky's suppression of the birth of his children. But the cosmic dimensions of Sky's castration are actually inexplicit in our version of it, whereas its consequences for the future are to the fore. As we shall see, the themes and issues of sovereignty that Detienne and Vernant consider the distinguishing factor between the first and the other episodes are embedded in the dimensions of family life, in the contrast of force with cunning, and in the dynamics of sexual difference that are present in all episodes of the story. As for Kronos's gulping down his children, I will explain it in metonymic terms as a step between Sky's hiding his children within Earth and Zeus's swallowing of Metis; see below, 69–70, 91–93. In fact, Vernant and Detienne are unable to keep to a model that really does disjoin Ouranos from his successors, cf. p. 101: "Par sa position médiate entre Ouranos et Zeus, Kronos . . ."

The Narrative Sequence of the Hesiodic *Theogony*   69

it applies only to key terms that the mythical narrative is concerned to define and justify; if it applied consistently to everything, could speech ever begin?

In any case, the first act of Kronos was to gulp down his children as each emerged from the *nēdús* 'womb' of its mother, Rhea, to her knees (460). Kronos *gulps down* his children; he does not eat them. The significance of this strange act is syntactic and not simply a matter of table manners. The word καταπίνω 'swallow whole' is used three times (459, 467, 473) to refer globally to what Kronos does to all the children.[42] For Zeus, the last-born child, for whom Rhea deceptively substitutes a swaddled stone, the poem uses the same word (497), but it also provides a more precise and specific description (487): τὸν τόθ' ἑλὼν χείρεσσιν ἑὴν ἐσκάτθετο νηδύν, "then taking it [the stone] with his hands, he put it down into his own *nēdús*."

In other words, Kronos has a *nēdús* 'womb' as well as Rhea. When he swallows the children, he is doing something very similar to but significantly different from what his father, Ouranos, had done with him and his siblings: Ouranos had taken his children and put them back, once they were born, into a *keuthmón* 'hiding place, hole, cave' of Gaia, a physical feature of the earth that functions as a kind of proto-womb/tomb from which the children could not emerge into light. This reversal of Gaia's procreative function was answered by Sky's castration and the birth of Aphrodite. Kronos has learned from his father's failure, of which he was the instrument. At the same time, the basic terms at issue have progressed and been transformed from the primordial spatial anatomy of Earth's cave to the relatively anthropomorphic notion of *nēdús*. The anatomical reference of the word *nēdús* is uncertain, but two things about it are clear: it is more or less the same body part with the same function in both Kronos and Rhea,[43]

---

[42] LSJ⁹ defines καταπίνω 'gulp, swallow down (solids or liquids)'; in other words, as Gregory Nagy suggests to me, it means to eat without chewing. Aside from its use here and in later retellings of this story (as in Plato *Euthyphro* 6a2 or Apollodorus 1.20.3, etc.), it is used by Herodotus to describe Egyptian plovers swallowing leeches from the mouths of crocodiles (2.68), by Aristophanes of bad poets wolfing down slices of fish (*Clouds* 388), and on two other occasions of swallowing people: Euripides *Cyclops* 219, where the Satyrs ask the Cyclops please not to swallow them as he will his full pails of milk, and Aristophanes *Knights* 693, where the Sausage Seller describes the angry Paphlagonian as a storm wave ready to swallow him up (to which compare Theognis 680: μὴ ναῦν κατὰ κῦμα πίῃ, "lest the wave swallow the ship"). It is also the regular Hippocratic term for swallow.

[43] It seems to me unlikely that it means "womb" for Rhea and "stomach" for Kronos, as LSJ⁹ would have it. The distinction is ad hoc and makes the reflexive possessive ἑήν 'his own' in line 487 pointless. If its function was not contrastive, why use ἑήν in the first place? Even if a contrast between womb and stomach is there on the surface, the point of the diction and the story is that in both Rhea and Kronos, the *nēdús* has essentially the same form and function. Specific (mis)conceptions concerning reproductive anatomy and sexual procreation that lie behind this notion are

and it is a procreative attribute similar in function to the *keuthmṓn* of Gaia,⁴⁴ but evolved from it. The difference between a spatial womb/cave and a *nēdús* is another aspect of the myth's metonymic logic, in that the personages of the myth now can operate within an emerged natural world and accordingly have body parts that are distinct from physical features of nature. So in order to preserve his masculine, kingly prerogative, whose existence is in itself a metonymic step forward from the blank role of Sky, Kronos is outdoing his father by reversing procreation and *actually adopting for himself a female procreative function* (concealment of the children before birth) because he now possesses within him a body part with procreation as its possible function. Ouranos had only reversed female procreation and asserted male sexuality at its expense, with the result that he was irreversibly detached from his male body part. By putting the children in his own *nēdús*, Kronos has turned the tables on Rhea and put himself in the position that the "winning" side had in the first episode of the myth. Though their father, he has hidden away the children inside himself! From this perspective, we can see yet another way in which Kronos's stratagem is an incremental improvement over the first episode. Gaia had succeeded in restoring her procreative function by using her cunning and allying herself with her youngest male child, who was trapped within her. So it was an additive combination of female with male that defeated the exclusionary maleness of Ouranos. Kronos has gone one step further by cunningly combining male and female at once inside himself and in his own self to forestall his wife from doing the same.⁴⁵

But in more ways than one, it is just another fruitless trick. Kronos's preemptive strategy demands constant vigilance (οὐκ ἀλαοσκοπίην ἔχεν, ἀλλὰ δοκεύων / παῖδας ἑοὺς κατέπινε [466]), a measure of his cunning.⁴⁶ In

---

not clear from the evidence in this text and are not necessarily relevant to its meaning, either. Skeptics about the concrete parallelism between male and female *nēdús* might wish to consider the concrete, exterior similarity between male and female breasts.

⁴⁴ The parallelism between *nēdús* and *keuthmṓn* extends to the reaction inspired in the female by the procreation-arresting act of the corresponding male in each episode: in Earth's case, the pain of childbirth and the grief of death (see above, p. 61 with n. 20); in Rhea's case, the suffering of πένθος ἄλαστον, 'unforgettable grief', an expression associated with ritual lament by women for the dead. See Nagy 1974b, 255–61, Alexiou 1974.

⁴⁵ Note that he does so on learning from *both* Sky *and* Earth that he risked losing his kingship to his own child (463). This is another instance of the male + female strategy, and it explains why Rhea as well must have the benefit of assistance from both (470). She must stay one step ahead of Kronos in the metonymic race, and therefore it is essential that no advantage gained be abandoned. (I note that, from our perspective, which is not metonymic, it is senseless for Sky and Earth to help each side against the other.)

⁴⁶ For alertness and watchfulness as an aspect of cunning, see Detienne and Vernant 1974, 21–22, 37–38.

her grief at this clever new way of "unbirthing" her children, Rhea implores both parents to devise a (by implication, better) *mêtis* 'cunning plan' so that the birth of her last child, Zeus, will escape Kronos's vigilance and so that she may repay (τείσαιτο) the *erīnûs* 'furies, spirits of vengeance' of her father, Sky, *and* of her swallowed children (472–73).[47] Two things are especially worth noting: this is the first instance of the common noun *mêtis* in the *Theogony*, a term of capital importance in the poem. Here is yet another instance of what I would call "metonymic nominalism," the principle that a concept is namable upon its recurrence, as against its first instance. Just as Kronos is a king in name, as against Ouranos, so the *mêtis* of Gaia in response to Kronos's cunning trick is the first named *mêtis*.[48] Second, a single reactive ploy intended to repay the *erīnûs* of the prior and the future generation is represented as the first instance of "moral" retribution in the myth. Kronos's repayment (τεισαίμεθα λώβην, "we could repay the hurt" [165]) of his father was a matter of directly reciprocating one bad deed with another. Here it is a matter not of directly repaying the hurt itself but of repaying agents or principles of repayment (the *erīnûs*) that emerged in nature as a result of Sky's castration.[49] In fact, the fundamental terms of a reciprocal, punitive, self-justifying moral order are coming into existence and, now, into play in the world, as a stable sovereign order is established.

But how Rhea actually restores the moral order and defeats Kronos's vigilance is not completely clear from the narrative, which is as follows:

[47] Note that Sky and the swallowed children have *erīnûs*, but that Rhea has *pénthos álaston*, "unforgettable grief," instead (467), surprisingly so in view of the later association of *erīnûs* with crimes against mothers. In general, this myth concerns itself with conflict and its resolution between generations, and conflict within a generation is ruled out. Even the "solidarity" of Sky and Earth is unimpeached by Earth's instrumental role in his castration. This is a myth about succession, after all. It is important and significant that internal conflict within the solidary group of gods comes later, as a metonymic consequence of the establishment of a stable cosmic order. In Chapter 4 I take up the transformation of these themes into the *Iliad* into stories of intragenerational conflict among the Olympians. The only example of conflict over sovereignty by two members of the same generation in the *Theogony* is the conflict between Zeus and Prometheus, discussed below. But Prometheus is clearly not a member of a solidary kin group to which Zeus also belongs. He is a rival born of Zeus's collateral kin, like the hateful χηρωσταί 'heirs of a vacant inheritance' who win out when a mortal man dies intestate (*Theogony* 600ff.). In fact Prometheus's challenge to Zeus takes place before Zeus has any children! The kind of conflict that the *Iliad* can discuss, for instance, between Zeus and Poseidon, does not arise in the *Theogony*.

[48] It is true that the goddess Metis herself is born at *Theogony* 358 as one of the fifty Okeanids, but I note that she is not a functioning goddess in the myth until *after* the current episode. In more theoretical terms, my assumption must be that her birth *there* is related to a sequence that does not intersect with the one being played out *here*.

[49] As I have said, the logic of that sequence is apparent in that the castration was the first deed requiring "justifiable" repayment. But since it was the zero case, it was not carried out in answer to the claims of the *erīnûs*, for the simple reason that the *erīnûs* did not yet exist; or, to translate the language of the myth, the first act of "justifiable" revenge actually generated the *erīnûs*.

οἱ δὲ θυγατρὶ φίλῃ μάλα μὲν κλύον ἠδ' ἐπίθοντο,
καί οἱ πεφραδέτην, ὅσα περ πέπρωτο γενέσθαι 475
ἀμφὶ Κρόνῳ βασιλῆι, καὶ υἱέι καρτεροθύμῳ·
<u>πέμψαν δ' ἐς Λύκτον, Κρήτης ἐς πίονα δῆμον,
ὁππότ' ἄρ' ὁπλότατον παίδων ἤμελλε τεκέσθαι,
Ζῆνα μέγαν· τὸν μέν οἱ ἐδέξατο Γαῖα πελώρη
Κρήτῃ ἐν εὐρείῃ τρεφέμεν ἀτιταλλέμεναί τε.</u> 480
ἔνθα μιν ἷκτο φέρουσα θοὴν διὰ νύκτα μέλαιναν,
πρώτην ἐς Λύκτον· κρύψεν δέ ἑ χερσὶ λαβοῦσα
ἄντρῳ ἐν ἠλιβάτῳ, ζαθέης ὑπὸ κεύθεσι γαίης,
Αἰγαίῳ ἐν ὄρει πεπυκασμένῳ ὑλήεντι.
τῷ δὲ σπαργανίσασα μέγαν λίθον ἐγγυάλιξεν 485
Οὐρανίδῃ μέγ' ἄνακτι, θεῶν προτέρων βασιλῆι.
τὸν τόθ' ἑλὼν χείρεσσιν ἑὴν ἐσκάτθετο νηδύν,
<u>σχέτλιος, οὐδ' ἐνόησε μετὰ φρεσίν, ὥς οἱ ὀπίσσω
ἀντὶ λίθου ἑὸς υἱὸς ἀνίκητος καὶ ἀκηδὴς
λείπεθ', ὅ μιν τάχ' ἔμελλε βίῃ καὶ χερσὶ δαμάσσας</u> 490
<u>τιμῆς ἐξελάαν, ὁ δ' ἐν ἀθανάτοισιν ἀνάξειν.</u>
καρπαλίμως δ' ἄρ' ἔπειτα μένος καὶ φαίδιμα γυῖα
ηὔξετο τοῖο ἄνακτος· ἐπιπλομένου δ' ἐνιαυτοῦ,
Γαίης ἐννεσίῃσι πολυφραδέεσσι δολωθείς,
ὃν γόνον ἂψ ἀνέηκε μέγας Κρόνος ἀγκυλομήτης, 495
νικηθεὶς τέχνῃσι βίηφί τε παιδὸς ἑοῖο.
πρῶτον δ' ἐξήμησε λίθον, πύματον καταπίνων·

They really heard and obeyed their dear daughter,
and the two of them revealed to her as many things as were destined 475
to happen to Kronos the king and his stout-hearted son:
<u>they sent her to Luktos, to the rich land of Crete,
when she was about to give birth to the youngest of her children,
great Zeus; huge Earth received him
in broad Crete to ripen and rear him.</u> 480
*There she came, bringing him through black night,*
*first to Luktos; taking him in her hands she hid him*
*in a steep cave down in the caverns of earth,*
*in the wooded, covered Aigaian mountain.*
Then she swaddled a stone and handed it over to 485
the son of Ouranos, mighty lord, king of the former gods.
Then taking it with his hands he put it in his belly,
<u>pitilessly, but he did not understand with his wits that</u>

> instead of a stone his own son remained behind, undefeated and free from
>     woe,
> soon to subdue him by violence and hands and 490
> to drive him from his rank, and he in turn would rule among the
>     immortals.
> *Starting right then the courage and shining limbs*
> *of that lord grew; and as the year came round,*
> *tricked by the clever instructions of Earth,*
> *great devious-devising Kronos let back up his own offspring,* 495
> *defeated by the wiles and violent deeds of his own son.*
> *First he vomited out the stone that he swallowed down last.*

The first difficulty in this passage is stylistic. Instead of telling the story in linear fashion, it tells it teleologically; that is, it cannot keep from foretelling the conclusive events of each episode (477–80, 488–91) before it actually gets to them (481–86, 492–97ff.). This sort of sequencing is appropriate and even dramatic to an audience that knows and in fact anticipates the conclusion to its stories. As we have seen, it is also a typical feature of the metonymic style of thought, which is at once linear and goal oriented.

Indeed, in this case, it seems as though the poet is too interested in getting to the expected result. Commentators supply missing information from Apollodorus or the Orphic tradition about how Kronos was actually made to vomit up his children.[50] But the absence of such instrumental details is at least mitigated once we appreciate the reason for it. The birth of Zeus is like a stanza near the end of "The House that Jack Built" in that it explicitly recapitulates every step of the birth processes in the episodes that precede it. Zeus is born from his mother; then, like Kronos and his siblings, he is reinserted into the womb/cave/hiding place of Earth, and at the same time his father believes he is swallowing him down as he did Rhea's other

---

[50] See West (on line 494) and Detienne and Vernant 1974, 71–72 and n. 48, who cite Apollodorus (1.2.1). His account is that Zeus had Metis administer a *phármakon* 'drug' to Kronos that made him vomit (in support of which they cite appropriately *Odyssey* 4.227, φάρμακα μητιόεντα 'cunning drugs'). But the Hesiodic text calls for a combination of τέχνη 'trickery' and βίη 'force', which is, as West notes (on line 494), apparent only in the Orphic version (*Orphicorum Fragmenta* [Kern] 154), in which Zeus makes Kronos drunk on honey, ties him up, and castrates him. This story provides the requisite violence and cunning, but it still does not explain how Kronos came to vomit up his children. West (on lines 481ff.) also finds Hesiod "curiously noncommittal about where the birth [of Zeus] actually occurred." What concerns West is whether the child was born inside or outside the cave in Crete. This may be interesting from the standpoint of the next episode in the myth, but it is not an issue in this episode, in which the point is that the birth of Zeus was hidden, from us as well as Kronos.

children; then, by his own violence and cunning and with instruction in cunning from Gaia, exactly as in Kronos's case, he overcomes his father and so frees himself and his siblings.[51] The myth is more interested in recapitulating all these steps than in presenting all the details. In other words, its concern is with the metonymic logic and consistency of the story, not "realism." That logic demands that Zeus defeat his father by doing what the father had done and doing him one better: an act of concealment to outdo and undo Kronos's concealment of his children within himself, namely, the concealment of a stone in swaddling clothes and of Zeus in Earth. The fact that Zeus's way of restoring his siblings to the light is not explained but only named (νικηθεὶς τέχνῃσι βίηφί τε παιδὸς ἑοῖο, "defeated by the wiles and violent deeds of his own son" [496]) is another example of the metonymic "nominalism" I spoke of, whereby a notion such as kingship is capable of being named on the occasion of its second manifestation. Moreover, there is now a third in the series of verbal metonymies that mark the decisive steps in the progress of this myth. Previously noted were:

πρότερος γὰρ ἀεικέα μήσατο ἔργα

"he [Ouranos] was the first to devise [*mēsato*] unseemly deeds"

(166)

φίλου δ'ἀπὸ μήδεα πατρὸς/ἐσσυμένως ἤμησε

"he [Kronos] harvested [*ēmēse*] his father's genitals/devisings"

(180)

Now we have:

πρῶτον δ' ἐξήμησε λίθον, πύματον καταπίνων

"first he [Kronos] vomited out [*exēmēse*] the stone that he gulped down last"

(497)

---

[51] West assumes that the ἐννεσίαι 'instructions' of Gaia mentioned in line 494 are "given to Rhea." There is no such advice given to Rhea (*pace* West on 481ff., the narrative anticipation of the episode in lines 477–80 is not "the arranging of [the episode] between Rhea and her parents"); there is only the one μῆτις 'cunning plan' Rhea asks of Gaia at line 470, which encompasses the whole episode from the hiding of Zeus to the vomiting of the stone. The ἐννεσίαι of Gaia here are instructions to Zeus that fool Kronos (analogous to the ὑποθῆκαι of Gaia to Kronos in the first episode) and that are then combined with the violence that Zeus used to overcome his father; the violence is mentioned three times as his specific contribution (73, 490, and here, at 496).

This is the only attested instance in Greek of an aorist of the root ἐμέω with its final -ε- lengthened to -η-; elsewhere the form is always ἤμεσα.⁵² The line itself has a metonymic function, in that it evinces no need to speak of the subsequent vomiting of the other children: the freeing of one stone stands for the rest. It is unnecessary to add that the vomiting of the stone is Kronos's repayment for the castration with which Kronos repaid his father Ouranos's devious prior deed. Vomiting the stone also represents Kronos's loss of sovereignty to Zeus as well as his defeat by him and by Gaia in a contest of trickery, but instead of losing his masculinity, as Ouranos had, he loses his attempt at femininity, his ability to conceal his own children in his *nēdús*. The additive, metonymic verbal progress from *mésato* to *émēse* to *exémēse* echoes the metonymic learning process of the myth itself. The principle of feminine procreation, instanced here by no less than two female wombs for the youngest child, both Rhea's and Gaia's, wins out as before, but it must again be combined with the violence that apparently only males contribute. At least thus far, the myth evinces a rule of sexual difference that is expressible in terms of the Prague School distinction between marked and unmarked categories: females and males are both capable of exercising cunning, which is the unmarked member of the opposition, but only males are capable of exercising violence or physical force, the marked member of the opposition.⁵³ Each of the two qualities can be used either to foster or to prevent the procreation of children. Kronos's attempt to prevent the birth of his successor by cleverly discovering his own infertile femininity is surpassed by the procreative cunning of the older generation combined with the decisive, if inexplicit, force and cunning of the newer generation—in other words, by a combination of male and female personages and attributes across generations. The underly-

---

⁵² Ultimately, West on line 497 seems justified in defending ἐξήμησε, which is the reading of the mss. (except *k*, which has an impossible ἐξήμεσε). The form with -ε- is original, that with -η- secondary and analogical, assuming that the handbooks are correct that Gr. ἐμέω is cognate with Skt. *vámiti*, Latin *vomere*, and Lith. *vémti;* then the -ε- is the reflex of an original -*h₁-. The problem with this etymology is the absence of dialectal or epic evidence in Greek for an initial digamma; see Schwyzer 1968, 1:222 n. 5, 260 and Chantraine 1968–79, 2:343 s.v. ἐμέω for two ways to account for its disappearance: by dissimilation or as a substandard term taken over into epic. For a single stem attesting -η- as well as -ε- in the sigmatic aorist, compare Attic/Ionic ᾔνεσα with epic ᾔνησα. West points to such morphological alternatives in support of the manuscripts' reading, but I know of no other word exhibiting *both* forms within epic, which is really what is needed to support his purely philological argument; see Chantraine 1958, 1:346–53, for a survey. All things considered, I think that the form ἐξήμησε is best considered an example of "poet's grammar," on which see Jakobson 1968; in other words, it is a grammatically plausible form motivated by poetic factors (namely, the metonymies posited), not just grammatical ones.

⁵³ For the marked/unmarked distinction, see Nagy 1990b, 5–6, citing Jakobson 1957; Jakobson 1939; and Waugh 1982.

ing goal is that the right mixture of violence with cunning, old with young, and male with female will someday produce the ultimate in cosmic power.

The poet's next words present a problem:

λῦσε δὲ πατροκασιγνήτους ὀλοῶν ὑπὸ δεσμῶν,
Οὐρανίδας, οὓς δῆσε πατὴρ ἀεσιφροσύνῃσιν·
οἵ οἱ ἀπεμνήσαντο χάριν εὐεργεσιάων
δῶκαν δὲ βροντὴν ἠδ' αἰθαλόεντα κεραυνὸν
καὶ στεροπήν· τὸ πρὶν δὲ πελώρη Γαῖα κεκεύθει·
τοῖς πίσυνος θνητοῖσι καὶ ἀθανάτοισιν ἀνάσσει.

And he [Zeus] set free his father's brothers from their destructive bonds,
the sons of Ouranos, whom their father[54] had bound;
they were grateful for his benevolent deeds
and gave him thunder and the blazing thunderbolt
and lightning; previously, huge Gaia had hidden it within herself:
trusting in them he rules over mortals and immortals.

(501–6)

The poet seems to be referring to the binding of the Cyclopes by their father (οὓς δῆσε πατήρ, "whom their father bound") "as if he had already told the story,"[55] but it is not apparent that he has. A similar passage shortly hereafter (617ff.) alludes to the binding of the Hundred-Handers by Ouranos and Zeus's subsequent release of them as well; in their gratitude, they become Zeus's allies in the battle of the Olympians against the Titans. West adopts the solution of H. Buse to this apparent inconsistency.[56] Buse guessed that Hesiod "originally" conceived the story of the castration of Ouranos about the Titans alone, without including the Cyclopes or the Hundred-Handers in lines 139–46. That would explain why the "youngest child," who is the hero of the episode, is the youngest of the Titans, not of all the children (Titans, Cyclopes, and Hundred-Handers are consistently distinguished in the text). Later, Buse continues, when the poet found that the story of Zeus required that the birth of the Cyclopes and the Hundred-Handers be told, he reintroduced them into the myth by having them born

---

[54] The word πατήρ here could refer to Zeus's father, Kronos, and was apparently so understood in antiquity (Apollodorus 1.1.5, 1.2.1) and by Tzetzes (see West on *Theogony* 502); but the consensus now seems to be that it refers to Ouranos, on the basis of the parallel passage concerning the liberation by Zeus of the Hundred-Handers in 617ff. in which the word πατήρ has no such ambiguity, and given the isofunctionalism in other regards of the Cyclopes, who seem to be referred to here, with the Hundred-Handers. See Detienne and Vernant 1974, 80.

[55] West on 502.

[56] Buse 1937, 27–28.

The Narrative Sequence of the Hesiodic *Theogony*  77

at the same time as the Titans, not realizing that this adjustment created a new problem. For if they were born at the same time as the Titans, they were also imprisoned in Gaia along with them; and when the Titans are released after the castration of Ouranos, the audience assumes, as West puts it, that "the castration which liberated the Titans would naturally also liberate anyone else concealed with them."[57] We are asked, then, to believe that Hesiod had the Cyclopes and the Hundred-Handers born precisely in the middle of the story of the birth and imprisonment of the Titans by Ouranos, that he next speaks of them again in the context of their liberation from imprisonment by their father, but that he was unaware that his audience would think of them as imprisoned and therefore liberated along with the Titans. How could a poet be so unaware of what he was saying? This explanation accounts for one inconsistency by asking us to believe that it arose from the poet's bumbling attempt to correct another (supposed) inconsistency and that the correction entailed an even worse inconsistency. One may wonder whether the poet was so inept or the explanation is faulty.

I doubt that there is an inconsistency here to begin with. At issue are both a metaphor and a metonym. The language of binding (usually with the words *déō* and *desmós*, but also with *dámnēmi* / *damáō* / *damázō* and *pēdáō*) is metaphoric for the "killing" of an immortal. The epic tradition can speak of a thunderbolt as *binding* a warrior (*Iliad* 13.434–37, etc.) just as the confinement of Ares to a bronze jar is *binding* (*Iliad* 5.385ff.) or the hiding of creatures from the light (underground, in a cave or hollow hiding place) is *binding* (*Theogony* 717–21; Pindar *Pythian* 1.27); so also their release (always with forms of the verb *lúō*) from bonds can be described as being brought to light, in using the language of birth (*Theogony* 625–26).[58] The reference to the release of the Cyclopes and then the Hundred-Handers from binding is a precise allusion to their release from the hiding place within Earth in which Sky confined them in the first episode of the myth.[59] As to the

---

[57] West on 139–53.

[58] This and much more evidence is collected and presented by Detienne and Vernant (1974, 86–98); they cite the passage in Aeschylus *Prometheus Bound* 235 in which Prometheus, past master of unbinding and being bound, boasts of having unbound (ἐξελυσάμην) men and kept them from descending to Hades, but they do not make explicit the symbolic connection between the binding of gods and the death of men. They also note (87 and n. 92) the possible connection between the bronze jar in which Ares is confined and the δειρή 'neck' (cf. Latin *cervix*) of the prison in Tartarus where the Titans are ultimately hidden in darkness (*Theogony* 726–31). There is a clear analogy between both of these and the *keuthmôn* (womb/tomb) within Gaia in which her children are confined and from which they ultimately emerge.

[59] Detienne and Vernant (1974, 76) maintain that Ouranos is not a binding god, that he is without *mêtis*, just as he is not a king; but once again, his is the zero case of binding. Using the

objection that they, too, must have been released from that prison by the castration of Ouranos, it depends on a physical or "cosmogonic" model for the interpretation of the first episode of the myth that it may once have had but that is no longer an explicit or a functional part of it. Sky's castration is a metonymic event that is a symbolic antidote to his prevention of the birth of his children, as the birth of Aphrodite from his genitals shows; and just as Kronos himself, the youngest of the Titans, stands for his siblings, so is the castration itself tantamount to their liberation and no one else's. Some scholars assert that Hesiod could or would or should have said "and so the Titans were freed; but the Cyclopes and Hundred-Handers were not freed yet, and remained below the earth."[60] But since Hesiod does not even see fit to say explicitly that anyone at all was freed by the castration of Ouranos, I question the validity of their assumption. Instead, the narrator seems to assume that his audience understands the extent of Kronos's metonymic power, a power that we extend too far in thinking that it implies the liberation of the Cyclopes and the Hundred-Handers even when we are directly informed otherwise, as here.

In any case, the liberation of the Cyclopes is as much the last element of this episode as the first element of the next one, and the next episode is actually the culmination of the narrative. In it, Zeus establishes his sovereign order and withstands threats to his supremacy by finding a way to square the circle, to maintain his own political and procreative powers without suppressing feminine sexuality and procreation. For that is clearly one of the myth's pressing dilemmas. Another is also coming into focus, namely, how is it possible for a stable sovereign order to be established when the principle of succession—which is nothing more or less than a particular

---

words *déō* and *desmós* of what he did to his children at this later point in the narrative, when it is a term used of Zeus, is somewhat anachronistic, as though Ouranos could now be called a king, but it suits the way that metonymy functions in myth. In this respect, the myth is like *a train that stops only to take on passengers and never leaves any off*. It cannot go backward, so it must describe a prior event, when it is compelled to, in terms established by present ones. Such a principle goes a long way toward explaining rules of epic narrative such as Zieliński's law, which states that "if the poet did not wish to leave out anything in two [simultaneous] accounts, he reported them both not as parallel but as sequential accounts" [Wenn der Dichter von den beiden Handlungen . . . keine missen wollte, so berichtete er sie beide, aber nicht als parallel, sondern als einanderfolgende Handlungen] (Zieliński 1899–1901, 405). Also pertinent and explicable is Tilman Krischer's corollary to Zieliński's law (Krischer 1971, 91): "the Homeric narrative never passes through the same time (of an account) twice and that this is a characteristic of the epic style" [die Homerische Darstellung niemals dieselbe Zeit (der Handlung) zweimal durchläuft und . . . dies eine Eigenschaft der epischen Stiles ist].

[60] So West on *Theogony* 139–53; and Detienne and Vernant 1974, 77: "Hésiode aurait du dire ce que nous apprendrons seulement plus tard."

manifestation of the metonymic rule, whereby the next episode is built upon the previous one—always obtains? If the sovereign is a patriarch, then son succeeds father as episode succeeds episode, in which case the order of the day is *cumulative change,* not Zeus enthroned forever. In fact, these two aspects of the puzzle that the myth is trying to solve are closely related. The functional distinction between the sexes is intertwined with the competitive contest between them and with the principle of son succeeding father.[61]

But in the episode of the Cyclopes we can begin to glimpse how the myth will solve its puzzle, for what Zeus is doing by liberating them is nothing less than incorporating the past into the future. Instead of leaving his grandfather's generation buried in the depths of an underworld to which they were consigned by Sky, he is "bringing them forth" (that is, actually getting them born into the world) as part of his sovereign order, and they in turn provide him with a weapon that is, like the sickle of Gaia with which Kronos overthrew his father, a tricky tool that was heretofore hidden in the depths of the Earth (505). Like the "birth" of the Cyclopes and also of Zeus himself from Gaia, the "birth" of the thunderbolt bridges the great gap between cunning and force as well as the one between past and future, since it is the product of the Cyclopes' skills (μηχαναί) and the ultimate weapon of force.[62] The thunderbolt is also yet another "child" of Gaia, but this time her offspring is an instrument of the current patriarch's power provided by a previous generation rather than a threat to it placed by Gaia in the hands of the youngest child of the next generation. The difference is a sort of seal on this tool's success as well as another mark of its superiority to its prior analogues. In the end, then, the episode of the liberation of the Cyclopes and the award of the thunderbolt to Zeus is little more than a concrete example of metonymic "learning," that is, of learning from previous episodes' successes and failures. The Cyclopes and their

[61] For an explicit and vivid expression of the dilemma that this state of affairs presents on the mortal plane, see lines 600–612, in which the poet expounds on the conflict between a patriarch's need for heirs and the pains that women inevitably bring. According to Hesiod, a man is damned with or without a wife, since dying intestate means surrendering one's properties to hateful collateral kin.

[62] On the meaning of the term μηχαναί, see Martin 1983. The Hesiodic variant of the Cyclopes as cunning fabricators of the ultimate weapon of fiery force who are liberated from hiding places beneath the earth stands in suggestive contrast to its counterpart in the *Odyssey,* where one Cyclops attempts to confine Odysseus's men within a cave, only to be defeated by a primordial fiery weapon created by the more cunning but much weaker adversary, who thereby brings his men forth from the darkness. Odysseus has learned how to do the Cyclops one better, effectively beating him at his own game.

thunderbolt are clear analogues in origin and function to Zeus himself, and as such they are appropriate tokens of his identity as king.

As mentioned above,[63] Kronos's stratagem is the first event to call up the word *mêtis*, which is the name the text assigns to his stratagem's antidote, the tricky plan of Gaia and Ouranos to conceal the baby Zeus. If Kronos is the first explicit king, he is also the first person to devise a (still not so called) *mêtis*, on the principle, formulated above,[64] that the second occurrence of a discrete concept, in this instance the antidote to his tricky plan, is the one that evokes its proper name. We may be tempted to anticipate that the divinity who incarnates *mêtis* will now appear in the sequence, as was the case for *móros* and *kếr*.[65]

## Learning Metonymically, Part 2

The subsequent episodes of the myth are events with variants that will, in principle and in fact, continue for the rest of mythic time, beyond the *Theogony* itself. They are nothing more or less than testing challenges to the sovereignty of Zeus, a sovereignty that is never static or lightly borne by those upon whom it is imposed, since it is a dynamic part of the emergent world of myth.[66] In fact, the myths portray Zeus's sovereignty as inherently unstable and unbearable, along with the ordered structure of the world itself. Both are in constant need of reinforcement or reassertion or recalibration. This is true even if Zeus seems eternally able to meet all challenges. It is almost as though Zeus's power over the world would end if no one resisted it, or to put it another way, in this portrait of the world the need to test and challenge the authority that rules the world is as irresistible and unclosable and constitutive of experience as the need for that authority to resist subversion and so persist.

Despite the open-endedness that is ultimately built into the myths in this way, these particular episodes in the *Theogony* have a structure like that of a breaking wave. They are still concerned with the initial establishment, however unsteady, of Zeus's power, in contrast to the failure of his predecessors to survive even a single contest, a factor that makes it possible for

---

[63] Above, 71.
[64] Above, 68.
[65] Above, 66–67.
[66] For challenges to the sovereignty of Zeus beyond the *Theogony*, see below, 114–16, 118–20, and, for a remarkable instance, Ovid *Fasti* 3.796–808; see also Lang 1983 on a set of variants that constitute a subtext to the whole *Iliad*.

this particular myth to have a structure and even an apparent end. In other words, the myth's form is based upon its prior episodes and oriented toward a goal that they have already implicitly (and, in the prologue, at least, explicitly) defined, namely, the establishment of one and the same male in continuing power over the world. It may also be true that the challenges to Zeus after the *Theogony* are intrinsically different from those within it (I shall return to this subject).[67] In either case, it is important from the standpoint of method to realize that the issue here is a contrast between the significance of mythical episodes within the structure of a single myth as against a sequence of myths. This issue will arise again later.

To say that the myth's form in this last episode is based on prior episodes and implicitly defined in them is only to assert yet again the validity of the rule of metonymy, but in this case it seems to be a deceptive formulation. On the basis of prior episodes, we would expect this one to begin, as did the others, with another recapitulation, perhaps in the even greater detail that suits the climax of a myth told in epic style, of the birth of a new sovereign's children from his spouse. This time, however, it would incorporate a clever and successful method of regulating their birth without the sovereign's surrendering power to the youngest. Such a tale is indeed the climax of the myth, but it is retarded by no less than three apparently digressive episodes. Retarding a climax by means of digression is hardly an unexampled strategy in epic-style storytelling.[68] Moreover, the digressions themselves are intimately related to the climactic episode and to the previous episodes. All three are centered upon the twin themes of generational competition with respect to cunning and with respect to force, two notions that are at the heart of the myth's notion of kingship. In fact, the only thematic difference between the three digressions and the climactic episode is that the contest in them is not between Zeus and a female procreative partner over sexual cunning, the ability to create children, and a male child destined to become his successor, but between Zeus and a varied sequence of male rivals directly over the sovereignty of the cosmos. The confrontation with the female threat, the most dangerous of all, is left for last, and these other confrontations are apparently meant to prepare for it.

In fact, the notion of kingship itself is gaining in scope as the world has grown from a single nuclear family dominated by a patriarch who was its biological father into an extended family with collateral branches spanning

---

[67] See below, 118-20 on *Iliad* 1.397-405.
[68] The standard example is the story of Odysseus's scar, as discussed by Erich Auerbach (1953); see also the critique of Auerbach by Norman Austin (1966) and more recently by Michael Lynn-George (1988).

several generations. Zeus can no longer prove his sovereignty by simply resolving the problem of succession in the narrow sense, by asserting definitive superiority over his sexual partner and her male offspring. The supreme patriarch has been redefined as the winner of a contest among a set of male rivals arising from the members of his growing cosmic household.[69] The episodes that precede the expected resolution of strictly reproductive aspects of the myth are not digressions but places in which the narrative portion of the *Theogony* "catches up" with the metonymic progress of its catalog portion. Their very existence also makes it clear that the issue is not simply the narrow one of how a male can succeed in reproducing himself without ceding power to his offspring, but also the political and social issue of how to become king of the world. One can see, then, that inasmuch as Ouranos was a "zero-degree" king and Kronos a primitive one, Zeus is the "evolved" version, a true king, presiding over an evolved and proliferating domain.

The first of these digressive episodes is the exquisitely structured confrontation between Zeus and Prometheus, an excursus from the genealogy of Prometheus's family that begins at line 507.[70] Iapetos and Klymene have four children, in sequence, Atlas, Menoitios, Prometheus, and Epimetheus. The dreadful teleology of each of these births is then told in the same sequence (511–20), except that Prometheus's ultimate destiny is left for last (521–34)—a swerve that highlights his significance. Each has a symbolically equivalent end. Epimetheus receives the first woman; Menoitios is thunderbolted by Zeus; Atlas's fate (*moîra* in line 520) is to hold the heaven tirelessly under heavy constraint (*anánkē*); and Prometheus is bound in unbreakable bonds. I have spoken of the symbolic equivalence of binding and thunderbolting, and Atlas's fate is to be understood as a form of binding.[71] In exchange for Prometheus's gift of celestial fire to mankind, Epi-

---

[69] In other words, Zeus is now πατὴρ ἀνδρῶν τε θεῶν τε, "father of gods and men," since the father in this expression is not a biological but a social one. On the sociological meaning of this term attested in Greek and other Indo-European languages, see Ernout and Meillet 1959, 487–88 s.v. *pater;* also Risch 1944, 122.

[70] For the decoding of this episode, Vernant 1974 is fundamental despite the differences in my approach.

[71] It is an immobilization and a removal to the distant west, but also see the expression applied to him in line 517, "under mighty necessity," ὑπ' ἀνάγκης. Like the English word *necessity*, the word *anánkē* is etymologically related to an Indo-European root for binding (cognate with Latin *nex* 'bond, death by binding' and Hittite *ḫenk-an* 'fated death'): Benveniste 1935, 154–55. Note also that the same expression is applied to Prometheus's binding at lines 615–16, ὑπ' ἀνάγκης ... κατὰ δεσμὸς ἐρύκει, "the bond restrains him beneath necessity." Puzzlingly, Chantraine (1968–79, s.v. *anánkē*) claims that none of the etymologies that have been proposed accounts for the two

metheus accepts the gift of the first woman, an eternal cause of suffering with fiery origins and attributes who forever distinguishes mortals from immortals;[72] in fact she is presented as a punishment to Prometheus tantamount to his binding (585–615, esp. 613–15).[73] In other words, all Prometheus's siblings are either actually or metaphorically thunderbolted, and their destinies are united with those of the other rivals to Zeus in the retarding episodes that precede the marriage of Zeus and Metis. After all, his fiery thunderbolt is the symbol of Zeus's ultimate power.[74] Observe that in yet another instance of the metonomy of the myth's sequence, he has only just received it (in lines 501–6). So we are to understand the destinies of all the children of Iapetos and Klymene as the result of challenges to the sovereignty of Zeus and as occasions for absolute assertions of that sovereignty. The difference is not worth dwelling upon, especially since the narrator does not inform us as to the behavior that prompted Zeus's responses except in Prometheus's case. He is a metonym, then, for his three siblings.

At line 521, the poet takes up Prometheus's story at its conclusion, with him bound in chains, a column driven through, and an eagle eating his liver. This horrific tableau immediately gives way to another: Herakles' slaughter of the eagle and the liberation of Prometheus, which took place "not against Zeus's desire" (529) in order to augment the glory (*kléos*) of Zeus's son (Herakles) and also because by then he had relented from the *khólos* 'anger' he had harbored since Prometheus started competing (ἐρί-ζετο [534]) with him in *boulaí* 'trickery'. Having begun with the end of Prometheus's story, the narrator has proceeded to its aftermath and is

---

meanings attested for it, which he distinguishes as "constraint" and also "kinship." He says that the notion of bond should be the connection, as though no one had suggested such a thing, but he seems to reject Benveniste's hypothesis, which postulates exactly that connection; the passage from the *Theogony* I have cited (615–16) even attests to a functioning semantic connection (to say nothing of the symbolic one) between *anánkē* and the notion of bond.

[72] *Theogony* 570, 585, and compare *Works and Days* 57.

[73] The first woman, who is fabricated by the fire god (*Theogony* 571–72) and adorned with a golden crown of his devising (579–84), also has a tricky nature (589) that is analogous to fire itself (on the trickery of fire and of Hephaistos himself, see Detienne and Vernant 1974, 262–64) in its ability to subdue or seduce the force of men. Moreover, the definitive inability of mortal men to procreate without women and their critical need for children (*Theogony* 590–612) define the human condition in contrast to the divine. Mortal men are continually succeeded and replaced by their offspring, in contrast to the tense permanence of Zeus's reign (see above, 78–79 and n. 61).

[74] Overtly in line 505: "trusting in them [thunder and lightning and the thunderbolt] he rules over gods and men." See also Hesiod fr. 343.8 M–W, where Zeus swallows Metis not from fear that she will bear a child more powerful *than himself* but "lest she bring forth another thing mightier *than the thunderbolt*" δείσας μὴ τέξῃ κρατερώτερον ἄλλο κεραυνοῦ.

thence actually embarked on the story from the beginning, since he has to explain what caused Zeus's *khólos* in the first place.[75] The anger in Zeus caused by Prometheus's competition in trickery is in fact the trigger of the myth and its focal point, as we can see from the diction at its conclusion:

οὐδὲ γὰρ Ἰαπετιονίδης ἀκάκητα Προμηθεὺς
τοῖό γ' ὑπεξήλυξε βαρὺν χόλον, ἀλλ' ὑπ' ἀνάγκης
<u>καὶ πολύιδριν ἐόντα</u> μέγας κατὰ δεσμὸς ἐρύκει.

for not even the son of Iapetos, *akáketa*[76] Prometheus,
escaped from his [Zeus's] heavy anger, but under necessity
a mighty bond restrains him despite his multiple intelligence [<u>*kaì polúidrin eónta*</u>].[77]

(614–16)

The narrative's goal, then, is not the liberation of Prometheus but his binding as a result of Zeus's anger. The ring opened at line 521, where the genealogies end, is thus closed at line 617, whereupon the next episode begins. So this myth is an example—the first in the *Theogony*—of the anger of Zeus.

---

[75] For a similar way of beginning a story with a goal in mind and then tracking back to a cause of anger (also called *khólos*) which triggers the forward movement of the narrative toward its goal, see *Iliad* 1.9–11. The last clause there is introduced by the word οὕνεκα 'because of this' in line 11 just as it is in line 534 here.

[76] The meaning of this epithet is obscure, but everywhere else it belongs to that other epic tricky fire bringer and first sacrificer, Hermes. In this connection, West cites a gloss of Hesychius: Ἰθάς· ὁ τῶν Τιτήνων κῆρυξ, Προμηθεύς. τινὲς Ἴθαξ. Here Prometheus-Ithas/Ithax is the *kêrux* 'herald, go-between' of the Titans. Hermes is the herald of the Olympian gods. The key to the apparent competition between these two figures in mythical tradition may be that they fulfill the same function for two competing groups of gods. Their competition suggests that the present story is appropriate to the time before the Olympians proved their dominance over the Titans in the *Theogony*, which takes place in the next episode of the myth. As for the name Ithas/Ithax, it should be related to the root of αἴθω 'burn' (see Chantraine 1968–79, s.v., for its relation to ἰθαρός 'pure' and ἰθαίνω), which is contextually appropriate to Prometheus and supports an etymology of Ἰθάκη, Odysseus's island, suggested by Gregory Nagy. Odysseus, who identifies himself at one point as a mortal named Αἴθων (19.183), has important links with Hermes, such as being the only epic personage to share with him the epithet πολύτροπος (*Odyssey* 1.1; cf. *Hymn to Hermes* 13, 439; see Nagy 1990a, 34). As for his island, it is repeatedly associated in the *Odyssey* with the sight of fire and smoke (as in 10.30 or 1.58). There is another trickster figure named Aithon (= Erusikhthon), father of the shape-changing sorceress Mestra in Hesiod fr. 43b M–W, whom Sisyphos wooed unsuccessfully (Hesiod fr. 43a.36–57 M–W).

[77] This phrase "even though knowing many things" and its feminine variant (*kaíper polúidrin eoúsa[n]*) is attested at least three times and perhaps four, of tricky persons trying but failing in the attempt to outstrip Zeus in intelligence (here and in Hesiod fr. 43a.58 M–W, of Mestra whom Zeus denied to Sisyphos; fr. 343.6 M–W of Metis herself; perhaps also Alcaeus fr. B6.7 L–P, of Sisyphos).

What enrages Zeus first is being deceived at Mekone, where Prometheus offers him a choice between two sacrificial portions, covering one with a beef stomach (καλύψας γαστρὶ βοείῃ) that conceals its edible meat and entrails, and covering the other with a layer of fat (καλύψας ἀργέτι δημῷ) that conceals only inedible bones. Which one to pick? *Zeus knows the trick,* but he has a goal in mind, namely, woes for the whole race of mortals, and he will bring it to pass.[78] His goal is clearly the opposite of Prometheus's, which is to deceive Zeus and benefit men by providing them with the edible portions of the animal. So Zeus takes the fat-covered portion but gets very angry when he sees only the white bones within. The narrative repeatedly insists that Zeus "knows imperishable tricks," *áphthita médea eidós*),[79] but in his anger Zeus compliments Prometheus, saying that he knows imperishable tricks beyond all, ironically professing Prometheus's superiority. Then he defeats the whole purpose of Prometheus's division by "not giving," *ouk edídou*,[80] mortals sacrificial fire with which to cook the meat that Zeus's choice privileged them to consume. So Prometheus deceives Zeus and steals fire for mortal men. Seeing the blaze of fire among men makes Zeus deeply angry (δάκεν δ' ἄρα νειόθι θυμόν, "it bit his heart to the bottom" [567]). Now mortal men have two defining characteristics that distinguish them from gods: meat and fire to cook it with. So Zeus decides to give them a third, a bad thing in exchange for the fire (570), a

---

[78] West writes in his note on line 551, "It has long been recognized that in the original story Zeus did not see through the trick, but was thoroughly deceived." In his view, Hesiod wants to save Zeus's "omniscience and prescience." But the next episode immediately belies that explanation. The language could not be more plain in line 565: ἀλλά μιν ἐξαπάτησεν ἐὺς πάϊς Ἰαπετοῖο, "but the son of Iapetos thoroughly deceived him," and the same language for deception is repeated in the reprise of the story in *Works and Days* 48. There is an escalation here that West's historicism obscures. First, Zeus knowingly lets himself be deceived, a trick that one trickster might play on another and one that suits the goal of Zeus, as we are told; but then, in the next episode, Prometheus really does deceive Zeus and make him angry. Prometheus's trickery is improving in the pervasive metonymic fashion of the myth. First he succeeds in tricking a willing victim; then he tricks the same victim without prior detection.

[79] This formula also and simultaneously means "has unfailing genitals," a signification that is more to the fore in subsequent episodes. For the double meaning, see Nagy 1974b, 265–78.

[80] The language of gift exchange is exploited more fully in the version of the story told in the *Works and Days*, where the woman given (57) by Zeus as a gift (85) in return for the theft (the opposite of giving, since it is taking what is not given) of fire is called Pan-dora 'All-gift' (81–82); but the same undertones are present here as well. Zeus "did not give" the fire (*Theogony* 563); Prometheus "stole" it (566); and Epimetheus "received" (513) the maiden, who is a kind of poisoned gift. Gregory Nagy points out to me the parallel between such a gift and the meaning of *Gift* in German, namely, 'poison', a translation of the medieval Latin term *dosis* 'dose, drug, poison' that is itself a borrowing of Greek δόσις 'giving, gift'. Ambivalence is built into the notion of gift from the start. For another example of an apparently positive gift that bites its recipient, see *Iliad* 7.287–305. Ajax receives Hector's sword, with which he later commits suicide.

beautiful bad thing in exchange for a good one (585): the first woman. Hephaistos and Athena make her according to Zeus's tricky plans. She has a silver garment and a beautiful embroidered *kalúptrē* 'veil' to cover her head, with a golden wreath around it cunningly inscribed with marvelous creatures. These deceptive coverings for an evil recall the way that Prometheus deceptively 'covered' *kalúpsas* (541) portions of meat, the good one with the beef stomach, the bad with its fat. This maiden is even described as a drone who consumes the food produced by others' toil rather than a nurturer, a stomach that eats and does not provide (599), a means to take from men the meat that Prometheus gave them to cook and to eat. What Zeus has actually done is to give men as their inevitable companion δόλον αἰπὺν ἀμήχανον, "sheer cunning that cannot be tricked" (589). Without a wife a man has no children to care for him in old age or to inherit his property. Even with a good wife, a man's life is at best a balance of good and evil. With a bad one, it is ceaseless grief.

The significance of all this is not immediately transparent, and the narrative almost appears to have run away with itself, since it features the participation of divinities who have not yet been born.[81] But the basic point is simple: Zeus is angered at Prometheus's successful and threatening attempts to deceive him. He must prove that he is the winner not just by exercising superior force in binding Prometheus but in his ability to outwit him. So the crowning trick is Zeus's tricky award of trickery incarnate—woman— to mortal men. It undermines Prometheus's benefactions since it makes men eternally subject to the cunning of their wives, who are creatures they cannot do without and who will always be *other than themselves*. In this respect the tale contrasts radically with the destiny of Zeus himself, whose crowning act is to *become one with* the goddess of cunning. So the myth has several goals: to define mankind as distinct from divinity,[82] to define men as distinct from women, and to have Zeus in anger defeat the challenge to his cunning from Prometheus by the exercise of both superior force and superior cunning. That is a recipe for domination that men cannot hope to achieve. The anger of Zeus at Prometheus, then, makes the definition of

---

[81] Namely, Hephaistos and Athena. Significantly, although the narrative cannot go back in time to restart from an earlier moment, it can go forward in this way toward its goal. This is what explains the appearance of these gods here, that the explicit *télos* 'goal' of Zeus is woe for men (552).

[82] I agree with West that this distinction is explicit in the language at the beginning of the tale, lines 535–36: "at Mekone, where mortal men and gods were separated from one another," ὅτ' ἐκρίνοντο θεοὶ θνητοί τ' ἄνθρωποι / Μηκώνῃ. See also Nagy 1979, 215–16, on κρίναντο in *Theogony* 882 and *Odyssey* 9.220, where the same verb, διακρίνομαι, is used of the distinction between sheep and goats. See also 6 n.3.

the whole cosmos that much sharper. What has actually happened is that men have become distinct from gods. They cook meat with fire and eat it; they burn bones wrapped in fat for the gods;[83] and also, they have acquired an insurmountable sexual difference. Men cannot ever become androgynous like Zeus,[84] since Zeus set woman as the cunning portion and Epimetheus foolishly and unknowingly accepted her as such.

Before discussing its sequel, I have two final remarks to make about this tale: the notions of competition (*éris:* ἐρίζετο [534]) and exchange are its structuring principles, and they crystallize its metonymic logic. Each move is meant to top the next one, which it also includes and betters. That is why, for instance, Zeus "was not giving" fire to mortal men (563), as against taking it away, because the myth cannot remove aspects of reality that are already present and because it is a gesture to counter Prometheus's nongift to Zeus (the fat that contains only bones). *The logic of the myth is cumulative, not reversible.* Even the notion of aetiology explicit in this myth ("from then on men burn white bones [ὀστέα λευκά] for the immortals" [556]) is simply an application of the metonymic rule to the relation between myth and ritual. A single event in the myth becomes an everlasting part of reality, an eternally repeated ritual.

The Titanomachy is appropriately consequent upon the myth of Prometheus, the Titan whose cunning Zeus defeats one-to-one. It is a test of force between the divine communities each represents, and it is a test of the combined worth of each group as well as its particular members. One might expect that the next "logical" step after a one-to-one contest in cunning would be a one-to-one contest in force, but the myth is naturally concerned to present the extreme case of each possible challenge to Zeus in a cumulative sequence. Cunning is not a trait ascribable to or exercised by solidary groups in this tradition, whereas force is both an individual and a group trait.[85] So the battle challenge to the Olympians by the Titans is a test of Zeus's sovereignty, of his ability to maintain the existence of his solidary

---

[83] This definition of the divine portion is true of the descriptions of sacrifice in Homeric epic, but evidence from epichoric inscriptions proves that the gods did receive special cuts of beef. Whatever the reason for this distinction, my point here is only that the Promethean sacrifice is consistent with the prototypical sacrifice of epic and the definition of the human condition it implies. See Nagy 1979, 216–17 with sec. 7 n. 2.

[84] Zeus's androgyny consists in his combination of the masculine trait of supremely destructive force with the creative ability to give birth to a child; for a detailed demonstration, see below, 91–93.

[85] I base this statement on the *absence* in Greek myth and epic of a social group exercising cunning together as a group of warriors can exercise force. On the contrary, individuals are regularly the contrivers of ruses. There are indeed classes of animals that are known for their cunning, such as seals or cuttlefish, but that is not the point.

group, not just his own capacity for violence. Zeus's response to the test is an astute cultivation of solidarity with the past prompted by the *phradmosúnai* 'clever plans' of Gaia herself, the cunning mother of the Hundred-Handers, whom Zeus releases from the womb/tomb within her in which they have been imprisoned since the beginning of the myth. Thus he wins for his group allies of the requisite violence. The path to the Olympians' success at withstanding a test of force is adaptive and additive rather than static and one-dimensional. A simple exercise of force would be, by definition, inadequate to turn the tide. It is a question of acquiring superior force through cunning and of integrating past into present by heeding Gaia's counsel and restoring her offspring. This is, in fact, the final stage in the restoration of the myth's proper sequence. Of those whose creation Ouranos had reversed, the Hundred-Handers are the only children who remained unborn. Now all the arrested births—of the Titans, the Olympians, the Cyclopes, and the Hundred-Handers—have been undone (note the language of birth in regard to their release: ἀνήγαγον ἐς φάος, "brought back to light" [626]), and the broken sequence of mythical generation has been reconstituted, setting right the wrongs done by Zeus's patriarchal predecessors. Moreover, the restoration of the Hundred-Handers, like that of the Cyclopes, is a symbolic recapitulation of Zeus's own birth. There is, in fact, a symbolic equivalence among all these masters of force, the Titans, the Cyclopes, their thunderbolt (it, too, was hidden within the earth), the Hundred-Handers, and Zeus himself, who was also saved by the promptings of Gaia and nourished in her caves. In this context, it makes sense that the Olympians, who have, so to speak, greased the myth's wheels and whose combined force outweighs their enemies', win the confrontation with the Titans, since the side that best observes the principle of metonymic addition must prevail at each stage of the myth.

The stage is now set for Zeus to meet the ultimate masculine challenge, a youngest son whose attributes combine cunning and force, like Zeus's own. Typhoeus possesses the tireless hands and feet of a mighty god (κρατεροῦ θεοῦ), and like his recently reborn brothers, he is a multiple-headed monster. One hundred serpent heads spring from his shoulders, with darting tongues and fire sparkling from each pair of eyes. There are voices in every head that utter every sort of sound, from bulls to lions to gods to dogs. These multiple, mutating voices, which later tradition overlays with multiplicity of form, are tokens of his cunning.[86] This terrifying creature

---

[86] Detienne and Vernant 1974, 115–16. On multiplicity of form, see West on *Theogony* 831–35, citing Nonnus for actual metamorphoses. West points out that the different animals whose voices Typhoeus emits correspond to the typical animal metamorphoses, and that the use of the

must be single, since cunning, unlike force, is not a group trait, and he must be a child of Gaia, since in the context of the myth she has been either the biological mother or the "adoptive" mother of all the male children who supersede their fathers. So despite her apparent alliance with Zeus in previous episodes, including her physical "adoption" of Zeus as her own and heretofore her "youngest" child, it makes sense that this ultimate test be a new youngest child from within her. She does not, however, actively participate in a challenge to Zeus alongside her latest offspring, either because Zeus's strike against him is preemptive or because the myth is tactful in regard to her relationship to Zeus. The overall structural point is that the birth of Typhoeus completes the liberation of Gaia's femininity after its suppression by Ouranos. The release of the Titans, the release of the Olympians, the liberation of the Cyclopes and then of the Hundred-Handers—all have been steps along this path. In a sense, the birth of Typhoeus effects closure on the story of Gaia, the procreative principle, and makes it possible for Zeus's reign—including his own first procreative act—to begin in earnest as its sequel. In other words, Typhoeus is something like Zeus's protoson, in such a way that his attributes, a combination of trickery and violence, are bound up with his genealogy. Typhoeus is in fact an Anti-Zeus, his darker double, and there is a mythopoeic exchange of attributes between the two that reinforces this underlying theme.[87] The thunder and lightning with which Zeus preemptively strikes Typhoeus are accompanied by πρηστήρων ἀνέμων, "blazing winds," which are certainly appropriate to the lord of the thunderbolt.[88] Their presence is also motivated by the destiny of Typhoeus, who becomes the source of just such storm winds after his defeat by Zeus (869).[89] On the other hand, the poet can also speak of the πυρὸς τ' ἀπὸ τοῖο πελώρου, "fire from that monster" (845).[90] The

---

word ἄλλοτε in lines 833–35 is the standard formula with which to describe shape changing. This is a sign that changing shape and changing voice are mythological variants of each other, not that Typhoeus was "originally" a shape changer, as West argues on the basis of Near Eastern parallels.

[87] By mythopoeic I mean a thought process that is acceptable or common in myth but marginal in terms of scientific thought. A precise parallel to this exchange of attributes in a similar context lies in the confrontation in Vedic mythology between Indra Vṛtrahan and the monster he slays, the Vṛtra, as discussed in Renou and Benveniste 1934. There is also the moment in book 22 of the Iliad, esp. lines 193–201, when Hector of the glancing helm becomes swift-footed, precisely when he is wearing the armor of Patroklos, formerly Achilles'.

[88] For more on the historical and dictional association of Zeus with the storm winds, see Nagy 1979, 321–23.

[89] West on line 846 cites the association of πρηστήρ and τυφῶν in Aristophanes Lysistrata 974, and he also notes the underlying doubleness that the parallel points to: "It is impossible to allot one [wind or thunderbolt] to Zeus and the other to his adversary."

[90] West on line 845 supposes that this fire is arising from Typhoeus's scorched body (an

upshot is that when the poet precedes his detailed description of the confrontation with the words

Ζεὺς δ' ἐπεὶ οὖν κόρθυνεν ἐὸν μένος, εἵλετο δ' ὅπλα

And so since/when Zeus was capping his own *ménos* [mind-body energy],
   he took up his weapons

(853)

the language, typically, is subject to two interpretations.[91] On the one hand, the words mark his resolution of the conflict with Typhoeus as the climax of the suite of episodes in which Zeus withstands the challenges of male adversaries. In this sense, the language here harks back to the language of the Titanomachy, in which the same point in the narrative is marked by these similar words:

οὐδ' ἄρ' ἔτι Ζεὺς ἴσχεν ἐὸν μένος.

no longer was Zeus restraining his own *ménos* [mind-body energy].

(687)

On the other hand, Typhoeus is the embodiment of Zeus's *ménos*, his double, and the language of this expression can also be understood to mean that Zeus was mastering *ménos* manifestly his own but incarnate in his antitype.[92] So the contrast between the two expressions, "he was not restraining his own *ménos*" (subject to one interpretation only) and "he was

---

interpretation for which he cites line 859) and not the same as the fire from his eyes, which "are never actually said to burn anything" (though nothing is being burned here, either; he is referring to lines 826–27: ὄσσε... πῦρ ἀμάρυσσεν, "his eyes were flashing fire"). In this context, I would suggest that it is more likely that the tradition actually does envision fire flashing from the monster's eyes; Sappho, as elsewhere, has metaphorized epic violence into erotic imagery, hence the "flash" or ἀμάρυχμα in Anaktoria's eyes (fr. 16.18 L–P). Either way, the deeper point is that Zeus and Typhoeus are equals in the fiercest imaginable competition and that fire, like wind, is an attribute of both.

[91] On the subject of one code and two messages in Hesiodic poetry, see Nagy 1982, 43–73, revised in Nagy 1990a, 36–82.

[92] For a parallel, though contrastive, use of the word *ménos* 'mind-body energy', see Andromache's first words to Hector on the wall at Troy. Φθίσει σε τὸ σὸν μένος, "That *ménos* of yours will wither you" (*Iliad* 6.407ff.), she predicts. Unlike Zeus, Hector does not get the better of his own *ménos*; in fact he dies in a confrontation with a hero of whom he is the double (above, n. 87), not the other way around (in other words, he is "someone else's double," if it is possible to think in such terms); that explains why Andromache's remark is the inverse of Hesiod's, for Achilles—not Hector—is the one strictly analogous to Zeus.

capping his own *ménos*" (subject to two concurrent interpretations, one parallel to the former expression, one beyond it), is an icon of the metonymic advance from the previous episode to this one.

## Learning Metonymically, Part 3

All the metonymic sequences in the myth until now have been leading up to the first marriage of Zeus. It proceeds as one could predict. The youngest child—in this instance, the younger of only two—is foretold by Gaia and Ouranos to be a threat to his father's kingly rank. Hating all his children, Ouranos himself had returned them after their birth to their mother's womb/tomb, but a combination of trickery and violence on the part of the children's mother and her youngest son cost Ouranos his masculinity. They also resulted in the only birth thus far in the myth from something male: the generation of Aphrodite herself, the incarnation of productive feminine sexuality, from Ouranos's severed genitals. Learning from his father's destiny, Kronos had sought to avoid the threat to his succession posed by his children. He placed each of them in his own *nēdús* 'womb/tomb', but he was tricked into taking a swaddled stone for his youngest son, Zeus, who was secreted away and returned to Earth's womb as his own parents had been; then, by a combination of cunning and violence Zeus had succeeded in liberating his siblings and also those of his parents, in getting them to be born or, in the cases of the reversed births of the older generation, reborn.

Given these failed attempts to forestall the natural order of succession, what will Zeus do? He is facing the same sort of threat from his own offspring, and he must use the metonymic principle to counteract it. His first wife is herself the metonymic *télos* of all the mothers in the prior episodes: she is Metis, 'Cunning' herself, not just cunning tricks or their sequel, a trick named as *mêtis*.[93] Likewise, his response to her pregnancy and the threat it poses to him is the metonymic *télos* of the previous episodes: he keeps the children in their mother's womb and puts them in his own *nēdús*

---

[93] Along these same lines, one might expect the name of Zeus and Metis's next child to be Kingship. It is worth noting that in Aristophanes' *Birds*, which features a magnificent parody of the *Theogony* in its parabasis (lines 685–702) and whose plot is a wild sequel to it, the name of Peisthetairos's bride, in a marriage that marks his displacement of Zeus as the sovereign of the universe, is exactly that, Basileía 'Kingship' (*Birds* 1633, etc.), and she is even said to be Zeus's daughter! I suggest that Aristophanes is referring to a variant tradition that is consistent in respect to both the name and the gender of this child with the succession myth in the *Theogony*. On the child's gender, see below, 92–93.

at the same time by swallowing Metis herself after fooling her "with tricky words [*lógoi*]," αἱμυλίοισι λόγοισι (890). In other words, Zeus tricks Cunning herself, and then he performs the ultimate in tricks: he gives birth to a child. Putting the children within their mother within his own *nēdús* is metonymic in three ways at once. It incorporates the strategies of his predecessors within his own at the same time as it literally incorporates the mother and children within himself. Moreover, the myth is signifying that this act represents the incorporation by Zeus of *mêtis* within himself, in other words, his acquisition of the tricky intelligence that Metis incarnates (900). So Zeus's incorporation of Metis is his crowning gesture, the perfect pendant to his acquisition of the thunderbolt. As a result of it, he succeeds precisely where his patriarchal predecessors had failed. By putting Metis into his *nēdús* he accomplishes two things that neither of them had: he prevents the birth of one child (the son who was destined to deprive him of his kingship), and as he must, he succeeds in giving birth instead to a female figure who contrasts completely with Aphrodite in her generation and her nature. She is born from his head, that is to say, from himself *entire,* for the word *kephalḗ* 'head' is actually a synonym in epic language for an entire person.[94] In fact, the head is a metonym for the whole, the point being that Zeus has *not* lost the metonymic relationship between his head and the rest of himself, in contrast to Ouranos and his genitals: once severed, the metonymic relation between them and himself was irretrievably lost.[95] The vestiges of Ouranos's masculinity became the paradoxical and ironic birthplace of Aphrodite, whose birth represents the total failure of Ouranos's effort to suppress the generative feminine sexuality that she incarnates. For an instant in the story of the world's creation, Zeus undismembered is its only perfect androgyne. His ability to give birth signals his complete victory, and his daughter Athena is a nonthreatening mirror image of his own combination of cunning and violence, a reinforcement of his sovereignty rather than its undoing. She is nonthreatening because she is female, and in this myth power is transferred only to males, although her status as a female is in doubt or, more accurately, neutered. She is a virgin, and so an infertile, nonerotic female as well as a warrior. In short, she is a masculinized female unable to produce male heirs. So her gender traits are both a mirror to the androgyny of Zeus, who gave birth to her, and a sharp contrast to the fertile eroticism of Aphrodite. In a word, Zeus has become the first (and only)

---

[94] *Iliad* 8.281, 18.114, etc.; *kephalḗ* is a variant for *autós* 'dead body' in *Iliad* 1.3 (cf. 11.55); on the meaning of *autós,* see below, 99 n. 13.

[95] For the essentially sexual nature of Ouranos's existence, see Detienne and Vernant 1974, 67.

male mother of a female son. The mere fact of Athena's birth, moreover, is enough to enable Zeus to suppress the birth of the male child. It seems that the only successful strategy is for the male child not to be born at all and for the female one to be born in his stead. By the metonymic principle once more, he is the first male to give birth and to "unbirth" a child successfully—at one and the same time, in other words, to apply destructive force and creative cunning to solve the problem of ending his own succession. This pattern also explains why Zeus and Metis, unlike their predecessors, are fated to have only one child: more children could justifiably be expected to revolt with the help of their mother and the youngest son, but there are no groups of unborn children to bring to light, now or later.[96]

With Metis inside him, Zeus is literally the outermost of the dolls-within-dolls I used as a metaphor to account for the syntax of his myth. He himself has the mother within himself who has the child within herself, because the ultimate in cunning is, in the end, the metonymic principle itself. Metis is essentially the apprehension of logical connections between episodes and the consequent ability to foresee what the outcome, what the teleology, will be.

[96] The absence of other offspring in this case shows how the retarded births of the Cyclopes and the Hundred-Handers are consistent with the logic of the whole myth, as I argued above, 76–78.

CHAPTER 4

# The *Mênis* of Achilles and the First Book of the *Iliad*

It is possible to foresee a sequel to the *Theogony* from within my metonymic analysis of its myth.[1] The stage has been set for another myth whose central theme is the *mênis of Zeus*. Neither the word *mênis* nor the proper use of the term is conceivable until the *Theogony* is complete, at which point there is a relatively stable cosmic order presided over by Zeus, the wielder of the thunderbolt. While that order was being formed, it was tested by several potential successors and defended by the use of the thunderbolt. By its nature Zeus's order, now that it is established, will be threatened again by future potential successors.[2] Still, by finally swallowing Metis and giving birth to Athena, Zeus has once and for all put an end to the threat his predecessors were unable to surmount, and he will henceforth prevail, though never without a struggle. So at the end of the *Theogony* and not before then, a world order exists for Zeus to preside over and defend with the ultimate sanction, *mênis*. The word *mênis* is completely absent from the *Theogony*, but this is not the first time that we have witnessed the postponement of the proper term for a central theme of the mythical text until after the theme itself has been deployed in narrative. Such a postponement is consistent with the metonymic nominalism of the myth, whereby a

---

[1] I emphasize that such a sequel is foreseeable from within the text and its concerns and procedures; from a modern standpoint, a sequel contains explicit backward and forward cross-references that would violate the rules of linear progress in a mythical narrative. See above, 52–59, 87 along with 77 n. 59 on the metonymic nature of mythical narrative. I can cite as an independent parallel the attempt to view the *Theogony* and the *Homeric Hymns* as continuous in Clay 1989, though the continuity is not seen in terms of the metonymic rule given here.

[2] On the "instability" inherent in the "stable" regime of Zeus, see above, 80.

term is generated in mythical action and then named the *next* time it occurs.³ In terms of my analysis of the *Theogony*, the massive, violent defense of his order by Zeus in the episodes prior to the swallowing of Metis are "zero" instances of *mênis,* and the foreseeable sequel to the *Theogony* is a myth in which the word *mênis* will be explicitly attached to its referent for the "first" time.

If, then, as I argue, the *Theogony* is a *prooímion* 'prologue' to the *Iliad*, it is appropriate that the first word of the first line of the first book of the *Iliad* is the word *mênis;* but it is striking that the announced central theme of the *Iliad* is the *mênis* of Achilles and not the *mênis* of Zeus.⁴ On the other hand, if the *mênis* that is the subject of the *Iliad* were the *mênis* of Zeus, it would not be an epic poem—in the Homeric tradition's own terms, *kléa andrôn*—but a continuation of the *theôn génos,* "birth of the gods."⁵ The transfer of *mênis* from Zeus to Achilles is inevitable given the change of subject matter from the mythical narrative of the birth of the gods to a poem about epic heroes, which is another way of saying that the leap from the *mênis* of Zeus to the *mênis* of Achilles marks the transition to—or "re-presents" the creation of—epic poetry. Just such transfers of divine mythological themes to tales of mortal heroes have been shown by Georges Dumézil to generate epic from divine myth in other Indo-European traditions.⁶ My suggestion is that a sequential relation in performance between the *Theogony* and the *Iliad* recapitulated that ontogeny of epic.

A sequential relationship between Theogonic myth and Iliadic tradition is also consistent with a well-known myth about Achilles that the *Iliad* never explicitly acknowledges, namely, a variant of the myth about the point of departure of Greek epic, the marriage of Peleus and Thetis. According to a tradition first attested in Pindar,⁷ Thetis acceded to marriage

---

³ See the discussion above of the terms *basileús* and *mêtis* in Chapter 3, 71, 80, and 91 n. 93.

⁴ There exists no instance in attested epic tradition in which the adjectival genitive associated with the noun *mênis* is used as an objective genitive (in other words, where "the *mênis* of Achilles" would imply someone else's *mênis at him*) rather than a possessive genitive. I doubt therefore that there is any underlying ambiguity in the phrase, although the possibility cannot be ruled out completely. See also below, 131, on the hero who incurs *mênis*.

⁵ See further below, 118–20: the *Iliad* actually does refer to Theogonic themes on precisely this subject, but when it does so it actually adopts a Hesiodic style, as Laura Slatkin (1986) has shown. On the self-reflexive terms *kléos* and *kléa andrôn*, see Nagy 1974b, 1979. The phrase *theôn génos* is used in *Theogony* 44 and 105 to designate the song that catalogs the generation of the world.

⁶ I am referring to Dumézil's monumental work, *Mythe et épopée* (3 vols.). For the notion that *mênis* and terms related to it were contextually restricted to divinities and heroes, see also 126 n. 69, below.

⁷ Pindar *Isthmian* 8.27–55. See also Aeschylus *Prometheus Bound* 755–81 and 907–27 as well as Apollonius of Rhodes *Argonautica* 4.800ff. Pindar is the oldest surviving author to attest to this

with the mortal Peleus instead of Zeus in order to avert the birth of a son who would be stronger than his father. Pindar reports a prophecy of Themis herself that Achilles would have surpassed Zeus if his mother had not consented to a marriage beneath her divine status that neutralized the threat he constituted to Zeus's order. To put it another way, Achilles threatened to arouse Zeus's *mênis*, but Thetis's willingness to wed Peleus forestalled it. This myth is a recognizable sequel to the succession myth in the *Theogony*, and if Thetis had not wed Peleus—and even perhaps since she did—it could have been *the* sequel to it I have mentioned. Since Homeric epic has veered away from the Theogonic *mênis* of Zeus and toward the epic *mênis* of Achilles, it is not surprising that it does not acknowledge this myth despite at least one clear opportunity to do so.[8] The myth about Peleus and Thetis attests to an archetypal competition between Achilles and Zeus in Theogonic terms, which is inherent in the performance sequence I am suggesting. However, the plot of the *Iliad* deflects this competition in such a way as to render Achilles the Zeus of heroes with respect to his *mênis*, yet without marking him as Zeus's antagonist. Achilles' divine antagonist is Apollo instead.

Although the *prooímion* to the *Iliad* presents the *mênis* of Achilles as the initial subject of the poem, the narrative itself mitigates the transition from divine to heroic *mênis*. First, the *mênis* of Apollo precedes the *mênis* of Achilles as the story unfolds, and second, the *mênis* of Zeus himself lurks in the background and only wells up to the surface of the narrative in support of the *mênis* of Achilles at the conclusion of book 1. In other words, the epic has found a way to articulate its ontogeny, to bridge the gap between the inception of its central theme and the conclusion of the myth of the *Theogony*.

## From the *Mênis* of Zeus to the *Mênis* of Achilles via the *Mênis* of Apollo

In my view, to repeat, it is significant that the narrative of the *Iliad* does not begin with the *mênis* of Zeus *or* the *mênis* of Achilles; it actually begins with the *mênis* of Apollo, and there is even a variant prologue attested for the *Iliad* whose only content is to link the *mênis* of Achilles to Apollo's as the subject of the *Iliad*:

---

variant, but I treat with great caution attempts to see such random events as indicators of the age of a given tale.

[8] See below, 121–23.

ἔσπετε νῦν μοι μοῦσαι, Ὀλύμπια δώματ' ἔχουσαι,
ὅππως δὴ μῆνίς τε χόλος θ' ἕλε Πηλείωνα
Λητοῦς τ' ἀγλαὸν υἱόν· ὁ γὰρ βασιλῆϊ χολωθεὶς . . . [9]

Sing to me now, Muses who have homes on Olympus,
how *mênis* and *khólos* seized both the son of Peleus
and the glorious son of Leto; for he, angered at the king . . .

This was a variant prologue to the *Iliad* known to Aristoxenus, so its legitimacy cannot be simply dismissed. I do not maintain that it is preferable to the standard one, only that traditional poems are by definition multiform, so that an appreciation of the expressive and poetic value in textual variants like this one can enhance our understanding of the nuance of the received text and of the compositional process in general. It would be senseless to consider this variant the product of some secondary editorial intervention, since it is a prologue composed in traditional epic style whose content is simply different from that of the received text.[10] It raises these questions: What is the relationship between the *mênis* of Achilles and the *mênis* of Apollo? How and why are they linked in the narrative structure of the first book and in this alternative prologue? And why does the received text suppress the relationship between the *mênis* of Achilles and Apollo?

In my view, the *mênis* of Apollo serves as a bridge between the Hesiodic *mênis* of Zeus and the Homeric *mênis* of Achilles, a mortal epic hero. It has certain essential characteristics. First, it is caused by an offense to the *timế* 'prestige' of the old priest Chryses (*Iliad* 1.11), who approached the whole

---

[9] Text of the prologue variant from the critical apparatus to *Iliad* 1.1 (Allen).

[10] For parallels to the diction in this passage, compare 2.484, 11.218, etc. (= first line); 15.122 χόλος καὶ μῆνις; 4.23, 8.460, and 18.322 for χόλος + αἱρέω; 1.197 ἕλε Πηλείωνα#; for Λητοῦς ἀγλαὸν υἱόν, "glorious son of Leto," compare the expression, "genitive of masculine proper name + ἀγλα-ὸς / -ὸν υἱ-ός / -όν at line end," which occurs 18 times in the *Iliad*, plus one instance of this expression transposed, as here, to the line beginning: compare 10.196, ‖καὶ Νέστορος ἀγλαὸς υἱός# to 23.160, #Νέστορος ἀγλαὸς υἱός‖. Although rare for this expression, this metrical transposition is a standard "Severyns' law" variation (Severyns 1944–48, 2:96–97, 54). It is especially interesting that the phrase "son of Leto" is not only a traditional formulaic variant but also a relatively rare metronymic, whereas the form in the received text, Λητοῦς καὶ Διὸς υἱός "son of Leto and Zeus" is metrically equivalent to it, gives the names of both parents, and is formally less easy to parallel. Significantly, another metronymic for Apollo is actually attested in epic and lyric, Λητοΐδης 'son of Leto', in *Hymn to Hermes* 253; Hesiod *Shield* 479; Pindar *Pythian* 1.12, etc. The variant metronymic formula attested in the nonstandard prologue may well be more archaic than the bilateral name in the standard one; in any case, such a difference is difficult to motivate except as a genuine product of the evolving epic tradition. Another interesting feature of this prologue is its first line, which recurs four times in the *Iliad* (2.484, 11.218, 14.508, and 16.112) but always to introduce a catalog, whether of ships or fallen warriors; catalogs are a genre of Hesiodic poetry, and an almost identical line is also attested in the prologue to the *Theogony* itself, at line 114.

host of fighting men (καὶ λίσσετο πάντας 'Αχαιούς, "and he implored *all* of the Achaeans") [1.15] and in particular its leaders, the two sons of Atreus (named, pointedly, κοσμήτορε λαῶν "twin marshalers of the hosts" [1.16]), in the hope of effecting a transaction: to ransom his daughter. For Chryses, then, the "owner" of his daughter is the whole community, not just Agamemnon. His verbal offer of an exchange also takes the form of an implementation of the rules of reciprocal exchange. He expresses a kindly wish that the gods will favor the Achaeans in their attempt to sack Troy and return home, and in return he requests that they release his daughter, accept his ransom, and respect the god Apollo, whose priest he is (1.17–21). A clearer demonstration that exchange is, in Mauss's term, a total social phenomenon would be hard to contrive. Chryses' appeal to the group for an exchange of valuable goods under the protection of the god Apollo is at once social, economic, and religious. And the whole group—it is the same group that had presided over the distribution of goods and had awarded the priest's daughter to Agamemnon in the first place, as we soon find out (1.162, 276, 299, 367–69)—approves the transaction and commends respect for the status of the priest (1.22–23). There could not be a clearer indication that both the process of exchange and the value of the terms offered meet with social approval, as Mauss's theoretical principles would require.[11]

But the unthinkable takes place. Agamemnon dismisses Chryses, threatening him with violence if he persists and showing contempt for the priest's age and the tokens of his bond to Apollo. Chryses' offer of exchange had highlighted the social dimension of the transaction as against any link between the girl and Agamemnon's own status, but Agamemnon's response does the reverse. He sidesteps not only his role as leader but also any inherent obligations to the group's standards of behavior, in favor of his own desire (ἀλλ' οὐκ 'Ατρείδῃ 'Αγαμέμνονι ἥνδανε θυμῷ, "but it was not pleasing to Agamemnon, to his heart" [1.24]). Later, Agamemnon justifies himself by saying that he really wants (βούλομαι [1.112]) to have the girl at home, since he wants (προβέβουλα) her more than his own wife (1.113). Now there is ample reason to believe that a hero's wife in the Homeric hierarchy of value is the most costly and valuable of all exchangeable goods, in that she represents in her person the hero's own accumulated worth and prestige.[12] So Agamemnon's avowal that he prefers Chryseis to his wife

---

[11] See above, 36–37.

[12] Witness Helen and Penelope, but also the explicit statement in the *Odyssey* that whoever wins the hand of Penelope is the "best of the Achaeans," that is, becomes the hero of the epic and so wins the ultimate prestige. See Nagy 1979, 38–39 on 11.179. Penelope's power to confer *kléos*

amounts to a peremptory statement that she is not exchangeable for anything at all, including his wife. No little irony resides in Clytemnestra's corresponding preference of someone else to him, which makes her the negative ideal of a Homeric wife (*Odyssey* 24.199–202), but Agamemnon is unconscious of that irony, so that the face value of his statements in terms of the conventions of the Homeric society is worth bringing to mind. Agamemnon has taken leave of his social obligations and, on the basis of his own desire, valued this girl as an incommensurable piece of property. In doing so, he has made a grievous and obvious mistake about what she is (or is not) exchangeable for.

When the priest goes to the seashore and prays to Apollo Smintheus, he again uses the language of exchange to specify the appropriate return for his suffering: "May the Danaans pay [τείσειαν, literally 'pay'] for my tears with your weapons" (1.42). Apollo responds by shooting his arrows at mules, keen dogs, and then the bodies of men, the word for which, *autoísi* (51), anticipates their lifelessness.[13] Apollo's repayment is swift, massive, and indiscriminate, but the peculiar sequence of destruction calls for an explanation, since this is in fact the expression of Apollo's *mênis*. Heretofore the consequences of *mênis* have been indiscriminate, relentless devastation on a cosmic scale, usually manifested in celestial fire, not the death of mules and dogs.

The key to this variant of *mênis* is Apollo's invocation as Smintheus. It and two other well-attested epithets of Apollo, Parnopios and Karneios, all relate to the same semantic field. As Smintheus is an adjectival form of *smínthos* 'field mouse', so Parnopios derives from *párnops* 'grasshopper' and Karneios should derive from the gloss *karnós* 'louse that infests animals and plants (for instance, the vine)'.[14] Moreover, when the priest Chryses subse-

---

does not reflect some matrilocal tendency that would contradict the otherwise patrilocal rules of epic society but indicates that a wife is the embodiment of her husband's prestige; the same is true of the woman who serves as a hero's *géras*, as will be clear hereafter. From Nagy's standpoint, Penelope even represents the hero's *nóstos* 'return home', which is another name for the subject of his poem. Precisely the same notion about wives and poetic prestige was enacted when Agamemnon himself entrusted his wife to an *aoidós* 'singer' when he left for Troy—instead of bringing one along (*Odyssey* 3.267–68); note also the exile of this bard by the nefarious couple Clytemnestra and Aegisthus (3.270–71). See Nagy 1979 37–38, sec. 13 n. 5. On the other hand, in 24.196–97 Penelope herself may be construed as winning *kléos*, as discussed by Marilyn Katz (1991), which seems to me to complement the notion that she also confers it.

[13] For the meaning of the word αὐτός as 'dead body', see the contrast between αὐτούς and ψυχαί 'shades of the dead' in *Iliad* 1.3–4 and see Nagy 1979, 208.

[14] M. P. Nilsson (1968, 1:213, 535) made the connection between Apollo Smintheus and Parnopios and cites the evidence from Strabo (13, p. 604 etc.) to the effect that the cult image of Apollo at Chryse featured Apollo treading upon a field mouse; but in regard to Karneios, both he

quently refers to the damage Apollo has done in this instance, he says μέγα
ἴψαο λαὸν Ἀχαιῶν, "you greatly *ipsao* the host of Achaean fighting men'
(1.454), where the verb *ipsao* is a cognate of the noun *ips* 'woodworm found
in vines.'[15] Field mice, plant lice, grasshoppers, and woodworms—all are
small creatures capable of swelling to huge populations that inflict sudden
and massive devastation on vegetation. The usual translation of Apollo's
epithet Smintheus is "mouse killer," but the dictum of Martin Nilsson on
the way that gods function applies here in reverse: "He who wards off
disease can also send it."[16] The priest's invocation of Apollo Smintheus
means that his epithet can also be translated "mouse killer" in the sense of
one who uses mice to kill, just as on other occasions he may be the benevolent god who kills the mice.

As for the mules and dogs followed by the dead bodies of men, the
pairing corresponds to an archaic division of movable property into two
subgroups, the two-footed (humans) and the four-footed (animals), attested in a number of other ancient Indo-European languages and elsewhere in epic.[17] So the priest Chryses invokes Apollo in his capacity to
inflict massive devastation upon *plants* by the use of swarming, pestilential
creatures, and the god appears and attacks both forms of *nonplant* life, the
two-footed (humans) and the four-footed (animals). Apollo's epiphany as a
god who can wreak or arrest pestilential devastation upon plants has been

---

(1:533 n. 1) and Walter Burkert (1985, 235) speak of the second Hesychian gloss on the word
καρνός, namely, βόσκημα, πρόβατον 'flock of sheep or cattle' and gloss over the first one, φθείρ
'louse', because the Karneia included the sacrifice of a ram. The meaning 'flock of sheep' makes
sense in connection with the collective, swarming aspect of destructive insects; the ram in the
ritual may be a metonym for such a flock, or as I have just suggested, the name of the ritual may
pertain to the plant louse and not refer to the ram at all.

[15] Significantly, in its only other occurrence, Achilles uses exactly the same expression to refer
to Zeus's acts on behalf of his (Achilles') wrath right before he sends Patroklos into battle in
16.237. The meaning of the root from which ἴψ 'woodworm' and ἴπτομαι 'devastate' derive may
well have been the more general notion of 'devastate'. Specialization to one particular creature
that accomplishes devastation is a typical result of semantic competition: see Kuryłowicz 1966.
For a simple parallel to this common process, compare Latin *tegula* 'roof tile', which must once
have meant simply 'covering'.

[16] "Wer Krankheit sendet, kann sie auch abwehren," Nilsson 1968, 1:541. As instances of the
same syndrome, I am reminded by Gregory Nagy of the name of the California pest-control
mascot, Pestina, an angry caterpillar, and of the bear named Smokey who counsels Americans on
the prevention of forest fires.

[17] First described by Jacob Wackernagel (1910) on Sanskrit *dvipad-/cátuspad-* and Umbrian
*veiro pequo*, see also Schmitt 1967, 210–13; compare the parade around the body of Patroklos:
πρόσθε μὲν ἱππῆες, μετὰ δὲ νέφος εἵπετο πεζῶν, "in front of him were men on horseback, and after
him followed a cloud of foot soldiers" (23.133). This contrast is neither obvious nor universal. For
instance, there is another "totalizing" expression for animal life attested in Greek, namely, ἑρπετὰ
καὶ πετεινά, "things that walk (on the ground) and things that fly," Herodotus 1.140, etc.

extended into an ability to do so to animals and humans as well; in other words, Apollo can now destroy *all* living things, which is appropriate for a god inflicting *mênis* upon a social group. It is possible to explain this extension of Apollo's powers by examining the diction, for the effect of the onslaught of Apollo's arrows is in fact not sickness but fire:

οὐρῆας μὲν πρῶτον ἐπῴχετο καὶ κύνας ἀργούς,
αὐτὰρ ἔπειτ' αὐτοῖσι βέλος ἐχεπευκὲς ἐφιεὶς
βάλλ'· αἰεὶ δὲ πυραὶ καίοντο θαμειαί.
ἐννῆμαρ μὲν ἀνὰ στρατὸν ᾤχετο κῆλα θεοῖο.

First he went back and forth at the mules and the keen dogs,
and then, letting loose his pointed weapon at the bodies,
he struck: pyres were burning continually everywhere.
For nine days the shafts of the god went back and forth along the army.
(*Iliad* 1.50–53)

The narrative effect of the *kêla theoîo* 'shafts of the god' on the bodies is to cremate them. The expression *kêla theoîo* becomes still more relevant to its context when we realize that the noun *kêla* being translated 'shafts' is a plausible derivative of the same root as the verb in the previous line, *kaíonto* 'were burning'.[18] A variant of this expression, *kêla Diós*, "*kêla* of Zeus," is used at *Theogony* 708 of the thunderbolts hurled by Zeus at the Titans, and in *Iliad* 12.280 the phrase *tà hà kêla*, "those *kêla* of his (Zeus's)," describes aspects of a snowstorm. English lacks a generic term for weapons that are "thrown pieces of fire," if one can speak of such a thing, but in epic diction the association of this noun with fire is alive. It survives even in secondary derivatives of the noun *kêla*, such as *purì kēléōi*, "blazing fire," a phrase used four of the seven times it occurs to refer to fire as a weapon of war, specifically, the fire that the Trojans set to the Achaean ships (15.744, 8.217, 235, 22.374).[19] So "shaft" is not an accurate way to render either the

---

[18] The long vowel form the root of καίω 'burn' is attested in the epic aorist, ἔ-κη(ϝ)-α as well the adjective κήλεος 'burning'. There is no accepted etymology of κῆλον. Frisk 1970 and Chantraine 1968–79 withhold confirmation of such plausible cognates as Sanskrit *śara-*, *śarya-* 'arrow' and Middle Irish *cail* 'lance' because they exhibit a short vowel in their roots; but neither has anything better to suggest. The etymology I am proposing here is phonologically and semantically straightforward.

[19] In its three other attestations it is used of fire in the funerary ritual (compare the cremating fire in *Iliad* 1.52), the fire in which Andromache will burn Hector's garments even without his body (22.512), and the fire used to boil the water in which Patroklos's body is bathed (18.346).

connotations or the denotations of this term.[20] The closest word in English is perhaps *bolt*, which can be used of thunderbolts and also to denote crossbow arrows, or the word *firebrand*, which denotes a flaming piece of wood used as a weapon of destruction.

How to explain Apollo's bolts/firebrands with which he exercises his *mênis* upon the whole host of fighting men? These are surely a variant of the thunderbolt that functions as Zeus's expression of *mênis*, the ultimate weapon for the ultimate sanction. In other words, Apollo has taken over a function of Zeus, to exercise *mênis* in the human world, and the manifold symbolism that goes with it has been adapted to his own persona. I am not claiming that this is some ad hoc invention of a particular poet to suit an idiosyncratic circumstance; far from it. The adoption by Apollo of Zeus's attributes is a harmonious and traditional melding that recurs elsewhere and is consistent with the functional scheme of the epic pantheon, wherein Apollo regularly acts as the right hand of Zeus in concert or in parallel with Athena.[21] But the interpenetration of Zeus and Apollo also suits the context of a transition from divine myth to epic poem. Direct intervention in the human domain does not suit Zeus's style of rule, since he acts among mortals only through intermediaries. So the switch from Zeus's thunderbolts to fire-arrows shot by Apollo is a correlate to the leap from the *mênis* of Zeus to that of Achilles, a leap toward which it modulates. After all, it is one thing for another Olympian god (Apollo) to exercise a *mênis* that is analogous to Zeus's, and another for a mortal hero (Achilles) to do the same.

## The *Mênis* of Achilles or the *Mênis* of Agamemnon

Yet the *mênis* of Apollo is more than just a thematic intermediary between that of Zeus and that of Achilles. It functions as Achilles' model and

---

[20] West on *Theogony* 708 suggests that the traditional translation of κῆλα as arrow shafts stems from a false etymological connection with the noun κᾶλον 'firewood'; he notes the inappropriateness of the translation 'shaft', but not the etymological and contextual associations of κῆλα with fire. In fact, κᾶλον 'firewood' is also related to καίω 'burn' (see Chantraine 1968–79 and Frisk 1970, s.v.). If the etymology of κῆλα that I am proposing is correct, then they are parallel formations from the same root, perhaps at an earlier point dialectal variants of the same word that eventually became lexically distinct.

[21] These three gods in fact form a triumvirate cited as agents of the *admittedly impossible*. See Agamemnon's desire to have ten men as wise as Nestor (2.371–72) or Nestor's impossible wish to regain his youth (7.132–35) or Achilles' wish to survive and capture Troy with Patroklos and no one else (16.97). The implication seems to be that although these three constitute the most powerful coalition in the divine realm, even for them such a fantastic outcome is not possible. For Apollo as the instrument of *mênis*, see above, 10–18. For the complementary relationship between Apollo and Athena in the *Iliad*, see Nagy 1979, 144–50.

sets him into a relationship of identity and antagonism with Apollo that pervades the *Iliad*.[22] What triggers this relationship is Agamemnon's response to the realization that Apollo's *mênis* has confronted him with a decision about the relative value of the girl Chryseis as against the whole host of fighting men for whom he is responsible. In an assembly called at Hera's instigation by Achilles for the sake of the well-being of the whole host,[23] the priest Kalkhas informs Agamemnon that he must return the girl to her father without receiving anything in exchange for her other than the hope that by doing so the Achaeans *may* persuade Apollo to stop the devastation (called *loigós*, lines 67 and 97) of his whole social group.[24] The devastation explicitly ascribed to Apollo's *mênis* in line 75 is threatening the army's return home, to say nothing of its attempt to capture Troy, and even this reversal of Agamemnon's dismissal of the priest is not guaranteed to appease the god. In response, Agamemnon describes his preference for the girl over his wife, but then he says that he wants (using the verb *boúlomai* from line 112 once again at line 117) the host of fighting men to be safe rather than to perish, and so he is willing to give her back. In view of the incommensurable value he has just placed on the girl, he is portraying his willingness to give her up for the sake of the army's well-being as a sacrifice on his part, a loss that merits compensation from the group. As he says (1.119–20), it is "unseemly" (οὐδὲ ἔοικε) for him to be the only member of the group to be publicly deprived of his *géras* 'token of social esteem'. They should get him another one. Agamemnon is not saying that the army's welfare is more valuable to him than the girl; the point is rather that he will give up the girl for the army's sake but not without compensation for his loss. He does not contemplate for a moment the possibility of abiding the loss in status that goes with the uncompensated surrender of the girl, a surrender prescribed by an Achaean priest of Apollo that is intended to disgrace Agamemnon and the Achaeans, for the dishonor that Agamemnon paid the priest Chryses is being reciprocated by the god in an exchange of harm.[25] In fact, Agamemnon's response is a way of covering up for his mistake, of asserting his authority just when it is being eroded; but his initial

---

[22] For the essential features of this ritual antagonism, see Chirassi Colombo 1977; Nagy 1979, 142–50; Rabel 1990; Nagy 1994.
[23] Hera's concern is for the whole group of Danaans whose death she witnesses (56), and Achilles also speaks of the effects of war and plague on the Achaeans (61).
[24] The modal form of the verb meaning 'persuade' that Kalkhas uses at line 100, πεπίθοιμεν, admits the gravest doubt about that possibility without actually ruling it out. Indeed, until now we have only seen cases of *mênis* forestalled or incurred. Once incurred, it has never been arrested until its resulting devastation has run its course.
[25] For more on the theory and practice of "negative reciprocity," see Sahlins 1972, 185–275.

mistake about the girl remains a problem that will not go away. Now, in an effort to reverse the plummeting trajectory of his status, Agamemnon is about to make a second grievous error about the rules of exchange and the relative value of persons. It is once again rooted in his own desire and at the expense of his solidarity with the host of fighting men. It is important to note that an insistence on precisely that solidarity is a tellingly persistent feature of Achilles' response to Agamemnon's acts against him, just as it was built into Apollo's response to Agamemnon's acts against Chryses. Those who believe that Achilles is a hero without a social conscience have ignored a fundamental feature of his persona in this regard.

Achilles greets Agamemnon's demand for a new *géras* to replace the one he is willing to relinquish with disbelief (1.122–29). Since Agamemnon's discourse is teetering on the brink between praise and blame,[26] Achilles begins with a pair of superlatives for him, one honorific, the other critical—κύδιστε 'most glorious' and φιλοκτεανώτατε 'most attached to his possessions'[27]—and then reminds him that there is no storehouse of prizes or institution for reassembling and redistributing wealth, which would be truly "unseemly" (οὐκ ἐπέοικε [126]). Give back the girl to the god for now, Achilles says; the seemly way to get a new *géras* is to realize the ultimate goal of the warrior community and sack Troy. The distribution resulting from that victory will be more than sufficient to redress Agamemnon's present loss.

Achilles' response only exacerbates Agamemnon's status problem and pushes the discourse between them over the brink into unmitigated blame,

---

[26] On the functional contrast between praise and blame, see Dumézil 1943, Nagy 1979, 211–75, Martin 1989.

[27] The usual translation of this word is "most greedy for gain," but our notion of greed requires modification for a world where people as well as things are possessions invested with symbolic value. The difference between material and spiritual values does not exist, nor is Agamemnon a social deviant or revolutionary who has freed himself from the nexus of possessions and value in such a way as to prefer only the possessions; it is not plausible to consider Agamemnon overly attached to the physicality of his possessions. Since possessions are tokens of a person's social value, a desire to accumulate them is systemic, not vicious. The point of Achilles' epithet seems to be that possessions are exceptionally φίλο- 'near and dear' to Agamemnon since he is so reluctant to give them up and so eager for immediate restitution if he must do so. The insult would then be pertinent to both his rejection of the ransom for Chryseis and his present demand for restitution. Some degree of attachment to one's possessions is also a given in Homeric society; so Achilles' epithet may well have the ironically deprecating tone we take in calling a politician "ambitious." On the other hand, Agamemnon's rejoinder to *philokteanótate* in line 146, πάντων ἐκπαγλότατ' ἀνδρῶν, "most hostile of all men," is unambiguously pejorative, *pace* Kirk 1985, 68. The adjective ἔκπαγλος is continuously associated with dominant physical or sexual power in the epic, as is its verbal root, \**plēg*- (see Chapter 1, passim and passages such as *Iliad* 15.198–99). For the mirroring of epithets between Achilles and Agamemnon as a feature of Homeric speech exchanges, see Lohmann 1970, 183–212.

though not until the very end of Agamemnon's speech. Since to Agamemnon it looks as though Achilles is deceitfully outranking him by "bidding" (κέλεαι [134]) him, as one would an inferior, to give up his *géras* while Achilles would hold on to the one he received in the same distribution, Agamemnon offers two alternatives. The first is that the group award him a new *géras* that suits his desire and is a worthy exchange for the one he is giving up (135–36); failing that, he will himself take the *géras* of Achilles, Ajax, or Odysseus. The first alternative reasserts Agamemnon's rank with respect to the whole community; the second does the same with respect to its three best warriors, which makes it a more concrete and hostile assertion of his superiority to all. The first alternative is couched as the less likely of the two,[28] and if what Achilles has just said is correct, it is decidedly unlikely that the group can reconvene to award Agamemnon a new prize, since it has none to award. In proposing it, Agamemnon only makes the second alternative appear inevitable. In any case, he blithely postpones a decision as to what should happen in this regard and begins organizing the return of Chryseis to her father. In the process, he asserts his rank in the same vein by ordering the same group of warriors, this time augmented by Idomeneus, to furnish a captain for the ship that will bring her back. The inclusion of Idomeneus is just a way of rhetorically postponing and so highlighting his singling out of Achilles, whom he lists last and provocatively, with an insulting superlative epithet:[29]

> εἶς δέ τις ἀρχὸς ἀνὴρ βουληφόρος ἔστω,
> ἢ Αἴας ἢ Ἰδομενεὺς ἢ δῖος Ὀδυσσεὺς
> ἠὲ σύ, Πηλείδη, πάντων ἐκπαγλότατ' ἀνδρῶν,
> ὄφρ' ἡμῖν ἑκάεργον ἱλάσσεαι ἱερὰ ῥέξας.
>
> and let some man of counselor rank be the captain,
> either Ajax or Idomeneus or godlike Odysseus,
> or even you, son of Peleus, most hostile of all men,
> so that you may sacrifice and appease the far-worker for us.
> (1.144–47)

---

[28] At least, that is the way Agamemnon is presenting it. The first alternative is marked as the less likely one by the suppression of its conclusion (Chantraine 1963, 274–75) and by the grammatical mood of its verb δώσουσι (future), as opposed to δώωσι (subjunctive) in the second alternative, which the speaker considers more plausible. See Rijksbaron 1984, 70, for a close parallel in Herodotus.

[29] The rhetorical norm is a list of three names, with the third and concluding one preceded by an epithet; Agamemnon lists Ajax, Idomeneus, and godlike Odysseus, but once the list appears complete, he adds on Achilles.

Agamemnon is by now baiting Achilles and turning to the language of insult. It is possible for him to do so because the essential outlines of the conflict between them have already been defined. Agamemnon's resentment that his sovereign authority is under violent attack by a hero who is his social inferior is set off against Achilles' resentment of Agamemnon's disrespect for him and his contempt for the rules of exchange and communal distribution that sustain the social hierarchy itself.

It is also discernible that the source of each hero's grievance against the other is now bound up with the *mênis* theme. The verb derived from the name of the ultimate sanction is explicitly attached to each, to Agamemnon at line 247 and to Achilles at lines 422 and 488. As the quarrel unfolds, each uses links in diction with the order of Zeus established in the *Theogony* to lay claim to the supreme god's sanction. Zeus's order was based on a primordial division (called *dasmós* at *Theogony* 425–27) of prizes based on social esteem (called *géras* at *Theogony* 427) according to status or sphere (called *timê* at *Theogony* 421, 426), and we have seen in detail how violation of either Zeus's hierarchy or the *thémistes* that define and maintain it constitutes a threat to the world order punishable by massive, indiscriminate devastation.[30] In his speech responding to Agamemnon's provocation, Achilles speaks of the way Agamemnon has undermined the basis of his own authority (1.150–51), which is wedded to the system of distribution. He complains of the *dasmós* 'division' (166) of *géras* 'prizes' (161, 163, 167) and how Agamemnon's threat to remove even the relatively inferior prize that the group awarded him in disproportion to his major contribution to the battle is an offense to his *timê*, which in this context means "prestige" (171). He announces his return home to Phthia, since he was present in the first place not out of hostility to the Trojans but as a favor to Agamemnon and Menelaos, to restore their damaged *timê* (159). Having his own prestige damaged by those whose prestige he has come so far (156–57) to restore is evidently an unbearable contradiction. A little later, after Athena has appeared as Hera's surrogate and promised him triple the gifts if he refrains from actually killing Agamemnon, Achilles decides to remain in Troy but withdraw from the fighting.[31] Before doing so, he takes an oath on a scepter

---

[30] On the different meanings of *timê* in the divine and mortal realms, see above, 68 n. 39. For another instance of the *dasmós-géras-timê* structure on the divine level in Homeric epic, see the discussion of the beginning of *Iliad* 15 in Chapter 1, 28–30 and n. 48.

[31] Athena's appearance is not a manifestation of the *mênis* theme. Her role as Hera's surrogate, like Hera's prompting of Achilles to call the assembly in 1.55 in identical terms (compare lines 55–56 with lines 208–9), is to be referred to the Judgment of Paris, which allies the two goddesses on the side of the Achaeans against the Trojans and Aphrodite. Their concern to defuse the quarrel

wielded by the Achaeans who "have preserved the *thémistes* from Zeus" (οἵ τε θέμιστας / πρὸς Διὸς εἰρύαται [238–39]). Those *thémistes* have been trampled by Agamemnon and his "nobodies" (229–31), the Achaeans who put up with his voraciousness and are tacitly accepting, since they are not rejecting his order to take away the gift that they all gave Achilles (162). The content of Achilles' brief oath is at first surprisingly narrow. It voices only his conviction about the social dimensions of the devastation that his withdrawal will have and the powerless regret that will overtake Agamemnon when he realizes the mistake he is making about Achilles' value:

ἦ ποτ' Ἀχιλλῆος ποθὴ ἵξεται υἷας Ἀχαιῶν
σύμπαντας· τότε δ' οὔ τι δυνήσεαι ἀχνύμενός περ
χραισμεῖν, εὖτ' ἂν πολλοὶ ὑφ' Ἕκτορος ἀνδροφόνοιο
θνῄσκοντες πίπτωσι· σὺ δ' ἔνδοθι θυμὸν ἀμύξεις
χωόμενος ὅτ' ἄριστον Ἀχαιῶν οὐδὲν ἔτεισας.

at some point a yearning for Achilles is bound to come upon the sons of the Achaeans, on <u>all of them put together</u>; and then you [singular] will not at all be able to ward off [devastation] despite your anguish, when many fall dying beneath man-slaying Hector: but you [singular] will rip at the heart within yourself in your anger that you [singular] paid no honor at all to the best of the Achaeans.

(240–44)

But the underlying scope of this oath is clear in the perspective of the *mênis* theme. As in other instances of *mênis*, Achilles is specifying a whole solidary group as the object of the sanction his absence will impose, and he is expressly assuming Agamemnon's ultimate identity and solidarity with that group, just as Apollo had in punishing the whole host of fighting men rather than Agamemnon alone. Moreover, by blaming Agamemnon for another grievous mistake about a person's value—in this case, failing to respect and recognize Achilles' own value as "the best of the Achaeans"— Achilles is identifying the outrage done to him with the outrage done to Chryses. In other words, the oath is actually Achilles' claim to a *mênis* like Apollo's. Nor is it coincidental that Achilles overtly links it to the claim that he is the "best of the Achaeans," for in the first episode (1.91), Achilles

---

between Agamemnon and Achilles, like Hera's to end the *mênis* of Apollo, is in the interest of the success of the whole war effort and not for or against one or the other hero.

mentioned that Agamemnon asserts his right to that same title.³² Issues of relative status, as we have seen, are inextricable from the *mênis* theme. In this instance, if Achilles is indeed the best of the Achaeans, then Agamemnon has no grounds for *mênis* whatever—there is no tabu against treating an inferior as an inferior—and Achilles' grounds for anger at Agamemnon are even more imposing: to his violation of reciprocity obligations is added a breach of the social hierarchy.³³ What is especially striking is the oblique way in which Achilles suddenly asserts his absolute superiority, not as a direct, competitive assertion in propria persona³⁴ but as a tardy realization in the mind of Agamemnon. It is as though everyone but Agamemnon knows Achilles' value, just as everyone but Agamemnon knew Chryseis'.³⁵ At the conclusion of this short but potent oath, rather than hand on the scepter to the next speaker, Achilles hurls it to the ground. The gesture marks both his social detachment from the group of Agamemnon's Achaeans and that group's detachment from the divine and deathless *thémistes* of Zeus that the scepter represents.³⁶

In response, Agamemnon calls up his own *mênis*. He characterizes Achilles' threatened withdrawal as a symptom of defeat, a rout. Maintaining that his own sovereignty is intact, he claims *timḗ* from many, especially Zeus himself (1.175), the ultimate sovereign. As for Achilles' claim to superiority, Agamemnon dismisses it as violence (177) and physical prowess—calling him *karterós* 'strong' (178)—and divine gift only. The reference to divine gifts and thus to Achilles' mother is appropriate to this context, since genealogical status is a part of social rank, but Agamemnon is implying that Achilles' divine origin lessens the value of his prowess.³⁷ Then (182–84) he makes an explicit analogy between Apollo's depriving him of Chryseis and his depriving Achilles of Briseis, his *géras*. The implication is that Apollo's *mênis* was a response to an offense in the domain of status, and that as it

---

³² For the use of the verb *eúkhomai* 'say (proudly and accurately)' in line 91 to express the contentious assertion of a true claim, see Muellner 1976, 79–82.

³³ On the higher, poetic dimension of meaning in the title "best of the Achaeans," see Nagy 1979, 26–41, and passim.

³⁴ Indeed, Achilles has poignantly cast himself as a grammatical third person, as though he were already absent from the society from which he is about to withdraw. On the affect of the grammatical persons, see Benveniste 1966c, which cites Rimbaud's ungrammatical expression, "je est un autre," to convey the alienation implicit in third-person self-reference.

³⁵ For the overt validity of his claim, see again Nagy 1979.

³⁶ For the handing on of the scepter, see, for example, 2.185–86. My analysis of Achilles' oath does not exhaust its meaning; for more, see Lowenstam 1993, 59–143.

³⁷ Others do not share this view. For example, Nestor lists Achilles' divine birth along with his strength as an aspect of his status at 1.280–81.

justified Agamemnon's loss of Chryseis, so Agamemnon's *mênis* justifies the seizing of Briseis from the disrespectful Achilles:

> ὡς ἔμ' ἀφαιρεῖται Χρυσηίδα Φοῖβος Ἀπόλλων,
> τὴν μὲν ἐγὼ σὺν νηί τ' ἐμῇ καὶ ἐμοῖς ἑτάροισι
> πέμψω, ἐγὼ δὲ κ' ἄγω Βρισηίδα καλλιπάρηον
> αὐτὸς ἰὼν κλισίηνδε, τὸ σὸν <u>γέρας</u>, ὄφρ' ἐὺ εἰδῇς
> ὅσσον <u>φέρτερός</u> εἰμι σέθεν, στυγέῃ δὲ καὶ ἄλλος
> ἶσον ἐμοὶ φάσθαι καὶ ὁμοιωθήμεναι ἄντην.

> As Phoebus Apollo is depriving me of Chryseis,
> I will send her off with my ship and my companions,
> but I will go myself to your hut and get fair-cheeked Briseis,
> that *géras* of yours, so that you may know well
> how much better [*phérteros*] I am than you, and so that another
> would also dread to appear as my equal and be likened to me face to face.
>
> (182–87)

At the same time as Agamemnon is basing his *mênis* on Apollo's, he is using the same language that Zeus uses in book 15 to threaten Poseidon with *mênis* and make him stand down from his desire to be treated as an equal:

> φραζέσθω δὴ ἔπειτα κατὰ φρένα καὶ κατὰ θυμόν,
> μή μ' οὐδὲ <u>κρατερός</u> περ ἐὼν ἐπιόντα ταλάσσῃ
> μεῖναι, ἐπεί ἑο φημὶ βίῃ πολὺ <u>φέρτερος</u> εἶναι
> καὶ γενεῇ πρότερος· τοῦ δ' οὐκ ὄθεται φίλον ἦτορ
> ἶσον ἐμοὶ φάσθαι, τόν τε στυγέουσι καὶ ἄλλοι.

> Let him [Poseidon] consider then in his heart and spirit,
> so that strong [*krateros*] as he is he will not dare to await
> my onset, since I assert that I am much better [*phérteros*] than he in force
> and earlier in birth; yet his dear heart does not care about
> appearing equal to me, whom others also dread.
>
> (15.163–67)

In effect, Agamemnon is adducing both Apollo and Zeus, whose *timḗ* he claims at the beginning of his speech, as models for his *mênis*, although the comparison of his words to Zeus's suggests a problem that again evokes the succession myth in the *Theogony*.

Along with his birthright as the elder (sic), Zeus nakedly asserts that he is superior (*phérteros*) in *bíē* 'capacity for destructive force, violence' to Poseidon, strong (*karterós*) as he is.³⁸ In contrast, Agamemnon claims that Achilles is violent and strong (*karterós*), but that he himself is better (*phérteros*). In Zeus's rank assertion, *phérteros* 'better' and *karterós* 'strong' are not opposed but complementary. In fact his superiority principally resides in his greater strength. Accordingly, the distinction between *karterós* and *phérteros* in Agamemnon's rank assertion appears to be specious, for it is not clear from it *in what the superiority of Agamemnon can consist*.³⁹ In the absence of force, there is cunning and genealogy, but nothing suggests that Agamemnon prevails in those domains either.⁴⁰ The solution to this problem is implicit in Agamemnon's initial statement that he has *timế* from many and especially Zeus and in his contemptuous command to Achilles earlier in this speech. "Go home with your ships and your companions and rule over [your] Myrmidons" (179–80), he tells him, to highlight the contrast between Achilles' petty kingdom and his vast assemblage of subjects. The locus of Agamemnon's superior status is the extent of his domains and subject peoples. This becomes explicit when Nestor later restates Agamemnon's assertion of superior rank in an unsuccessful attempt to reconcile the two heroes: "You Achilles are strong [*karterós* again], and a goddess mother bore you, but he is better [*phérteros* again] since he rules over more people" (280–81). In this opposition, the fact of broader power advances Agamemnon's status beyond Achilles'.⁴¹ But that only poses the problem on another level, since that power of his appears to be a mere fact, without resonance in the Theogonic ideology of sovereignty based on one of two qualities, superior force or superior cunning. Agamemnon possesses and strives to preserve the scope of his sovereignty, but in terms of the myth of Zeus's kingship, he

---

³⁸ Zeus concedes that Poseidon is *kraterós* (line 164), κρατερός περ ἐών, "strong as you are" just as Poseidon concedes that Zeus is, κρατερός περ ἐών (15.195). To repeat, each is conceding *the other's* prowess. (The spellings *kraterós* and *karterós* are metrical alternates of the same word.)

³⁹ Perhaps such speciousness also accounts for the false parallelism in suffixation between the two words, since the *-teros* suffix of *phérteros* is a true comparative, whereas that of *karterós*, which sounds the same, is actually a simple adjectival suffix. Agamemnon only appears to be offering a balanced assessment of qualities in himself and Achilles.

⁴⁰ Nestor's conciliatory formula has both Achilles and Agamemnon superior to the rest of the Achaeans in counsel and fighting (1.258). On the other hand, there is Achilles' second oath, in which he expresses his opinion that Agamemnon "does not know how to think forward and backward at the same time" (343). Admittedly, Achilles is a biased witness, but the outcome of the first episode and of the *Iliad* as a whole seems to bear out Achilles' view; thinking forward and backward at the same time is a mark of cunning; as I have shown in Chapter 3, Zeus's *mêtis*, for instance, synthesizes past and present. On Agamemnon's genealogical status with respect to Achilles, see note 42 below and Segal 1971b.

⁴¹ For additional references by Nestor to the quantity of Agamemnon's subjects as the basis of his status, see *Iliad* 9.69–74, and 97: ἐν σοὶ μὲν λήξω, σέο δ' ἄρξομαι οὕνεκα πολλῶν / λαῶν ἐσσι ἄναξ, "in you will I end, and I will begin with you since you are lord of many hosts." Note also that by book 9, Nestor is calling Achilles ἄνδρα φέριστον, "the best man" (9.110).

appears to be a king lacking superior force, superior cunning, and probably superior genealogical status as well.[42] Can *mênis* modeled on that of Apollo and Zeus supervene to legitimate Agamemnon's kingship, or vice versa?

The quarrel between Agamemnon and Achilles really comes down to a single issue: who has the right to *mênis*? The converse should also be true: in order to halt the quarrel between them, each hero should cease his *mênis*. Nestor's speech of "reconciliation" concludes as follows:

'Ἀτρείδη σὺ δὲ παῦε τεὸν μένος· αὐτὰρ ἔγωγε
λίσσομ' Ἀχιλλῆϊ μεθέμεν χόλον, ὃς μέγα πᾶσιν
ἕρκος Ἀχαιοῖσιν πέλεται πολέμοιο κακοῖο.

Son of Atreus, you stop [παῦε] your *ménos*; and I personally
implore you to let go of your *khólos* at Achilles, who is a
great barrier in evil war for all the Achaeans.

(1.282–84)

Actually, Nestor only aims to put an end to Agamemnon's *mênis*; the words *ménos* and *khólos* are regularly attested as terms that cross-refer to it.[43] He tells him not to take away Briseis but to leave her as the Achaeans gave her, to Achilles. True, that would remove the cause of Achilles' *mênis*, but that is a consequence of his advice, not its primary goal. Nestor immediately tells

---

[42] In a parallel passage to this one, which will be further discussed later, at the conclusion of his offer of prizes to Achilles in Book 9, Agamemnon orders Achilles to assume an inferior rank—μοι ὑποστήτω, "let him stand beneath me" (160)—on the grounds that he is *basileúteros* 'more kingly' than Achilles; but then he actually adds that he is also *progenésteros* 'older [sic] in birth' (161). 'More kingly' refers again to the greater scope of his power, and the claim to be older than Achilles resonates with Zeus's assertion that he is superior in force to Poseidon and 'older in birth' (15.166). Zeus is older than Poseidon only in the sense that Poseidon was reborn after Zeus had been born and reborn. At best, the age ranking asserted by Zeus, added by Agamemnon in book 9, and omitted here, is a weak point. There is reason to doubt that Agamemnon's greater age commands more respect than Achilles' divine genealogy, including Nestor's statement here in book 1 (line 280). In epic genealogical jousting, the focus is on the contents of the genealogy, not the age of the contestants. See, for instance, the examples in Muellner 1976, 69–78. When Nestor invokes his own advanced age as grounds for respect from younger heroes, he adds other criteria as well (as in *Iliad* 1.259–61). Lastly, the *Theogony* attests to a fundamental ambivalence about the privileges of age, since the youngest regularly prevails, most significantly in the case of Zeus himself, who is youngest and eldest at once. That is another in the list of opposites that he implausibly and uniquely combines (see above, Chapter 3, 91–93).

[43] The words *khólos* and *ménos* can be used to *refer back* to *mênis*, but they do not carry the connotations of *mênis* in contexts that have not been previously defined as instances of the *mênis* theme. In fact, in contexts that are not previously defined as *mênis*, *khólos* has its own set of resonances and connotations. See Walsh 1989 and his forthcoming work based upon it. For other examples of *ménos* and *khólos* referring back to *mênis*, see the discussion of book 15 in Chapter 1, including 30–31 with n. 50, and Chapter 2, 41 n. 27.

Achilles not to rile Agamemnon on the grounds that he is his superior, so that the two injunctions establish a context of ending Agamemnon's *mênis* at Achilles, not vice versa. First Nestor reinforces Agamemnon's contrast between who is *phérteros* (Agamemnon) and who is *karterós* (Achilles). Then he concludes with the lines just quoted, a direct plea to Agamemnon to end his *mênis* and recognize Achilles' value in war to the whole social group.

Nothing here addresses the situation from Achilles' point of view, but by the time Nestor intervenes, Athena has already recognized Achilles' *mênis*, though *without anyone else's knowing of it*. After Agamemnon has stated definitively that he would himself deprive Achilles of his *géras*, Achilles tries to decide whether to demonstrate definitively his superiority in *bíē* and kill Agamemnon outright or whether to "restrain his *khólos*," as the poet puts it (192). As he is pondering these alternatives, he is actually drawing his sword, leaving no doubt as to which choice he will make. At that moment Athena comes down and appears from behind to him alone "to halt [παύσουσα] his *ménos*" (207). She promises Achilles triple damages if he holds back. In another demonstration of his strict adherence to the rules of exchange, he readily accepts her offer with a proverb about reciprocal obligations: ὅς κε θεοῖς ἐπιπείθηται, μάλα τ' ἔκλυον αὐτοῦ, "Anyone who obeys the gods, they really hear him" (218). The successful restraint of Achilles' *ménos* and *khólos* by Athena contrasts dramatically with Nestor's effort to do the same for Agamemnon. Nothing could be more private and intimate than Achilles' invisible and flattering encounter with the goddess, who promises him justifiable recompense if he will turn from an irrevocable action to words.[44] By contrast, *all the Achaeans* witness Nestor's humiliating and fruitless attempt to use words to deflect Agamemnon from taking an action that has in fact become irrevocable, since he has already announced it and will not further debase himself by recanting. All that Nestor can offer Agamemnon is a restatement of Agamemnon's view of his superior status vis-à-vis Achilles and a chastisement of Achilles for speaking up against his superior. So it is not surprising that Nestor's formulation has the effect of exacerbating Agamemnon's *mênis* instead of quelling it. He responds to Nestor with an aggrieved, exaggerated account of Achilles' desire to dominate him—that is indeed Agamemnon's fundamental problem,

---

[44] It is perhaps unnecessary to point out, after a work such as Richard Martin's *Language of Heroes*, that this conversion to words from acts is not as drastic in epic as it would be in our world. Words are a form of action in epic, and they can have the attributes and consequences of violent deeds. For instance, the word ἐκπαγλός 'violent' is used for deeds (above, n. 27) and for abusive speech (as in 15.198), or ἀντίβιος 'exchanging violence' is applied to physical and verbal exchanges (1.304 vs. 3.20, etc.).

who outranks whom—and then he asks, with unconscious irony, if Achilles has a divine license to abuse him with words just because the gods made him a warrior (291).[45]

As for Achilles, he answers Agamemnon, not Nestor, and in a way that closely resembles Poseidon's answer to Zeus's threat of *mênis* against him in book 15. That is, his speech is an aggressive concession to Agamemnon that flatly contradicts both the tenor and the content of Nestor's remarks. Achilles first denies that there is any impropriety in his speaking out against Agamemnon and refuses to give in to him, but then he concedes the girl:

ἄλλο δέ τοι ἐρέω, σὺ δ' ἐνὶ φρεσὶ βάλλεο σῇσι·
χερσὶ μὲν οὔ τοι ἔγωγε μαχήσομαι εἵνεκα κούρης
οὔτε σοὶ οὔτε τῳ ἄλλῳ, ἐπεί μ' ἀφέλεσθέ γε δόντες·
τῶν δ' ἄλλων ἅ μοί ἐστι θοῇ παρὰ νηῒ μελαίνῃ,
τῶν οὐκ ἄν τι φέροις ἀνελὼν ἀέκοντος ἐμεῖο·
εἰ δ' ἄγε μὴν πείρησαι, ἵνα γνώωσι καὶ οἵδε·
αἶψά τοι αἷμα κελαινὸν ἐρωήσει περὶ δουρί.

I will tell you [singular] another thing, and you store it in your mind:
For my part, I will not fight you [singular] hand-to-hand for the girl,
not you [singular] nor anyone else, since you [plural] who gave her to me
    took her away.
But as for the other things that I have beside my swift black ship,
you [singular] may not take a single one of them away against my will;
go on, try it, to let these others here know as well:
then your black blood will spurt up around my spear.

(297–303)

The solidarity here between the "you" (= the Achaeans) who gave Achilles his *géras* and the "you" (= Agamemnon) to whom Achilles is conceding her is being ironically reinforced by a growing social gulf between both "you-s" and Achilles. Achilles' reason for not fighting over the girl is that the same people who gave her are now taking her away. In societies that are governed by rules of exchange, taking away what is not yours is usually an unequivocal act of war that thenceforth defines the parties concerned as reciprocating enemies.[46] So the deadly violence with which Achilles initially wished to reciprocate Agamemnon's decision to

---

[45] As Douglas Frame points out (1978, 84–85), Nestor is a symbol of intelligence but not usually an effective user of it.
[46] On the rules of reciprocal exchange in archaic societies, see above, 35 n. 13.

take away Briseis was expectable and normal. In response to Athena's offer of recompense, however, Achilles restrained himself from violent action and turned to words. Now Achilles says that he will not fight Agamemnon over the girl, since the Achaeans who gave her to him are taking her away. The logic of Achilles' interpretation of his inaction, an interpretation which he makes as a consequence of his agreement with the goddess not to resort to physical violence, is that Agamemnon's action in taking away the girl unopposed institutionalizes a social gulf between Agamemnon and his Achaeans over against Achilles. It detaches them from one another socially just as the exchange of gifts or of harm attaches social groups or individuals to one another in positive or negative social contracts. Accordingly, it will take a *further* act of stealing to define them as actual enemies. The unopposed taking away of Briseis establishes a zero relationship between Achilles on one side and the Achaeans with Agamemnon on the other—a relationship that could become a negative one indeed if Agamemnon tries to take something else from Achilles or vice versa. The result of these events is precisely as Achilles defines it. Henceforth, he and the Achaeans with Agamemnon are neither friends nor enemies. No social contract whatever exists between them. In the end, Achilles' speech is no simple concession. It creates an extraordinary space in which Achilles will express *mênis* against the Achaeans and Agamemnon without interacting with them in any conventional way whatsoever. On the other hand, Achilles' contract with Athena has reinforced his ties to the divine community. It is even plausible to say that he has given up his ties to the Achaean community in the name of his ties to the divine one.

There are two strange things happening here, then. The first is Agamemnon's taking back a prize that his society gave to one of its members, and the second is that the person who is being deprived of that prize is not resisting the loss by the use of force or knuckling under to a superior but, by returning it, is zeroing out his relationship to the society that gave it to him on that basis. It is not that either of these two actions is prohibited or inconsistent with a system of reciprocal exchange but that they are not normally conceived or conceivable within it. The peculiar features of Achilles' response are especially clear from a comparison to the closely parallel response of Poseidon to Zeus's demand that he retire from battle. Zeus backs his demand with a threat of *mênis* based on an explicit assertion of his superiority in *bíē* 'capacity for physical violence, killing power'. Poseidon considers himself equal in *tīmē* to Zeus (15.186, 209–11), but unlike Achilles, who says that he would be rightly called worthless or cowardly if he were to "give" in (1.294, verb *hupeíkō*) to Agamemnon in everything and that he "will no longer obey him" (296), Poseidon explicitly "gives in" (15.211, verb *hupeíkō*):

ἀλλ' ἤτοι νῦν μέν κε νεμεσσηθεὶς ὑποείξω·
ἄλλο δέ τοι ἐρέω, καὶ ἀπειλήσω τό γε θυμῷ·
αἴ κεν ἄνευ ἐμέθεν καὶ 'Αθηναίης ἀγελείης,
"Ηρης Ἑρμείω τε καὶ Ἡφαίστοιο ἄνακτος,
Ἰλίου αἰπεινῆς πεφιδήσεται, οὐδ' ἐθελήσει
ἐκπέρσαι, δοῦναι δὲ μέγα κράτος Ἀργείοισιν,
ἴστω τοῦθ', ὅτι νῶϊν ἀνήκεστος χόλος ἔσται.
ὣς εἰπὼν λίπε λαὸν Ἀχαιϊκὸν ἐννοσίγαιος,
δῦνε δὲ πόντον ἰών, πόθεσαν δ' ἥρωες Ἀχαιοί.

Justly offended that I am, I will still give in [*hupoeíxō*];
but I will tell you another thing, and I will make this threat from the heart:
if without me and Athena who leads the host
and Hera and Hermes and lord Hephaistos[47]
he intends to spare steep Ilium and will not be willing
to destroy it utterly and grant great might to the Argives,
let him know this, that the anger [*khólos*] between us two will be incurable.
So speaking the earth-shaker left the Achaean host
and went and plunged into the sea, and the Achaean warriors missed him.

(15.211–19)

Achilles also retires to his own domain and is also missed by the Achaeans after his speech of aggressive concession, but Poseidon has neither detached himself from the divine community nor compromised his ultimate allegiance to the Achaeans' cause. He complains but backs down, and he decides not to fight Zeus on the issue of his superiority. Instead of fighting now, he draws the uncrossable line a little farther back, saying that if Zeus ultimately decides to protect Troy to the extent of undoing its destined destruction, at the expense of the Achaeans, then their anger (called *khólos*) will be incurable (217) along with that of the other gods who are on the Achaeans' side. In responding this way, Poseidon preserves his relationship to the Achaeans and to the divine community and in particular to the gods who are his allies within it. But Achilles divorces himself from the Achaean community by actually *giving back* the gift that they gave him and threatening violence if they try to take something else. By doing so and by not

---

[47] On such a constellation of Olympians ranged against Zeus, which is in itself an allusion to the *mênis* theme, see below, 118–20; cf. Lang 1983.

actively resisting Agamemnon, Achilles does preserve his ties to Athena, Hera, and the divine community. There is one additional significant difference between Achilles' and Poseidon's responses: Poseidon actually postpones his *mênis* until the unthinkable eventuality of a Trojan victory, whereas Achilles just states his readiness to respond violently to further provocation, which he menacingly invites. In no way does he relinquish his claim to *mênis* on the current issue. So the fundamental question in the quarrel between Agamemnon and Achilles, "Which hero has the right to *mênis?*" is still unresolved, though not for long.

### The Real *Mênis* of Achilles

The process of defining a mortal's *mênis* as distinct from the *mênis* of Zeus is finally about to reach the end of its first phase. Since Achilles' retort to Agamemnon effectively rules out interaction between him and the Achaeans other than his handing over Briseis, once his speech is over the two men who have been "fighting with exchange of violent words," ἀντιβίοισι μαχεσσαμένω ἐπέεσσιν (304), stand up—apparently the rule is that if more than one person stands, public speech is concluded, since normally one person, the speaker, stands while all others remain seated—and the assembly disbands. Achilles goes to his hut and ships "with Patroklos and his companions" (307), a detail that highlights the social exile he has imposed upon himself at the termination of the assembly. Henceforth, Achilles has only two domains in which to interact, that of the gods and that of Patroklos and the Myrmidons. For his part, Agamemnon orders Odysseus to return Chryseis and carries out a ritual purification of the Achaeans' camp. Then he sends his two heralds to Achilles' hut to collect Briseis.

The poet describes these heralds as unwilling (1.327), fearful (331), and respectful of Achilles to such an extent that upon their arrival they are even unable to address him a single word (331–32)—not the conventional behavior of heralds. Achilles understands (ἔγνω [333]) that their silence is a misapprehension, a mistaken fear that he thinks them responsible for their mission; so he breaks the silence and explains to them that he blames Agamemnon (335), not them. When a similarly fearful (76–83) Kalkhas had earlier conveyed the message to Agamemnon that he had to return Chryseis, Agamemnon did not restrain himself from voicing his hostility at the messenger (102–20). This scene with the heralds, in which Achilles graciously deprecates their fear of like treatment and hands over the girl without being asked, again marks Achilles' sociability. Moreover, the oath that he swears, with them as witnesses, focuses on Agamemnon's inability to defend the society for which he is responsible:

εἴ ποτε δὴ αὖτε
χρειὼ ἐμεῖο γένηται ἀεικέα λοιγὸν ἀμῦναι
τοῖς ἄλλοις· ἦ γὰρ ὅ γ' ὀλοιῇσι φρεσὶ θύει,
οὐδέ τι οἶδε νοῆσαι ἅμα πρόσσω καὶ ὀπίσσω,
ὅππως οἱ παρὰ νηυσὶ σόοι μαχέοιντο Ἀχαιοί.

if ever once again [dè aûte]
a need for me should arise to ward off unseemly destruction [loigós]
for these others: truly he [Agamemnon] is raging in his destructive mind,
nor does he know how to think [noêsai] at once forward and backward,
so that the Achaeans may fight for him safely beside the ships.

(1.340–44)

This time Achilles is swearing that Agamemnon is acting antisocially, without the intelligence to secure the safety of his fighting men, for he has failed to foresee that they will once again (dè aûte [340]) become the victims of the devastation (loigós) that is the result of *mênis*.[48] "Not knowing how to think at once forward and backward" is the opposite of Zeus's behavior in the *Theogony*, where we witnessed his intelligence (called *mêtis* there; here the word for 'think,' noêsai, is a derivative of its more archaic synonym, nóos),[49] bridging the past (forward) and the future (behind), anticipating what would happen on the basis of what had happened and learning from others' experience. Agamemnon is in fact making the same mistake twice and so not even learning from his own immediately preceding experience. Achilles will become his second Apollo, and Achilles even foretells how he himself will be called upon to ward off the consequences of his own *mênis*. In contrast to Agamemnon, then, Achilles does have the intelligence to foresee the disaster of which he will be both cause and cure. The narrative, however, does not choose to name this intelligence.[50] For the moment, it is more significant that Achilles' emphasis on Agamemnon's inability to safe-

---

[48] The word *loigós* 'devastation' and the expression ἀεικέα λοιγὸν ἀμῦναι, "to ward off unseemly *loigós*," are contextually restricted in epic to the devastation that is the result of *mênis*. See Nagy 1979, 73–76. This is another allusion to the parallelism between Apollo's and Achilles' *mênis*.

[49] On the historical and semantic relationship between nóos and *mêtis*, see Frame 1978, 71–72, 72 n. 65, and 82–85.

[50] On possible reasons for this reticence, see below, 130–31. Lacking a homecoming and excelling in bíē, Achilles cannot be categorized as a hero with nóos or *mêtis*.

guard his host already signals the devastating social dimensions that Achilles' *mênis* will have: so the hero with heightened social sensitivity who acted to save the Achaeans from a self-willed leader who was consuming his people will expressly inflict massive devastation on the very society he set out to protect. To be sure, Achilles is here anticipating his first goal; yet our notion of suspense only pallidly approximates the effect generated by anticipation of the *télos* or goal in traditional narrative. What preoccupy us now are the causal steps in the resolution of the struggle between Achilles and Agamemnon that a thoughtful person should be able to foresee.

Turning away from the Achaeans and the Myrmidons, Achilles at the seashore weeps to his mother, Thetis.[51] She responds to his suffering with an empathetic epiphany and another divine request for words, whereupon he elaborately retells the narrative of the *Iliad* up to this point. This retelling is conventional epic retardation before a decisive moment.[52] But it is also noteworthy that Achilles begins it at a new logical starting point, the sack of Thebe, an event that is actually prior to the beginning of our *Iliad*; moreover, the last narrative element in his tale, the old story of Thetis helping Zeus, is not part of Achilles' story at all. These added narrative elements that frame Achilles' recapitulation bespeak the metonymic principle whose operation we have witnessed in the Hesiodic succession myth, wherein narrative recapitulation rebuilds the causality between episodes in preparation for a new episode.[53] Restarting from the "true" beginning restores and strengthens the coherence of the narrative's sequence, whereas ending that sequence with another story altogether prepares for a significant new episode.

The other story that Achilles tells at the end of his own is especially interesting, since it appears to be digressive rather than integral.[54] At line 393 Achilles finishes retelling his own story; then he asks his mother to go to Zeus and beg a favor on her son's behalf. In order to ask a favor of someone, however, you must either offer compensation or the favor must be compensation for a favor you have done.[55] So Achilles retells his mother's story:

---

[51] For the displacement of the language of prayer by that of tears, see Muellner 1976, 23.

[52] On the retardation convention, see Auerbach 1953; and Austin 1966.

[53] On the metonymic recapitulation function, see above, 54.

[54] Some think it an ad hoc invention of the poet, but the whole concept of ad hoc invention is radically inconsistent with the principles of traditional poetic composition. For a landmark statement of the theoretical issue, see Nagy 1992. For more on multiforms of this story, see above, 80 n. 66, and below, 121–22.

[55] On the principles of reciprocity implicit here, see, for example, the variants in Homeric prayers, Muellner 1976, 26–31.

πολλάκι γάρ σεο πατρὸς ἐνὶ μεγάροισιν ἄκουσα
εὐχομένης, ὅτ' ἔφησθα κελαινεφέϊ Κρονίωνι
οἴη ἐν ἀθανάτοισιν ἀεικέα λοιγὸν ἀμῦναι,
ὁππότε μιν ξυνδῆσαι Ὀλύμπιοι ἤθελον ἄλλοι,
Ἥρη τ' ἠδὲ Ποσειδάων καὶ Παλλὰς Ἀθήνη·
ἀλλὰ σὺ τόν γ' ἐλθοῦσα, θεά, ὑπελύσαο δεσμῶν,
ὦχ' ἑκατόγχειρον καλέσασ' ἐς μακρὸν Ὄλυμπον,
ὃν Βριάρεων καλέουσι θεοί, ἄνδρες δέ τε πάντες
Αἰγαίων'—ὁ γὰρ αὖτε βίην οὗ πατρὸς ἀμείνων—
ὅς ῥα παρὰ Κρονίωνι καθέζετο κύδεϊ γαίων·
τὸν καὶ ὑπέδεισαν μάκαρες θεοὶ οὐδ' ἔτ' ἔδησαν.
τῶν νῦν μιν μνήσασα παρέζεο καὶ λαβὲ γούνων.

I often heard you speaking proudly of it in my father's halls,
when you used to say how you alone among the immortals
warded off unseemly devastation [*loigós*] for the dark-clouded son of Kronos,
when the other Olympians were wanting to tie him up,
Hera and Poseidon and Pallas Athene;
but you went to him, goddess, and set him free from the bonds,
swiftly calling up to great Olympus a Hundred-Hander,
one whom the gods call Briareos but all men
Aigaion—for he also is greater in strength than his father—
who sat beside the son of Kronos and exulted in his glory;
and the blessed gods feared him and no longer tied him up.
Reminding him of these things, sit beside him and take him by the knees.
(1.396–407)

Achilles goes on to specify what Thetis should ask Zeus to do on his behalf, namely, help out the Trojans and bottle up the Achaeans so that they will be killed. Then the Achaeans will all get the full benefit of their king, and Agamemnon himself will realize his mistake in paying no honor to "the best of the Achaeans" (408–12).

In other words, Achilles suggests that Thetis use this tale in asking Zeus to become the active agent of his *mênis*. In fact, this story, whose distinctive Hesiodic style has been noted by Laura Slatkin,[56] is about Thetis *averting* the *mênis* of Zeus by forestalling an attempt on his sovereignty by the other Olympians. It is therefore a sequel to the *Theogony*, an episode in the succession myth in which for the first time a group that includes members

[56] Slatkin 1991, 60–77.

of a sovereign's own generation undertake to overthrow him by binding. Binding is one of the traditional metaphors for immortal "death," as was clear in my survey of the contexts of *mênis* in Homeric epic.⁵⁷ I noted that there were instances in which martial and sexual offenses incurred divine *mênis,* but offenses in the third sphere, that of sovereignty itself, were lacking. The attempt to bind Zeus that Thetis thwarted is a direct attack on the sovereign of the world. This tale, which Achilles is presenting as related to his own situation and as justification for Zeus's assisting him and his mother, has two variant features—by which I mean features that are predictable multiforms consistent with the other episodes of the succession myth—that are reflected specifically in the *mênis* of Achilles. In both contexts, the issue is who occupies the top of the social hierarchy—king of the gods in the divine, Hesiodic context, "best of the Achaeans" in the heroic, Homeric one. In neither context does the threat to the existing hierarchy come from an elder generation. A revolt from within Zeus's own generation is well motivated, since by now Zeus has either demonstrated his ability to meet threats from members of other generations or made allies of them. That is also why one such ally, a Hundred-Hander from the primordial first generation, is the perfect and significant choice to suppress this threat from Zeus's peers. His presence at the divine table is itself a mark of Zeus's success in bridging past and present, in outdoing his predecessors. From this perspective, a fundamental achievement of Zeus in the *Theogony* was to end conflict between generations (over succession) and so make the world stable enough for conflict within generations (over status).⁵⁸

So Achilles argues that just as his mother intervened to help Zeus enforce his status and so avoid the devastation that would arise from his exercising *mênis* to put down an attempt to displace himself from power, so Zeus should help enforce Achilles' superior status and actually inflict the devastation of *mênis* upon the Achaeans. The asymmetry is as striking as the symmetry. Whereas Thetis "alone averted devastation" (398) and protected both Zeus and her fellow immortals from *mênis* by forestalling their revolt, Achilles is expressly demanding that Zeus take part in the social devastation that will inevitably accompany the exercise of *mênis*. It is noteworthy that this asymmetry between Achilles' and Zeus's situations would disappear if

---

⁵⁷ See above, 7, 23, and 77 with n. 58.
⁵⁸ There is another variable element that emerges in the tests of Zeus in the *Theogony*: whether the party threatening the top of the hierarchy is an individual, like Prometheus or Typhoeus, or a group, like the Titans. Here Agamemnon and the Achaeans match a group of Olympians in revolt against Zeus, an imperfect social analogy that strongly suggests that Thetis's story is a genuine variant independent of the *Iliad* and not one "devised" for this particular context.

Achilles were Agamemnon, a leader threatened by a stronger subordinate; thus, it implies the legitimacy, or at least the potential seriousness, of Agamemnon's claims.[59] Yet there is one key factor that strongly entitles Achilles to invoke the story of Thetis's intervention on Zeus's behalf: the category "best of the Achaeans" transcends political sovereignty and pertains to traits that may or may not be a basis of political power, such as *mêtis* 'creative cunning', *bíē* 'destructive force', and their associated faculties, symbols, and consequences.

In telling his mother's tale, Achilles himself is asserting the continuity that I wish to identify and articulate between the *Theogony* and the *Iliad*, between his *mênis* and the *mênis* of Zeus. To be sure, the link is oblique. Achilles does not explicitly refer to Zeus's own assertion of dominion over his rivals in the *Theogony*; rather, using distinctly Hesiodic language,[60] he refers to an event that is discernibly related to the succession myth and also subsequent to it. A direct backward reference to the *Theogony* would not suit this context in any case, wherein Achilles is justifying a course of action for his mother, and it would also construct a direct analogy between himself and Zeus. Instead, Achilles draws a delicate and precise parallel between Zeus and Thetis as enforcers of the social order in which Achilles has the *mênis* and Zeus seconds it. The text is in fact negotiating a sensitive issue. Earlier we witnessed warriors surpassing the limits of the human condition who are both admirable and in danger of incurring nothing other than divine *mênis* itself.[61] For a hero to have *mênis* without incurring it at the same time, Zeus must conspire with him rather than against him. By telling this story and ultimately winning Zeus's allegiance to his cause rather than presenting himself as his equal, Achilles makes his own *mênis* as much an aspect of Zeus's cosmic status as of his own. There lies the precise link between Achilles' *mênis* and Zeus's that bespeaks the metonymic relationship between the whole *Theogony* and the first line of the *Iliad* that was my point of departure.[62]

Another Theogonic variant that would have suited the immediate demands of this context very well is the tradition that explains why Achilles himself is a mortal hero and not king of the universe: how Thetis averted the *mênis* of Zeus against herself and Achilles by submitting to marriage

---

[59] That Agamemnon's claim is eventually nullified by the *Iliad* also suggests that there is an antagonism built into this narrative against central political authority and a bias in favor of excellence at the social margins, at least in the human domain.
[60] I am again referring to the work of Slatkin (1991, 60–77).
[61] Above, 10–18.
[62] For more on the danger of *mênis* implicit in a hero's *mênis*, see Chapter 5.

with a mortal, Peleus, instead of becoming Zeus's consort. Once again, this alternative implies a more antagonistic and competitive model of the relationship between Zeus and Achilles than the *Iliad* permits on its surface, although aspects of just such a competition may not be far beneath.[63] To repeat, the risk is that Achilles' superior status will become fatally dangerous rather than admirable, that it will incur *mēnis* rather than legitimate its expression. As we shall soon see, the *Iliad* does not suppress the fatally dangerous aspect of Achilles' superiority: it displaces it from Achilles to Patroklos, just as it displaces Achilles' (and, for that matter, Patroklos's) divine antagonist from Zeus to Apollo. The choice of the Thetis tale in our *Iliad* over this variant, if it was actually available to Homeric tradition, may well reflect the same intent as those displacements. At the beginning of this chapter, I identified that very intent with the transition from divine (Hesiodic) myth to heroic (Homeric) epic, that is, with an ontogeny of epic itself that the beginning of the *Iliad* is actually recapitulating.

Thetis responds with warmth and sadness to Achilles' request, and she promises to go to Olympus when Zeus returns from his sojourn among the Ethiopians, who dwell on the world-encircling river. In the meantime, she tells him:

ἀλλὰ σὺ μὲν νῦν νηυσὶ παρήμενος ὠκυπόροισι
μήνι' Ἀχαιοῖσιν, πολέμου δ' ἀποπαύεο πάμπαν.

Sitting beside your swift-going ships
have <u>*mēnis*</u> at the Achaeans and cease completely from war.

(1.421–22)

After a digression describing in detail Odysseus's trip to hand over Chryseis, the ritual performed on Chryse to appease Apollo, and the voyage back to Troy, the narrator returns once again to Achilles before taking up the episode of Thetis's trip to Olympus on his behalf:

αὐτὰρ ὁ <u>μήνιε</u> νηυσὶ παρήμενος ὠκυπόροισι
διογενὴς Πηλῆος υἱός, πόδας ὠκὺς Ἀχιλλεύς·
οὔτε ποτ' εἰς ἀγορὴν πωλέσκετο κυδιάνειραν
οὔτε ποτ' ἐς πόλεμον, ἀλλὰ φθινύθεσκε φίλον κῆρ
αὖθι μένων, ποθέεσκε δ' ἀϋτήν τε πτόλεμόν τε.

---

[63] See the work of Slatkin (1991) on Thetis in the *Iliad*; also Holway 1989.

And sitting beside his swift-going ships he had *mênis*,
the Zeus-descended son of Peleus, swift-footed Achilles.
Neither was he visiting the man-ennobling assembly
nor was he going to war, but he was wasting away his own dear heart
staying there, and he was longing for the war cry and the battle.
(1.488–92)

Thetis's prescription and its narrated enactment verbally legitimate Achilles' *mênis*, but the exceptional, even paradoxical nature of that *mênis* as against the *mênis* of all other epic personages emerges now with special clarity. Achilles is to exercise his by sitting beside his ships, depriving himself of social interaction with his peers, ceasing from the one activity that embodies his status in the community, the practice of warfare. Withdrawal from the social group that is the object of one's *mênis* is a given,[64] but Achilles' *mênis* is passive, motionless self-denial and self-restraint, whereas the *mênis* of all others—even including the *mater dolorosa* Demeter's grieving withdrawal from the divine community—is the most active of socially destructive and self-confirming pursuits. In Achilles' case, the mechanism whereby an extraordinary individual appropriately and indiscriminately chastises a social group is being turned over to Zeus, leaving Achilles an aggrieved hero emptied of himself, even disempowered by "his own" cosmic rage. In the *Theogony*, Zeus's ability to enforce the world order in prototypical exercises of an as yet unnamed *mênis* depended on his transcendent *bíē* 'capacity for physical destruction' as embodied in the thunderbolt; in Achilles' case, it is actually the suppression of his exceptional *bíē* that characterizes his *mênis*. At least, that is the point of departure in its epic telling.

## Book 1 and the *Mênis* of Zeus

That is not the last manifestation of the *mênis* theme in the first book of the *Iliad*. When Thetis ascends Olympus and supplicates Zeus on Achilles' behalf, she justifies her request not with the tale that Achilles heard her tell but on the basis of whatever help she provided him among the immortals (1.505–6), a vaguer claim that certainly does not exclude that episode. Her plea is focused on Achilles' *timê* (505, 507, 508, 510) and Agamemnon's

---

[64] The extreme case and closest parallel is Demeter: above, 23–29 (with n. 37).

abuse of it in depriving him of his *géras*. When Zeus exhibits some reluctance to assent to her request that he honor Achilles by helping the Trojans (511–12), she tells him archly to be candid and either assent or, by refusing, confirm that her own *timḗ* is least among the gods' (516). Finally, after an outburst of vexation at the *loígia érga*, "deeds of devastation" that he foresees from a confrontation with Hera (518), Zeus makes a grandiose verbal and physical gesture of assent (524–30) that puts a cosmic seal on Achilles' *mênis* and commits him, the king of the gods, to bring about the social devastation that should accompany it (509–10). In effect, Zeus is guaranteeing the *mênis* of Achilles to be also his own, and in effect the *Iliad* is bridging itself to the *Theogony* by distributing Zeus's massive power to sanction tabu behavior among Achilles, his antagonist Apollo, and his ally Zeus.

As soon as Thetis departs and Zeus enters his home to dine with all the other gods, Hera asks him whom he has been plotting with and rebukes him for keeping secret counsels (540–43). He responds by assuring her that no one will be informed before her of any counsel he wishes to share (547–50); on the other hand, it is his prerogative to hide what he wishes to keep hidden from the gods. She should not importune him with questions about those matters. Hera takes offense at the notion that she is ever importunate, and in defense of her question she reports her righteous fear that he has promised Thetis "to honor Achilles and destroy many Achaeans at the ships" (558–59). Being only too correct, she gets the following threat from her spouse in response:

ἀλλ' ἀκέουσα κάθησο, ἐμῷ δ' ἐπιπείθεο μύθῳ,
μή νύ τοι οὐ χραίσμωσιν ὅσοι θεοί εἰσ' ἐν Ὀλύμπῳ
ἆσσον ἰόνθ', ὅτε κέν τοι ἀάπτους χεῖρας ἐφείω.

Now sit down and be silent, and obey my command,
lest all the gods on Olympus be of no help to you
coming nearer, when I lay my untouchable[65] hands upon you.

(565–67)

Once again Zeus asserts his authority to punish a rebellious member of the divine community without fearing the response of her peers: he is prepared to take on all comers. The context and the diction recall several instances of

---

[65] Or "unspeakable" according to the variant preferred by Aristophanes of Byzantium, ἀέπτους; see Chantraine 1968–79, s.v. ἄπτος. In either case, whether Zeus's hands are "untouchable" or "unspeakable," the underlying point is the same: they are tabu. On why the hands of *mênis* are tabu, see the Appendix.

the *mênis* theme, especially the sequence in *Iliad*, book 15, that began with Zeus's threat to repeat his punishment of Hera despite her support from others and concluded with Poseidon's backing down to Zeus's superior force while threatening to activate the pro-Achaean gods against him if he went so far as to cancel the sack of Troy. The situation that Hera fears is also beginning to resemble the one in Achilles' tale of his mother's achievement: an alliance between Thetis and Zeus over against an alienated faction of the divine community consisting once again of those who favor the Achaeans in the war.

It is not Thetis, however, but Hephaistos, the son of Hera, who quells the dispute between Zeus and his mother that is about to erupt into violence. It is not irrelevant that the conclusion to the *Theogony* describes the "virgin" birth of Hephaistos as Hera's competitive response to the "virgin" birth of Athena from the head of Zeus:

> αὐτὸς δ' ἐκ κεφαλῆς γλαυκώπιδα γείνατ' Ἀθήνην,
> δεινὴν ἐγρεκύδοιμον ἀγέστρατον ἀτρυτώνην,
> πότνιαν, ᾗ κέλαδοί τε ἅδον πόλεμοί τε μάχαι τε·
> Ἥρη δ' Ἥφαιστον κλυτὸν οὐ φιλότητι μιγεῖσα
> γείνατο, καὶ ζαμένησε καὶ ἤρισεν ᾧ παρακοίτῃ,
> ἐκ πάντων τέχνῃσι κεκασμένον Οὐρανιώνων.

> He himself gave birth to sparkling-eyed Athena from his head,
> frightening strife-stirring host-leading tireless
> mistress whom noise and wars and battles please;
> but Hera gave birth without having sex to Hephaistos,
> since she was very angry and competed with her husband—
> Hephaistos, who surpassed all the children of Ouranos
>     in cunning arts.
>                                        (*Theogony* 924–29)

This passage about Zeus's last wife (λοισθοτάτην... ἄκοιτιν [921]) as against Metis, his first, polarizes the distinction between their respective offspring as well as their deviant begetting. Athena is presented in her aspect as a goddess of war and violence, a masculinized female born from a male, whereas Hephaistos is an "unfathered" male who excels in cleverly contriving cunning things, in other words, in *mêtis*, a trait that the Theogonic myth persistently associates with females, specifically with the creation of children. If this male with *mêtis* cannot procreate a child as Zeus did upon swallowing Metis, he is at least a master of noncelestial fire whose craftsmanship is such that he can even create objects that move by themselves.[66] His genealogy as yet another potentially dangerous son of Zeus—and he is Zeus's son despite the absence of sexual relations between his parents—makes his role in this context in the *Iliad* especially appropriate. As an effort to quell the dispute between his parents, his speech is a variation on Nestor's prior attempt to end the quarrel between Agamemnon and Achilles. But unlike Nestor, Hephaistos succeeds. Recalling the language of Zeus's foreboding to Thetis, he first speaks with regret of the *loígia érga,* "deeds of devastation," that are about to take place if the quarrel continues,[67] and he points out to his mother what Zeus can do if he wishes:

> εἴ περ γάρ κ' ἐθέλῃσιν Ὀλύμπιος ἀστεροπητὴς
> ἐξ ἑδέων στυφελίξαι· ὁ γὰρ πολὺ φέρτατός ἐστιν·
> ἀλλὰ σὺ τόν γ' ἐπέεσσι καθάπτεσθαι μαλακοῖσιν·
> αὐτίκ' ἔπειθ' ἵλαος Ὀλύμπιος ἔσσεται ἡμῖν.

> If the Olympian lightning-hurler just wishes to, he could
> smite us from our seats; for he is by far the best;
> instead restrain[68] him with gentle words;
> then the Olympian will immediately be gracious[69] to us.

(1.580–83)

---

[66] For objects made by Hephaistos that move by themselves, see *Iliad* 18.372–77. Both Athena and Hephaistos in fact have aspects that reflect the complementary traits as well: Athena's wiles and tricks are legion in the *Odyssey,* and Hephaistos's capacity for violence is featured, for instance, in a battle of Achilles' at the conclusion of the *Iliad* (21.367, etc.) as well as in his skill at creating the weapons of war. But the Theogonic myth at this point is interested in the contrast between Athena and Hephaistos, not in their ability to bridge the opposites that their father Zeus bridged once and for all.

[67] See above, 116–17 with n. 48 for the specialization of the word *loigós* (now to include its adjectival derivative) to the devastation consequent upon *mênis*.

[68] LSJ⁹ translates all instances of the middle voice of καθάπτω in Homer as "accost" or "assail," but no one can "accost" or "assail" a person with "gentle words" (again in *Odyssey* 10.70 and 24.393). The underlying notion here and in all other epic instances of the verb is "get hold of, grab" and so "restrain." For instance, the same verb is used of Athena's restraint of the crazed Ares in the beginning of *Iliad* 15 (line 127), when he is about to incur the *mênis* of Zeus.

[69] The adjective used here to mean 'gracious'—Ἵλαος—and the verb ἱλάσσω or ἱλάσκω 'render gracious, appease' that is derived from it have until now been used five times in book 1 in the same context: the Achaeans' efforts through ritual to undo the *mênis* of Apollo and make him 'gracious' (1.100, 147, 386, 444, 472). Of the five other examples of the words in the *Iliad,* two apply to Achilles himself in the context of undoing his *mênis* (9.635 and 19.178). In fact the distribution of Ἵλαος and its cognates recovers the link I am postulating between the *mênis* of Zeus, Apollo, and Achilles. The other attestations of the word and its derivatives in the *Iliad* pertain to the Trojans' fruitless ritual attempt to appease Athena in *Iliad* 6 (lines 380 and 385) and the Athenians' yearly sacrifices to appease her symbiotic cult hero, Erechtheus, in the shrine she established for him in Athens (*Iliad* 2.550). The use of the word Ἵλαος is especially interesting in

The diction of the passage already marks it as another occurrence of the *mênis* theme, but in order to avoid helplessly witnessing (588–89) his mother's being struck by lightning,[70] Hephaistos goes on to describe how he was once cast down by the foot from the divine threshold to the island of Lemnos, scarcely breathing. In other words, he alludes to yet another sequel to the *Theogony*, to a time when Hephaistos challenged Zeus— which explains his remark, ἀργαλέος γὰρ 'Ολύμπιος ἀντιφέρεσθαι, "It is painful to stand up against the Olympian one" (589)—and underwent the consequences of Zeus's *mênis*. In Hephaistos's case, Zeus's *mênis* took the form of inflicting a violent demotion from the divine to the human domain that functions elsewhere as the immortal equivalent of death.[71] The story may also explain his limp, for being cast down from the divine threshold by the foot is equivalent to being struck by lightning and can result in difficulty walking, as in the case of the hero Anchises.[72] After reminding his mother of this story, Hephaistos raises a mocking laugh from all the gods as he limps

---

connection with Erechtheus, since he and Achilles are the only nondivinities to whom this word applies: both are heroes, one of epic, the other of cult even inside epic, and there are other parallels in diction and function between the two; see Nagy 1979, 182–83 and 183, sec. 11 n. 5, and below, 131–32. Outside of the *Iliad*, the same adjectival and verbal forms are used three times of Demeter, a goddess with *mênis*, in reference to the effect on her of ritual actions that are known aspects of her cult. First, at *Hymn to Demeter* 204, the jokes of Iambe make Demeter laugh and so appease her; second, at *Hymn to Demeter* 274, Demeter, angered upon being discovered while she is hardening the baby Demophon in fire, instructs the daughters of Keleos and the people of Eleusis to build her temple and conduct her cult rituals (ὄργια [273]) to appease her; third, at *Hymn to Demeter* 292, the same daughters of Keleos attempt to appease her with night-long rituals, including baths, etc. There is a fourth example at *Hymn to Demeter* 368, when punishment awaits those who neglect the sacrifices needed to appease Persephone's *ménos* (on the substitution of *ménos* for *mênis*, see above, 111 and n. 43). This time the reference is to Persephone, not Demeter, but the change is only an aspect of the symbiotic relationship between mother and daughter that marks the whole hymn. In the *Odyssey*, there is just one attestation. Nestor uses the verb ἰλάσσω at 3.419 to describe the effect on Athena of the ritual sacrifice he is about to perform. Shortly before, he told the story of her *mênis* against the Achaeans after the capture of Troy (lines 135ff.): on Athena's *mênis*, see Clay 1983. On the basis of these passages, I would propose the following rule about the distribution of the word *mênis*, to supplant the older view that only gods and Achilles have *mênis* (as stated, for example, in Irmscher 1950). That view is to my mind contradicted by adjectival and verbal derivatives of *mênis* and should be restated as follows: only gods and heroes have *mênis*, just as only gods and heroes can be made 'gracious' or ἵλαος through ritual appeasement thereafter. This rule does not contradict my view that the application of *mênis* to heroes is from a historical standpoint an extension of its application to divinities; in fact it justifies it as a putative restriction of *mênis* to gods and to Achilles alone would not. On the dangerous nature of *mênis* in heroes, see below, 131–32.

[70] The verb Hephaistos uses in foreseeing his mother's punishment is θεινομένην 'smitten' (line 587), which in epic is used for the action of a thunderbolt on its target; the same is true of its cognates in other Indo-European poetic traditions: Sanskrit, Armenian, etc.; see Watkins 1986.

[71] See above, 22, for another example of the same phenomenon.

[72] See above, 21–22 with n. 30.

around serving them all their wine—a pointed way of cooling the tension between his parents and preserving the integrity of the divine community that is menaced by their quarrel. Preserving that integrity is the ultimate purpose of Zeus's *mênis* in the first place, and we can see its having that effect here in three different representations: an actual threat by Zeus, an admonitory narrative example of the carrying out of such a threat, and a nervously humorous spectacle illustrating the point of the previous narrative.

Hephaistos's success imputes a measure of restorative social power to the mere narration of *mênis* that is akin to the activity of Apollo and the Muses, who sing responsively to the divine community (603–4) after Hephaistos serves them wine and before each god or goddess departs the gathering and goes off to sleep. Significantly, a poetic performance was also the sequel to the distribution of wine during the ritual appeasement of Apollo's own *mênis* that was enacted on Chryse earlier in the first book of the *Iliad* (471–74). Furthermore, as we shall see, poetic performance also plays a part in the appeasement of Achilles' *mênis* in book 9. Finally, this moment links the poem's audience to the divine audience, since both are attending a *mênis* narrative that is simultaneously a poetic performance. The conjunction coincides with the end of the first book and seems an appropriate point of closure—if in fact the book divisions have something to do with the conventional boundaries of a narrative performance, as at times they appear to.[73]

The simple underlying structure of the whole narrative in book 1 is coming into focus as it concludes. It consists of three intertwined instances of the *mênis* theme. First is the *mênis* of Apollo: Agamemnon incurs it, Apollo exercises it on the Achaean host, and finally, at Achilles' instigation with instructions from Kalkhas and under orders from Agamemnon, the Achaeans under Odysseus successfully appease it. While the Achaeans are devising this appropriate and successful response to the *mênis* of Apollo, a quarrel breaks out between Agamemnon and Achilles in which each righteously lays claim to *mênis* against the other. In fact, it is Achilles' *mênis* that Thetis persuades Zeus to validate—that validation being patently indispensable—but in so doing he knowingly arouses in Hera an urgent and appropriate fear of the consequences for her protégés, the Achaeans. In attempting to suppress her foreseeable protest, Zeus threatens Hera with *mênis*, but the threat is averted by Hephaistos's cautionary narrative about Zeus's *mênis* against him. Thus, Apollo's *mênis* proceeds through a complete

---

[73] On the structural value of some of the book divisions, see Broccia 1967, 45–66; Muellner 1990; and Nagy 1996, 182.

cycle, the incipient *mênis* of Achilles is incurred and validated by Zeus, but the potential *mênis* of Zeus against Hera is averted.[74] The goal of the narrative in book 1 is, to be sure, to set into motion the *mênis* of Achilles, but it also serves to reveal, in three thematically coherent and interlaced examples, how *mênis* can be appeased, incurred, and averted, for those are the exact points at which each of these first instances of the *mênis* theme concludes. The *mênis* of Achilles is now clearly situated between its two models, that of Apollo and that of Zeus.

## *Mênis* in the Hesiodic and the Homeric Tradition

*Mênis* is dangerous to incur. Once incurred, its appeasement is uncertain and costly. One's best course is to avert it if possible. In epic diction the word *mênis* is the formulaic complement of verbs meaning "fear," "cast off," "shun," "watch out for," and "renounce."[75] Actions that incur *mênis* include leaving the dead unburied, neglecting one's reciprocal obligations as a guest or host, transgressing the cosmic boundary between humans and divinities, and threatening the sovereignty of Zeus. In a system of thought in which the structure of human society is continuous with the order of the world as a whole, such violations take on cosmic dimensions. *Mênis* is an emotion, but it is not some pure feeling distinct from the specific actions that it inevitably entails. In fact, it is nothing less than the *nomen sacrum* for the ultimate sanction that enforces the world-defining prohibitions, the tabus that are basic to the establishment and perpetuation of the world of Zeus and the society of mortals he presides over. Like the offenses that provoke it, *mênis* may once have been a tabu word to utter.[76] But whatever its history as a word, it also has a mythical history in epic tradition. As we have seen, Zeus's crowning achievement in the *Theogonic* tradition is to acquire divine sovereignty by establishing his dominance in two complementary spheres of action that are by definition essential for governing the world: destructive force and creative intelligence, *bíē* and *mêtis*. The token of his acquisition of the ultimate *bíē* is the gift of the thunderbolt from his grandmother,

---

[74] Richard Martin points out to me that Zeus's forestalled *mênis* is metonymically consumed by the "Will of Zeus" theme announced in the proem to the *Iliad*; I add that it is there described as a process being "completed," *eteleleto*, a verb derived from the noun *télos* (*Iliad* 1.5: "and the will of Zeus was being completed"). On the Will of Zeus theme and its cosmic aspects, replete with fire storms and thunderbolts, see Nagy 1979, 333–37.

[75] As observed by Calvert Watkins (1977a, 193).

[76] Watkins (1977a, 1977b) makes a case that *mênis* is still a tabu word in epic. On the whole question and the word's etymology, see the Appendix.

Gaia. Since the thunderbolt is the ultimate violent weapon, its function is to defend the sovereignty of Zeus through his *mênis*. Likewise, the token of Zeus's acquisition of the ultimate *mêtis* is the swallowing of his first wife, Metis herself, and the birth of the goddess Athena from Zeus's head. Athena is herself defined in terms of these two alternative sovereign attributes. She presides over cunning and violence, which are either female or male attributes until herself and her father. As Zeus is an androgynous father, so she is the androgynous daughter born from him. Her combination of the two attributes would be a threat to Zeus's power were she not, in this male-biased universe, a fundamentally female yet of necessity infertile goddess—in her case at least, virginity signifies a benign qua unforced suppression of femininity.

When it comes to the two male heroes of the two principal epics, the distribution of these two complementary traits is in strict sequence with the Hesiodic *Theogony*. Achilles and Odysseus each surpass all other mortals in one of the two, either destructive force or creative cunning, but neither can combine the two traits as Zeus does.[77] In other words, the differentiation between the two great heroes is a structural consequence of the nature of the world that emerges in the Theogonic tradition, just like the division of sexual functions among mortals between the two genders. No mortal man can give birth to a child from his head; likewise, no mortal man can prevail in both *mêtis* and *bíē*.[78] From this standpoint, it is implicit in Achilles' nature as the hero who excels in *bíē* that he lay claim to *mênis*, the ultimate expression of the ultimate in *bíē*. Also implicit in Achilles' *bíē* is his failure to achieve a homecoming, since, as Douglas Frame has shown, the ability to achieve *nóstos* 'return home' is predicated upon exceptional *nóos* 'cunning intelligence'.[79] Each of the heroes has *kléos* 'immortal glory embodied in song' as a consequence of being the "best of the Achaeans" in his own epic, but only Odysseus achieves *nóstos* as the result of his exceptional *mêtis* and *nóos*, and only Achilles has the consequence of his superlative *bíē*, *mênis*.[80] In

[77] To state what is perhaps obvious, once Zeus has broken the respective gender associations of *mêtis* and *bíē*, they are lost forever. It cannot be a token of femininity that Odysseus and Hephaistos excel in cunning if the lord of all gods also excels in that trait. To put it another way, Zeus's sovereign androgyny has translated sexual difference from a polar opposition between violence and intelligence to a more complex differentiation among varying degrees of violence and intelligence.

[78] Gregory Nagy reminds me that this statement requires qualification: no mortal *of this generation* can prevail in both. From the previous generation, there is Herakles, who comes closest to Zeus in this regard. See Nagy 1990a, 13–17 with reference to Dumézil 1971, 17–132, esp. 117–24.

[79] On the absence of *mênis* in the *Odyssey*, see above, Chapter 2. I have in mind here not just Odysseus's ability to return to Ithaca, but to return "to light and life" from the land of the dead.

[80] This formulation of a balance between the destinies of Odysseus and Achilles is not contra-

other words, the progress from Zeus to Apollo to Achilles, on the one hand, and from Zeus to Athena—for it is she, not Poseidon, who is Odysseus's underlying divine antagonist[81]—to Odysseus on the other, is a mythical account of the human condition. As such, it is not a view of the world that breeds resigned acceptance of the diminished abilities of mortals in comparison with those of the gods. Instead, it defines the boundaries between gods and mortals at the same time as it promotes admiration for heroes who defiantly and dangerously transgress them, as though a category cannot exist and function until and unless it is subverted, in the same way that rules of prohibition imply or even generate the existence of a concomitant need to contravene them.[82]

This context in turn makes it possible to understand why the standard *prooímion* to the *Iliad* was preferred to the variant known to Aristoxenus. The variant highlights the parallelism between Apollo's and Achilles' *mênis*, but the received text flagrantly accentuates the paradoxicality of Achilles' *mênis*. In fact, it attributes to it a tabu-breaking offense *that in itself normally incurs mênis*, namely, leaving bodies unburied as prey for dogs and birds (1.4–5). A mortal with *mênis*, a mortal wielding the ultimate cosmic sanction, is a paradox by definition, since he is both an enforcer of the order of Zeus and also a threat to that order.[83] In this regard I would formulate a further role about *mênis*, namely, that *heroes with mênis are just as likely to incur it as to express it*.[84] As a parallel to Achilles, I cite a figure who can be considered the only "son" of the goddess Athena, the hero Erechtheus, even though his father Hephaistos's ejaculate missed its mark and landed upon Gaia instead.[85] From the standpoint of Theogonic tradition, this hero's genealogy predestines him for *mênis* irrespective of his mother (Athena or

---

dicted by Achilles in book 9, when he speaks of his mother's offer of the *dikhthádiai kêres*, "twin destinies," one featuring *kléos* without *nóstos*, the other *nóstos* without *kléos*. That is a context in which Achilles is highlighting the contrast between himself and Odysseus (see Nagy 1992); to go on and portray Achilles as the overall loser in a comparison with Odysseus, since he wins only *kléos* while Odysseus ultimately wins both it and *nóstos*, is a step that I am reluctant to take. My editor puts it this way: "A monolithic hero can only win with a clear choice, but a polytropic hero can win by having it both ways."

[81] The terminology of *mênis* is not used of the relationship between Odysseus and Poseidon; on the "hidden" antagonism between Odysseus and Athena, see Clay 1983.

[82] For the way in which prohibitions function in comparable social settings, see the work of Mary Douglas (1966) discussed in Chapter 1, 26–28.

[83] For a demonstration that the *mênis* of Achilles is metaphorized in the *Iliad* as a thunderstorm of Zeus, see Nagy 1979, 317–47, esp. 346–47.

[84] See also the discussion above, 121–23 and below, 144–46. I consider the death of Patroklos in Achilles' guise after crossing Apollo's limits to be another instantiation of this rule, although with significant variations.

[85] For Erechtheus's status as the son of Athena, see Burkert 1985, 143.

Gaia), just as the myth about Thetis deferring to Zeus and marrying Peleus implies *mênis* for Achilles irrespective of his father (Zeus or Peleus). On the one hand, Homeric epic tells us that Erechtheus is the object of recurrent appeasement through sacrifice—using the word *hiláontai* 'appease (through ritual)', a term restricted to gods with *mênis*, to Achilles, and to Erechtheus[86]—presumably because of *mênis* against the Athenians (*Iliad* 2.550). Yet, on the other hand, it is also attested that Erechtheus *incurred* the *mênis* of Zeus (Hyginus 46) and was struck by the thunderbolt. Being struck by a thunderbolt is actually a means to achieve immortality in hero cult that is tantamount to being transported to the *Elúsion pedíon* "Elysian plain," a phrase that is itself also applied to a place that has been struck by lightning and so become sacred.[87]

In the meantime, however, we have left Achilles blessed by Thetis and Zeus with a most passive *mênis*. It remains to discuss its teleology within the *Iliad*.

---

[86] See above, n. 69.
[87] See Nagy 1979, 190, 203; for other parallels between Achilles and Erechtheus, see Nagy 1979, 182–83. It is surely no coincidence that both Poseidon and Thetis are sea divinities: see Nagy 1979, 347. Given this parallel between Erechtheus and Achilles and the function of poetry within epic itself to achieve the appeasement of persons with *mênis*, one cannot rule out a link between poetic performance of the *Iliad* and the sacrifices specified in *Iliad* 2.550.

CHAPTER 5

# The *Mênis* of Achilles and Its Iliadic Teleology

This book began with an assumption that terms for emotions such as anger have meanings and resonance that are specific to their culture, so that it could be informative to reconstruct the sense of an epic word such as *mênis* within its own poetic context. By now it is clear that this highly specialized social term denoting the cosmic sanction against tabu behavior is a far cry from any shared, secular notion of anger specific to contemporary Western culture. On the basis of the hypothesis of Albert Lord that more or less crystallized constellations of poetic formulas called themes are essential elements in the composition of traditional poems, the method of semantic reconstruction in this book has been systematic contextual analysis of occurrences of the word *mênis* and its derivatives, including the diction regularly associated with them, so as to determine and comprehend the essential, recurring features of the theme in which the word *mênis* is embedded within the epic tradition. At the same time as the terms of analysis have gone beyond individual words and formulas to themes, so my purpose has gone beyond a desire to "redefine" *mênis* and instead become a matter of rebuilding the poetic function of the *mênis* theme in the epic tradition. To that end, I have attempted an intensive study of the mythical syntax of the Hesiodic *Theogony* and suggested a sequential relation between it and narrative elements of the first book of the *Iliad*. From that perspective, the first book of the Homeric *Iliad* contains variations on a *mênis* theme whose prerequisites were generated in the Hesiodic *Theogony*. It remains to extend this study to the teleology of *mênis* within the *Iliad* as a whole.

In book 16 when Patroklos has put on the armor of Achilles and is about

133

to lead the Myrmidons onto the Trojan plain in Achilles' armor, he whips them up with a speech that evokes the themes of the first book of the *Iliad*:

Μυρμιδόνες, ἕταροι Πηληϊάδεω Ἀχιλῆος,
ἀνέρες ἔστε, φίλοι, μνήσασθε δὲ θούριδος ἀλκῆς,
ὡς ἂν Πηλεΐδην τιμήσομεν, ὃς μέγ' ἄριστος
Ἀργείων παρὰ νηυσὶ καὶ ἀγχέμαχοι θεράποντες,
γνῷ δὲ καὶ Ἀτρεΐδης εὐρὺ κρείων Ἀγαμέμνων
ἣν ἄτην, ὅ τ' ἄριστον Ἀχαιῶν οὐδὲν ἔτεισεν.

Myrmidons, companions of Achilles the son of Peleus,
be men, friends, and concentrate on flashing courage,
so that we may honor the son of Peleus, who is by far the best of the
Argives beside the ships, he and his close-fighting companions,
and also so that the son of Atreus, wide-ruling Agamemnon, may know
his *átē*, in that he paid no honor to the best of the Achaeans.

(16.269–74)

On withdrawing in book 1, Achilles had made it his explicit goal that Agamemnon learn painfully of his *átē* 'derangement' in dishonoring the "best of the Achaeans," namely, Achilles himself (244). At the decisive moment when Patroklos is returning to the fighting as Achilles' stand-in to save the Achaeans from certain disaster, his explicit goal is, paradoxically, still the same. Presumably, Achilles' supreme value was made plain by the devastating consequences of his subtraction from society; now the same message will again be conveyed to Agamemnon by the restorative consequence of his addition to it in the persona of his best friend. In lines 271 and 272 the speech also expresses an essential assumption behind this notion, namely, the identity in value between Achilles and his *therápontes* 'companions, sidekicks', a term that connotes more than association but less than incarnation.[1] Since Patroklos is repeatedly identified as Achilles' singular *therápōn*, the plural he uses here includes himself as well as the rest of the Myrmidons. It emphatically expresses the identity and solidarity between Achilles, Patroklos, and the group of *phíloi* 'friends' (270) that they lead.[2] As Achilles is the best, so are Patroklos and the other Myrmidons the best, since they are all Achilles' *therápontes*; it follows that their achievement will also be Achilles'.

In its stated purpose, then, the return of Patroklos to the fighting in book

---

[1] On the meaning of *therápōn* as 'ritual substitute', see Lowenstam 1981 and below, 160 n. 54.
[2] On the *phíloi* in this connection, see Sinos 1980; and Nagy 1979, 103–10. On the meaning of *phílos*, see Benveniste 1969, 1:338–53. On the etymology of *phílos*, see Schwartz 1982.

16 is the equivalent of Achilles' withdrawal of himself and his men from it in book 1. But from another standpoint, one that is actually ascribed by the narrator to the Trojans a few lines later when Patroklos appears on the field of battle, it is also the polar opposite of Achilles' withdrawal:

> Τρῶες δ' ὡς εἴδοντο Μενοιτίου ἄλκιμον υἱόν,
> αὐτὸν καὶ θεράποντα, σὺν ἔντεσι μαρμαίροντας,
> πᾶσιν ὀρίνθη θυμός, ἐκινήθη δὲ φάλαγγες,
> ἐλπόμενοι παρὰ ναῦφι ποδώκεα Πηλεΐωνα
> <u>μηνιθμὸν</u> μὲν ἀπορρῖψαι <u>φιλότητα</u> δ' ἑλέσθαι·
> πάπτηνεν δὲ ἕκαστος ὅπῃ φύγοι αἰπὺν ὄλεθρον.

> When the Trojans saw the brave son of Menoitios,
> him and his <u>therápōn</u>, with their armor blazing bright,
> the spirit in all of them churned, and their ranks were disturbed.
> They guessed that beside the ships the swift-footed son of Peleus
> had thrown away <u>mēnithmós</u>, had chosen <u>philótēs</u>;
> so each of them looked around for a place to escape sure death.
>                                                     (16.278–83)

Nestor intends the Trojans to be deceived by Patroklos's wearing Achilles' armor (11.799–801), and so does Patroklos (16.40–43), but Achilles expresses no such intention. He even prays to Zeus that Hector learn that his *therápōn* knows how to fight on his own (16.242–43). And actually, the Trojans' supposition as stated in the text is no illusion. In answer to a direct appeal to his friendship, Achilles had earlier told his friend Ajax that he would (9.650–55) set aside his *mênis*—for which the word *mēnithmós* is a formulaic alternative[3]—when the ships were set on fire. Repeating his promise to do so (16.61–63), he sends out Patroklos precisely when the first ship is set on fire (16.121–29), thus choosing *philótēs* 'friendship, solidarity' in several senses at once: by accepting his best friend Patroklos's plea that he allow him to return to the fighting, by sending his best friend out *as though he were himself,* and by doing so exactly when Ajax himself is retreating before the onslaught of the Trojans (16.119–26) and the first ship is set on fire. Although Nestor's idea of substituting Patroklos for Achilles was intended to induce in the Trojans a mistaken identification of one for the other, for Achilles and Patroklos both it is a true identification of one with

---

[3] Achilles himself uses the synonym in 16.63 in reaffirming his commitment to Ajax to cease his *mênis.* Watkins (1977a and b) asserts that it is a euphemistic substitute for it, but I believe his argument in this regard requires qualification. See Appendix.

the other and of both with the Myrmidons as a group, a ringing assertion of Achilles' supremacy as a fighter, and a profound gesture of friendship that signals the undoing of Achilles' *mênis*.[4] Aristotle's question-and-answer definition of the noun *phílos* is directly relevant: τί ἐστι καὶ ὁποῖός τις ὁ φίλος; τοιοῦτος οἷος ἕτερος εἶναι ἐγώ. "What and of what kind is a friend? Such as could be another I."[5] Aristotle's answer is ungrammatical, since an adjective that can only apply to third persons, "other," qualifies the first person pronoun; therein lies the fundamental notion behind Achilles' substitution. Patroklos is a third person whom Achilles identifies with himself, a "he" who is an "I." The teleology of Achilles' *mênis* is actually to become such *philótēs* 'friendship, solidarity', which is in every way its opposite.

## *Mênis* versus *Philótēs*: Alienation

The moment at which Patroklos goes out in Achilles' own armor to fight the Trojans is an act of solidarity on Achilles' part, a solidarity that was manifest in Achilles' first action in the whole epic, his calling of an assembly of the whole host of fighting men to face the devastating consequences of Apollo's *mênis* on them all (1.55). The poet tells us there that Hera put the suggestion in his mind out of her concern for the Danaans, but given the reciprocal, interactive nature of divine intervention in epic,[6] that concern must be thought of as shared by Achilles as well. His awareness, as against Agamemnon's disregard of the welfare and the detriment of the whole group, is a theme of the quarrel in book 1.[7] Yet, as I have maintained, figures with *mênis* characteristically lose solidarity with their social group. The personage who comes to mind as an example is Demeter bereft of Persephone, a mourning goddess who descends from Olympus and conceals herself in her shrine at Eleusis while the world withers. Demeter is in exile

---

[4] It is not apparent or explicit that a single Trojan ever mistakes Patroklos for Achilles. On the contrary, Sarpedon describes him as τοῦδ' ἀνέρος, "this man" (16.423), as though he were a warrior otherwise unknown to him, and Glaukos unhesitatingly names Patroklos as the slayer of Sarpedon (16.543). Wearing Achilles' armor has symbolic rather than literal value for Patroklos.

[5] *Magna Moralia* 1213a11–13. There is a reformulation of this question and answer in Diogenes Laertius's life of Zeno (7.23): ἐρωτηθεὶς τίς ἐστι φίλος, "ἄλλος," ἔφη, "ἐγώ," "When asked who is a friend, he said, 'Another I.'" This answer, ἄλλος ἐγώ, ultimately gave rise to the Freudian term *alter ego*, by way of Erwin Rohde and Friedrich Nietzsche.

[6] I am referring here to so-called Homeric double motivation, as described, for example, by Cedric Whitman (1958, 221–48, with n. 83), which is an aspect or a consequence of the reciprocity rules that govern the relationship between heroes and gods. On reciprocity in divine and heroic interaction, see Muellner 1976, 26–31.

[7] See above, 96–102.

from the whole divine community, a group against whose interests she is explicitly seeking to act.⁸ In other words, there is a profound and painful desire on the part of a personage with *mênis* to act indiscriminately against a solidary group on the basis of a violation of the very rules responsible for the coherence of that group.

In Achilles, this loss of solidarity coincides with the oath on the scepter in book 1, when he explicitly foresees the devastating consequences for the group of his withdrawal from it:

ἦ ποτ' Ἀχιλλῆος ποθὴ ἵξεται υἷας Ἀχαιῶν
σύμπαντας·

I swear that a yearning for Achilles will come over the sons of the Achaeans, all of them put together.

(1.240–41)

Yet his language also immediately betrays the cost of the loss. For Achilles refers to himself not as "me" but in the third person, as though he were himself imagining and identifying with the other Achaeans' desire for him in his absence. Moreover, since a third person is by definition an absent person, as Emile Benveniste has pointed out, alienation from self is inherent in such a third-person self-reference.⁹ In fact, the tradition is soon explicit about the lasting destructive consequences of Achilles' *mênis* upon himself:

αὐτὰρ ὁ μήνιε νηυσὶ παρήμενος ὠκυπόροισι
διογενὴς Πηλῆος υἱός, πόδας ὠκὺς Ἀχιλλεύς·
οὔτε ποτ' εἰς ἀγορὴν πωλέσκετο κυδιάνειραν
οὔτε ποτ' ἐς πόλεμον, ἀλλὰ φθινύθεσκε φίλον κῆρ
αὖθι μένων, ποθέεσκε δ' ἀϋτήν τε πτόλεμόν τε.

---

⁸ See the discussion of Demeter's *mênis* in Chapter 2, 23–25 above, and Loraux 1986.

⁹ The defining example is "Je est un autre" (Rimbaud, in Benveniste 1966c). There are three other occasions known to me in which persons other than Achilles in the *Iliad* refer to themselves by name in this way: Hector does so in 7.75, and Zeus does so twice, in 8.22 and 470. The expressive value in all three instances is the converse of Achilles'—and Rimbaud's. It is betrayed by the honorific epithets that Zeus applies to himself in line 22. The personage at the top and center of the social hierarchy is asserting his superiority over the group ("I am so far beyond the gods and beyond human beings" [8.27]), which in Zeus's case is actually preceded by a threat of the ultimate sanction (the *mênis* theme, not the word itself) against the other gods if any disobey his order (8.10–18). In other words, these are self-aggrandizing third-person references, like those in the war memoirs of Xenophon, Julius Caesar, and Napoleon. There is certainly a dangerous potential for alienation in such self-conscious grandeur, but that danger is hidden. The primary goal of this kind of third-person self-reference is to assert the status accruing to exceptional excellence.

> Meanwhile he had m&#275;nis sitting beside the fast-streaming ships,
> Zeus-descended son of Peleus, swift-footed Achilles;
> neither was he ever occupying himself in the glorious assembly,
> nor ever in war, but he was hurting his dear heart
> waiting there, and he was yearning for battle cry and war.
>
> (1.488–92)

The first victim of Achilles' *mênis* is in fact his own *phílon kêr*, "dear heart,"[10] and long before there is any yearning (ποθή [1.240]) for him on the part of the Achaeans, there is his own yearning (ποθέεσκε [1.492]) for the social occupations of a warrior male. *Mênis* is the opposite of *philótēs* not simply in that Achilles when he has it suffers from the loss of ties to the wider world but also in that he is thereby harming his own self. A distinction between inner and outer self does not exist for him, so that *mênis* is in the first instance the opposite of *philótēs* because it is the *absence* of *philótēs* even for one's self. It is also the inverse of *philótēs*. Just as Achilles' extreme gesture of friendship is literally to identify himself with a third person, his friend Patroklos, so the boldest mark of his alienation is actually to perceive himself as a third person, as an other. The opposition between *mênis* and *philótēs* has significant consequences from the standpoint of lexicography or translation. The conventional translation of *mênis* in English by the word "wrath," an epic term for a violent emotional response by a powerful personage, divine or human, does not suit a word whose opposite term is "friendship." In English, the opposite of friendship is enmity, and of wrath, delight. The essential problem is the distinctions that we draw between emotional and social terms. For us emotions are primarily individualized and internal, and their social dimensions are semantically secondary. With *mênis*, however, its social dimension is neither secondary to its emotional one nor divisible into inner and outer aspects. What English word is the opposite of both friendship and delight yet also includes alienation?

So how and why can Achilles' *mênis* become *philótēs*? The ninth book of the *Iliad* represents both the acme of his alienation and the beginning of its attenuation. When the embassy arrives (9.186–90), Achilles is singing the *kléa andrôn*, "songs of heroes" to a treasured lyre won when he sacked Eetion's city.[11] Singing to the lyre is conventionally opposed to fighting

---

[10] Compare Thetis's summary description of Achilles' response to the loss of Briseis: ἤτοι ὁ τῆς ἀχέων φρένας ἔφθιεν, "He really withered his mind in his grief for her" (18.446). For another parallel, see Archilochus's description (fr. 129 West) of his alienated *thūmós*—σὺ γὰρ δὴ παρὰ φίλων ἀπάγχεαι, "You are being choked off from the *phíloi*"—as discussed in Nagy 1979, 243–45.

[11] On the meaning of the expression κλέα ἀνδρῶν, see Nagy 1979, 102–3. Since the sack of

hand-to-hand, but twice before it has also been a way to appease *mênis*, so Achilles' performance is at least epicene and at most ambivalent. It signifies his *mênis* (whose expression is withdrawal from fighting) and simultaneously an attempt on his part to end it.[12] When he greets two of the five members of the embassy first as *phíloi* 'dear friends' (9.197) and immediately thereafter describes them twice as *phíltatoi* 'dearest friends' (198, 204), the scene appears to be set for the transformation of his *mênis* into *philótēs*.[13]

Instead, Achilles expresses his resistance to the compromise the embassy offers him with such passion that all his listeners are stunned into prolonged silence when he finally stops speaking (9.430–32). This reaction on Achilles' part is a consequence of Odysseus's unexpected but characteristic intervention and address. The plan had been for Phoenix to take charge (9.168–70), if indeed he and Ajax are the two *phíloi* to whom Achilles was pointing at line 196.[14] Furthermore, in the speech that Odysseus misguidedly makes to Achilles, after telling him to consider warding off the evil day for the Danaans (251), he actually reminds Achilles of what his father Peleus had told him on the day he sent him off to join Agamemnon: that his honor among all the Argives would increase (256–58) in proportion to his *philophrosúnē* 'solidarity' (256), and so he should be sure to restrain himself from internecine strife. Again, near the end of his speech, he says:

---

Eetion's city represents the true narrative point of departure for the *Iliad* (as is apparent when Achilles retells the events of the first book to his mother, 1.366) as well as the origin of the scarce sources of prestige—Chryseis and Briseis—which are the engine of dispute within it, the lyre may be a metaphoric acronym of the epic song being sung on it by Achilles: his own. For the use of another sort of acronym, first lines, as titles of Serbo-Croatian epic songs, see Lord 1960, 286 n. 2, citing Lord and Parry 1954, 266–67, a discussion by Parry's informant Nikola with a singer, Sulejman Makić, about identifying a song performance translated on 277–84. Makić's way of identifying his song is by its first line, "Two pashas spent the winter . . ."

[12] On the conventional opposition of battle and dance, see Muellner 1990, 83–90, including 85 n. 47; for the appeasement of *mênis* with song, see 1.472–74 (*mênis* of Apollo) and 603–4 (*mênis* of Zeus, with Chapter 4, 128). In contrast to those instances, note that Achilles' song is expressly a heroic epic.

[13] The sacrificial meal that Patroklos cooks is also noteworthy as the only one in the *Iliad* in which the meat is explicitly salted before being cooked (line 214). This is one of only two occurrences of the word ἅλς 'salt' in epic in which it is not a metonym for 'sea'; the other is in *Odyssey* 17.455, where Odysseus disguised as a beggar complains of the ungenerous Antinoos οὐ σύ γ' ἂν ἐξ οἴκου σῷ ἐπιστάτῃ οὐδ' ἅλα δοίης, "You wouldn't even give salt to your own home-born servant." Although postepic sacrificial ritual distinguishes between the unsalted entrails that were cooked on a spit and eaten by intimates and the salted boiled meat eaten by everyone else (Detienne 1979, 75–77), the otherwise unmentioned salt on spit-roasted meat might be another token of intimacy among *phíloi* in this context.

[14] Nagy 1979, 49–55, and 1992, 321–26.

εἰ δέ τοι Ἀτρείδης μὲν ἀπήχθετο κηρόθι μᾶλλον,
αὐτὸς καὶ τοῦ δῶρα, σὺ δ' ἄλλους περ Παναχαιοὺς
τειρομένους ἐλέαιρε κατὰ στρατόν, οἵ σε θεὸν ὣς
τείσουσ'· ἦ γάρ κέ σφι μάλα μέγα κῦδος ἄροιο.

If the son of Atreus is too hateful to you in your heart,
he and his gifts both, then at least take pity on the others,
the whole army of hard-pressed Achaeans, all of whom will honor you
like a god; then you might really win great glory in their sight.

(9.300–303)

In other words, in the two passages in which Odysseus invokes Achilles' social obligation to the host of fighting men, he emphasizes the honor and the glory that Achilles will acquire among them as though they were separate from Agamemnon and even if Agamemnon remains his enemy,[15] whereas Achilles' standpoint from the beginning has been that "all the Achaeans" are in solidarity with Agamemnon and he with them. Such a view is, as I have shown, consistent with the nature of *mênis* itself. The position to which Odysseus is asking Achilles to accede is the one that Agamemnon took from the beginning, that his own interests could be separated from those of the host of fighting men whom he leads. It is noteworthy that Odysseus identifies no one to Achilles as his *phílos*, including himself. The single reference to *philophrosúnē* 'solidarity' is to a quality toward others that Odysseus finds lacking in Achilles, not to one that Odysseus professes to be feeling or expressing for him. We have seen that having *mênis*, Achilles is not *phílos* even to his own self, let alone the *Panakhaioí* 'all the Achaeans' against whom he explicitly took action in book 1. In other words, Odysseus is asking Achilles to relinquish his *mênis* without acknowledging that it is the opposite of *philótēs*, that its basis is not just the group's estimate of his own transient prestige but the whole society's rules of exchange and solidarity and those of the natural world to which they are connected.

As Cedric Whitman has pointed out, Achilles seems to know that Odysseus has left out the conclusion from Agamemnon's speech charging the embassy, a conclusion in which he made explicit his actual goal in offering such massive compensation to Achilles:[16]

---

[15] The word ἀπήχθετο 'is hated' in 9.300 incorporates the root of *ekhthrós* 'enemy', the opposite of *phílos*. As Laura Slatkin points out (1988, 130–31), *ekhthrós* designates a personal, not a wartime enemy.

[16] Whitman 1958, 192.

δμηθήτω—'Αΐδης τοι ἀμείλιχος ἠδ' ἀδάμαστος·
τοὔνεκα καί τε βροτοῖσι θεῶν ἔχθιστος ἁπάντων—
καί μοι ὑποστήτω, ὅσσον βασιλεύτερός εἰμι
ἠδ' ὅσσον γενεῇ προγενέστερος εὔχομαι εἶναι.

Let him be subdued—Hades is unlovely and inflexible;
that is why he is the most hateful of the gods to mortals—
and let him take his place beneath me, inasmuch as I am more kingly
and inasmuch as I declare that I am older in my engendering.

(9.158–61)

The stated goal of Agamemnon's offer of gifts is not to recognize Achilles' value and acknowledge a face-losing error, but to assert Agamemnon's superiority in rank to Achilles, which is what he was attempting to do by taking Briseis from him in the first place. Achilles understands this motivation despite Odysseus's omission because of the sheer quantity of compensation being offered. His list of prizes is not a sign of friendship or a tangible recognition of Achilles' value, but a potlatch, the emulous offer of gifts as an assertion of the *giver's* prestige.[17] If Achilles were to accept these gifts from Agamemnon, he would effectively accept subservience to him for life, because they are intended to be beyond Achilles' ability to reciprocate.[18] That is why, when Achilles actually does receive even a reduced portion of these gifts in book 19, he does not receive them from Agamemnon himself. At Odysseus's suggestion—by then he has apparently understood what is at stake—Agamemnon brings them into the middle of the *agorḗ* 'assembly' where all can witness the transaction (19.173–74, 249), and the Myrmidons then take them from there to the ship of Achilles (19.278–79). As Marcel Detienne explains, property that is placed "in the middle of the assembly," like speech "in the middle," is common property that belongs to the whole group.[19] So the compensation of Achilles in book 19 binds the social group

---

[17] On the nature and function of potlatch as practiced by the Indians of the Pacific Northwest, see Mauss 1925 (English translations, Mauss [1967, 1990]). Note that Achilles in his response to Agamemnon's offer is at some pains to assert that he and his father have many possessions of their own at home and at Troy—minus Briseis, of course (9.364–65, 393–400).

[18] Whether or not Achilles has the material resources to equal such a list of gifts is not the issue. The point here is Agamemnon's intention and Achilles' apprehension of it. The circumstances and their results suggest that Agamemnon's list of items represents an overwhelming offer, a conspicuous consumption that might devastate even his own resources but which he has the bravado to imply he can easily replace.

[19] Detienne 1973, 83–98, esp. 88, which includes the following statement in its discussion of this passage: "La procédure préconisée par Ulysse permet donc de recréer les conditions d'un

as a whole to Agamemnon and then reinforces Achilles' bonds to the group; in fact, this exchange is a distribution to Achilles by the group, not a gift from Agamemnon to Achilles.[20] In this way, the final exchange is a reinforcement of Achilles' consistent point of view on the solidarity among Agamemnon, himself, and the society as a whole.[21]

No wonder Odysseus's speech in book 9 backfires: it exacerbates Achilles' *mênis* instead of arousing his *philótēs*. In his response (9.308–429), Achilles highlights one bitter facet after another of his alienation. Since Agamemnon abuses the system of distribution and reward (328–35), the only true reward for his bloody days and sleepless nights of fighting for other men's wives (325–27) will be a death indistinguishable from any coward's (317–20). Agamemnon, he says, having marshaled a huge army in Troy to retrieve his brother's stolen beloved, Helen (339–40), has now made off with the beloved of another, his ally Achilles, even though Agamemnon already has a wife. Achilles loved (*ephíleon*) Briseis "from the heart," as any decent man loves his spouse (341–42), but now he will not take her back from Agamemnon. Achilles says that he has no interest in fighting Hector and none in Agamemnon's gifts, which are *ekhthrá* 'hostile' (378). No quantity of gifts is exchangeable for one's life's breath (408–9). So he is returning to Phthia, having abandoned the choice of *kléos* in favor of a long life (359–61, 415).[22] At this point, Achilles' alienation has even come to the

---

partage" ["The procedure stipulated by Odysseus makes it possible to re-create the circumstances of a division of spoils"].

[20] See the previous note, and on the workings of the *dasmós* 'division of spoils', see above, 103–108, esp. 106.

[21] There is another, similar feature to this exchange process in book 19. When Agamemnon makes his "apology" to Achilles (78–144), the narrator calls attention to the fact that he makes it "right from his seat" and not "standing up in the middle" (77). Normally, the listeners in the assembly sit, and only the speaker "in the middle" stands. Presumably, Agamemnon remains seated because he is wounded and calling attention to the fact (47–52). He begins his speech by explaining that he is addressing Achilles himself (83–84) in such a way that others can listen, having a kind of public conversation with Achilles, whom he in fact addresses only in the third person, never in the second, throughout this scene (84, 89, 188), even though Achilles repeatedly addresses him in the second person (55, 146, 199). This quasi-withdrawn, remote way of speaking to Achilles seems to be an indication of just how difficult it is for Agamemnon to admit that Zeus (*sic*) is to blame for his mistakes, and he scarcely begins to interact socially with Achilles. Note also that Agamemnon is the last person to arrive at the assembly (51–52). Contrast Achilles' complaint in book 9 (372–73) that Agamemnon is too shameless to look him in the face; this inability on his part may already be implicit in the insulting word κυνῶπα 'dog-face' that Achilles uses of him at 1.159, since dogs avert their eyes if humans stare them in the face.

[22] On the association of the name of Achilles' homeland, Phthia, with the opposite of his *kléos*, which is *á-phthi-tos*, see Nagy 1979, 184–85. For more evidence of dictional sensitivity to the meaning of the name Phthia, see 24.856 (cf. 16.461) of Sarpedon ἔμελλε φθίσεσθ' ἐν Τροίῃ ἐριβώλακι, "he [Achilles] will perish in very fertile Troy," vs. Φθίῃ ἐριβώλακι (1.155, etc.), "very fertile Phthia."

point of extinguishing his desire to realize his heroic identity and win the ultimate prize of *kléos,* the imperishable glory embodied in epic poetry itself. The Achaeans will have to find another *mêtis* 'cunning trick' to save themselves, he says, since this *mêtis* is not working (423–25). This particular word in the conclusion to his speech, a word so strongly associated with Odysseus and his gift for deception and manipulation, is another pointer to the fundamentally hostile relationship between him and Achilles that constitutes the context of their interchange.[23] As Achilles says at the beginning of his speech (312–13), he "hates like the gates of Hades a man who hides one thing in his mind and says another." The mastery of just such duplicity characterizes Odysseus,[24] even as the hatred of it characterizes Achilles.[25]

The current cunning trick to which Achilles is referring is an attempt to persuade him to relinquish his *mênis* and adopt Agamemnon's point of view on their quarrel. For Achilles to do so would be to fall victim to a deceptive show of Agamemnon's "generosity" and a false notion of solidarity that would subjugate him to Agamemnon and cost him his heroic prestige and identity. Trouble is, Achilles' decision to leave has the same cost. Neither choice is consistent with the goal-driven progress of the *Iliad.*

## *Mênis* versus *Philótēs:* Incurring Friendship

From another standpoint, that of the metonymic syntax of myth, the interaction between Odysseus and Achilles is a recapitulation of the quarrel between Achilles and Agamemnon in book 1, and it results in the same impasse. Now, once the recapitulation is complete, the impasse should be broken by a new step forward in the sequence. That is in fact what happens. Achilles concludes his response to Odysseus with an invitation to his teacher, Phoenix, to spend the night with Achilles and decide in the morning whether or not to join him on his return home (9.427–29). After the prolonged silence that greets Achilles' speech, Phoenix wipes off a tear and answers the invitation. How could he do otherwise than join Achilles, his *phílon tékos,* "beloved child," on a trip home? Then, over the next sixty-one

---

[23] It is also strongly associated with Nestor, whom the narrator describes as "the very first to start weaving the *mêtis*" (πάμπρωτος ὑφαίνειν ἤρχετο μῆτιν) at 9.93 and also playing a special role in instructing the ambassadors, particularly Odysseus at 9.179–81. On the *nóos*/*mêtis* of Nestor, see Frame 1978.

[24] For instance, see *Odyssey* 13.254ff. For the connection of Odysseus's *mêtis* with deceptive communication, see Nagy 1979, 52–53.

[25] For Achilles as the hero of *bíē,* the traditional opposite of *mêtis,* see the discussion of this passage in Nagy 1979, 45–48.

lines, Phoenix explains why he calls Achilles his "beloved child." To defend his mother's honor and in response to her pleading, Phoenix had slept with a young girl to whom his father had been making love. Having so angered his father, who invoked the Furies and cursed his own son, Phoenix was forced to flee into exile. But he was welcomed by Peleus, who loved (*ephílēse* [9.481]) him as a father loves his only son. Phoenix, in turn, adopted Achilles and "loved him from his heart" (*ek thūmoû philéōn* [486], the same expression Achilles had used at line 343 of Briseis). In fact since the gods were to give him no offspring of his own, Phoenix considered him his own son (494–95), so that Achilles might one day "ward off unseemly devastation for me" (μοί ποτ' ἀεικέα λοιγὸν ἀμῦναι [495]). This fixed diction for dispelling the devastation (*loigós*) of *mênis* closes off the first part of Phoenix's speech, which therefore amounts to a profession of *philótēs* for Achilles upon which to base an as yet unstated demand that Achilles in return end his *mênis*.[26] Up to this point Phoenix has diverged from Odysseus. Instead of chastising Achilles for his lack of *philophrosúnē* 'solidarity', Phoenix is expressing his own *philótēs* and trying to evoke Achilles' as an antidote to his *mênis*. Since Achilles' alienation has just been exacerbated by Odysseus, that is no small task.

Now Phoenix elaborates on the divine virtue of being able to change one's mind. Even the gods themselves are *streptoí* 'flexible' and change their minds when human beings pray and sacrifice to them for respite from punishment of their overstepping (497–501). The *Litaí* 'Pleaders for respite', Zeus's own daughters, are the squinting, wrinkled, and clumsy spirits of such pleading, while wiry, nimble *Átē* 'Moral insensitivity' lurks to punish those who are rigid and resist them (ὃς δέ κ' ἀνήνηται καὶ . . . στερεῶς ἀποείπῃ, "whoever denies and . . . rigidly refuses"). So Achilles should honor these daughters of Zeus and let his honor of them "bend his mind" as it has the mind of others who are noble and true (ἐπιγνάμπτει νόον ἐσθλῶν [514]). *Streptaí* 'flexible' is the term that Iris uses for the minds of the noble and true (φρένες ἐσθλῶν) when recommending to Poseidon that he yield to Zeus and so prevent *mênis* from erupting between them in book 15 (line 203). Moreover, "bending her beloved heart" (ἐπιγνάμψασα φίλον κῆρ [1.569]) is what Zeus makes Hera do in his effort to stop *mênis* from erupting between them in book 1.[27] What Phoenix means, then, is that

---

[26] On the contextual fixation of the *loigòn amûn*- phraseology with the *mênis* theme, see Nagy 1979, 75, and above, 117 n. 48 and 126 n. 67.

[27] These two attestations each of στρεπτός and ἐπιγνάμπτω are their only metaphorical usages in the *Iliad* (and neither word occurs in the *Odyssey* or elsewhere in the epic corpus). Otherwise, ἐπιγνάμπτω is used of Asteropaios's fruitless attempt to bend Achilles' ashen spear (21.178) and

Achilles is now being appeased as one would appease a god with *mênis,* but if he is inflexible, then he is in danger of falling victim to *Atē.* The implication may be that such *átē* would lead, as Agamemnon's did (1.412, 9.18, 115–16, 16.274, 19.88) and Patroklos's will, to punishment by *mênis.*[28] In this context, then, Phoenix is implicitly invoking the rule about heroic *mênis* I have formulated: *heroes with mênis are just as likely to incur it as to express it.*[29] This paradoxical aspect of the *mênis* theme is an overt element even in the theme's very first Iliadic formulation, in the prologue itself, when Achilles' *mênis* is said to entail the devouring of bodies by dogs and birds, which is, as we have seen, a tabu violation that in itself calls down *mênis* upon its perpetrators.[30] Nor is it difficult to gauge the danger attendant in *mênis,* in view of the cosmic destructive power that it entails. In Achilles' case, however, that power is unleashed upon the Achaeans by a combination of his self-denying, inactive absence and Zeus's will. A compensating consequence of this disempowering empowerment seems to be that for Achilles, the conventional threat that he will incur *mênis* can become an invitation to defiance with impunity. For instance, the *Iliad* actually belies its own fronted assertion that dead bodies would be maltreated as a consequence of his *mênis.* In fact no one's corpse is so maltreated in the text, despite Achilles' intense desire to do so to Hector's.[31] A danger inherent in the

---

στρεπτός of men's tongues (20.248) and their tunics (5.113, 21.31). In other words, the metaphorical usage of both of these words is contextually restricted to the *mênis* theme. Likewise, the simple adjective γναμπτός 'flexible' also has only one metaphorical usage in the *Iliad,* by Apollo of Achilles' inflexible temperament as reflected in his maltreatment of the corpse (*sic*) of Hector, a *mênis*-worthy offense (24.40–41); see below, 185–87, and Nagy 1979, 109–10.

[28] For the death of Patroklos at Apollo's hands as an expression of *mênis,* see above, Chapter 1, 13–17, and for the hero's *átē* in that context, see 16.685, 805. The link to Patroklos is especially significant in view of the identification of the description of Patroklos's death with Achilles' own (see below, n. 54), but this does not contradict the principle I shall formulate that within the *Iliad,* Achilles is immune to *mênis.* Still less should it be taken for a sign that Patroklos dies because of Achilles' "mistakes." Patroklos's *átē* is specified as his failure to do what Achilles had told him. Insofar as Patroklos is a ritual substitute for Achilles, his death as the victim of Apollo's *mênis* is a reflection of the rule that heroic *mênis* incurs *mênis,* but insofar as the *Iliad* is at pains to establish Patroklos's responsibility for his own death and the glory due to him, it is also a reflection of the rule that Achilles cannot himself incur *mênis.* These two aspects of Patroklos's death appear to be contradictory. They are in fact complementary and fundamental to the significance of his death in the poem, which makes clear to Achilles the identity of friends and the difference between them (not the individuality of single persons but the divisibility of friends). After all, when he learns of Patroklos's death, Achilles does not feel guilty for having sent him out to fight; he regrets not having been at his side to ward off the harm (*Iliad* 18.98–126). For more on this question, see below, 161–62 with n. 56.

[29] See above, 125–28, 131–32.
[30] See the discussion in 32–33.
[31] For Achilles' attempts at corpse mutilation, see Segal 1971a and below, 168–73.

possession of *mênis* has been suspended for Achilles in the *Iliad*, and the reason for this suspension is not far to seek. Without it, Achilles could not have *mênis* in the first place, since the danger of incurring *mênis* would disable his antagonistic identification with Apollo, and Apollo is the model for Achilles, inasmuch as he is the god who presides over the limits whose transgression incurs *mênis* in the first place.

Now, finally, but still indirectly, Phoenix makes his plea. He would not be telling Achilles to jettison his *mênis* (μῆνιν ἀπορρίψαντα [9.517])—as though he had been telling him before!—unless Agamemnon had ceased his *khólos* 'anger', offered many gifts now as well as more later, and had sent the *phíltatoi* 'most friendly' of the Argives to Achilles to plead with him (515–22). Phoenix's belief in Agamemnon's good faith and his warning about *átē* do not necessarily bode well for the success of his attempt at persuasion, but the conjunction of pleading best friends offering gifts from someone relinquishing his *khólos* 'anger' brings to Phoenix's mind something that is decisive for the story of Achilles, namely, one of *tôn prósthen kléa andrôn heróōn* "the songs of the former warrior heroes," who were *dōrētoí*, "accepting gifts," and *parárrētoi epéessi*, "dissuaded by words" (524–26). We are about to be treated to a heroic tale about friendship from the most refined of epic teachers.

The old song that Phoenix tells among "all you *phíloi*" (528) is the story of one Meleagros of Aitolia. Within the epic Phoenix describes it as an epic song, but the remarkable study carried out by J. T. Kakridis in 1949 understands it instead as a folktale that has been discernibly transformed for insertion into its epic context.[32] According to Kakridis, the variations among

---

[32] Kakridis 1949. In fact, Meleagros's name is more often attached in antiquity to stories that resemble the folktale and its variants than to the tale told in Homer. For an Indo-Europeanist's point of view on Meleagros, see Watkins 1986a and 1986b. I disagree with the historicist arguments of Jan Bremmer (1988), whose search for the original version of the Meleagros myth leads him to believe that there was no tale about him in antiquity prior to the epic one (44–45). Any given myth is multiform from the beginning, or to put it another way, even the supposed "first version" of a myth, were it recoverable, would only be one variant among many. Bremmer's search for the original version of the myth is an imposition of Darwinism that depends on arguments from silence as well as the random and small proportion of texts that have survived from antiquity. What Bremmer explains away as semiliterate Greek "tolerance" of multiformity (50–51) was in its own context not tolerance of something peculiar but inexperience of any other situation. Nor is his narrow definition of folktale as lacking a clear protagonist (44) justifiable or pertinent; his rejection of the connection between the epic tale and the Aitolian folktale adduced by Kakridis rests upon that definition and upon his conviction that there is one recoverable, datable original version of the story. Bremmer also chooses to ignore the thematic parallels that Kakridis observes between the folktale and the epic tale, in particular, the one that he called "the ascending scale of affection." On the level of content as well as form, such parallels are not to be ignored as evidence that the epic tale and the folktale are variants of each other. See also below, 153 n. 42.

the story's parallels in worldwide folklore can be reduced to different treatments of a basic motif that he calls the theme of the ascending scale of affection. Some variants are based on the notion that an individual in society is surrounded by a hierarchy of persons of whom the nearest and dearest—in other words, the most irreplaceable—are one's blood relations; others represent the diametrically opposed view, that the nearest and dearest persons are those whom one chooses as friends. Meleagros is a hero who actually kills his own maternal uncle in a dispute over the distribution of the skin and head of the Calydonian boar (9.548, 567). The dispute's violent outcome results in a war between the city of Meleagros and that of his uncle, a war from which Meleagros angrily withdraws because his mother, in her anger at the killing of her brother, invokes the Furies and curses her own son (566–72). In other words, an alienation of affection between certain blood relations—in this case, the ties between brother and sister are honored at the expense of those between uncle and nephew and mother and son—precipitates a crisis in which the whole society of Meleagros is threatened. Phoenix even describes how Meleagros "in anger at his beloved mother lay beside his wedded wife, the fair Kleopatre" (556–57). The episode recalls how Phoenix himself, in response to his mother's pleas (451), lay with her rival and caused his father to invoke the Furies and curse him, just as Meleagros's mother had done. In fact, Phoenix's whole life story is, by no coincidence, a case of the complete alienation of affection between blood relations and their replacement by friendship ties.

As the enemy throngs the gates of Meleagros's city, a sequence of pleaders[33] comes to the doors of his bedroom to ask him to return to the fighting: first the elders of the people; then the best priests, who offer him a large piece of fertile land of his own choosing; then Oineus, Meleagros's father, followed by the hero's sisters and even his mother (574–85). Finally, the hero's companions, the dearest and nearest to him of all put together (*hoi hoi kednótatoi kaì phíltatoi . . . hapántōn* [586]), come to persuade him, but to no avail. Success is reserved for the hero's wife, who, as their city is being set afire, catalogs to him the *kḗdea* 'collective griefs' (591) that befall the people of a captured city: the burning of the city, the killing of the men, and the enslavement of the women and children (592–94). Her account persuades Meleagros to don his armor and save his city from imminent destruction at the last possible moment. So the sequence of pleaders passes from relatively remote persons in authority who command social respect to

---

[33] Verbal forms of the root of the word *Litai* 'Pleaders' recur four times in the passage, at 9.574, 581, 585, and 591.

family members, and from there to best friends and thence to the one friend whom the hero most prizes and who can convincingly portray to him the need for action on behalf of the whole social group. Both in its culminant structure and in its outcome, the story attests to the greater value of ties to *phíloi* as against ties of blood.[34] Phoenix does not deign to define the specific application of this paradigm to Achilles' situation, but it is not unclear. For Achilles, too, the choice the embassy presents to him can be construed as one between solidarity with the Achaeans and solidarity with his family, since his mother has been the agent of his social withdrawal by obtaining Zeus's validation of his *mênis,* and since his lonely father, Peleus, resides at the ultimate goal of his imaginary withdrawal from the heroic world and all its assumptions, his *nóstos* 'return home'.

In fact, Achilles formulates his response to Phoenix in terms of just this contrast. Intending Meleagros to be a negative model, Phoenix tells Achilles that the Achaeans will honor him like a god if he accepts the gifts now but that, like Meleagros, he will lose *timế* 'honor, prestige, respect' if he waits until the last moment to return and fights without the gifts (597–605). But for Phoenix to hold out the promise of *timế* to Achilles is to echo Odysseus's concluding statement (9.301–3); nor has his speech provided any cogent answer to Achilles' argument about the ultimate value of one's life's breath, namely, that no quantity of gifts can be exchanged for it. So it is not at all surprising that Achilles begins his answer to him by dismissing the value of *timế* from the Achaeans:

Φοῖνιξ, ἄττα γεραιέ, διοτρεφές, οὔ τί με ταύτης
χρεὼ τιμῆς· φρονέω δὲ τετιμῆσθαι Διὸς αἴσῃ
ἥ μ' ἕξει παρὰ νηυσὶ κορωνίσιν, εἰς ὅ κ' ἀϋτμὴ
ἐν στήθεσσι μένῃ καί μοι φίλα γούνατ' ὀρώρῃ.

Phoenix, revered father, Zeus-nourished, I do not need that
honor (*timế*); I consider that I am honored (*tetimḗsthai*) by Zeus's decree,

---

[34] More precisely, it attests to the greater value of *phíloi* who are not blood relatives as against those who are. Blood relatives are included among the *phíloi* in epic society (the word *phílos* is even used of Meleagros's mother in line 555, when she is the object of his anger), but that does not mean that the distinction the story is drawing is inoperative. The *phíloi* who are family members are a distinct solidary group within the *phíloi* in general. For examples of tales in which the opposite hierarchy is validated, see Kakridis 1949. The contrast between family and social solidarity is built into the traditional representation of the great Homeric heroes. See Muellner 1990, 70–71, on the similes in which heroes are conventionally likened to family-centered predatory animals, as against the wider army's representation as the gregarious creatures who are their prey.

which will keep me beside the beaked ships as long as the breath
remains in my chest and my limbs still have some spring in them.

(9.607–10)

Since the decree of Zeus that honors Achilles and keeps him breathing and beside the ships is nothing other than his validation of Achilles' *mênis* at Thetis's request in book 1, the contrast between these two kinds of *timé*, one from the Achaeans and the other from Zeus, is just a version of the contrast between ties to friends and ties to blood relatives. Moreover, *philótēs* and *timé* are interdependent if not synonymous in epic society and diction. It is heinous to dishonor one's *phíloi*; it is inevitable that those whom one loves dearly be the objects of *timé* 'honor, respect, prestige'.³⁵ As Agamemnon says earlier in book 9 in acknowledging his error with Achilles before the council of kings:

ἀασάμην, οὐδ' αὐτὸς ἀναίνομαι. ἀντί νυ πολλῶν
λαῶν ἐστὶν ἀνὴρ ὅν τε Ζεὺς κῆρι <u>φιλήσῃ</u>,
ὡς νῦν τοῦτον <u>ἔτισε</u>, δάμασσε δὲ λαὸν Ἀχαιῶν.

I was deranged, nor do I myself deny that he is worth many hosts
of fighting men, any man whom Zeus <u>loves</u> in his heart
as he has now <u>honored</u> this man³⁶ and subdued the host of the Achaeans.

(116–18)

The statement corrects a misapprehension that first Agamemnon (1.175), then Odysseus had articulated about the current object of Zeus's affection and esteem: <u>τιμὴ</u> δ' ἐκ Διός ἐστι, φιλεῖ δέ ἑ μητίετα Ζεύς, "His <u>timé</u> is from Zeus, and counsellor Zeus <u>loves</u> him" (2.197). Odysseus was referring to Agamemnon, but even by then the *timé* of Zeus had deserted him in favor of Achilles. In general, Homeric affection (or enmity) comes from the heart, but it is publicly expressed in unequivocally social words.³⁷ So

---

³⁵ For the link between *timé* 'honor, prestige, respect' and *philótēs* 'friendship, affection' and their verbal and adjectival relatives, see *Iliad* 5.325–26, 17.57, 18.81ff. (N.B., these three concern the *timé* that Aeneas, Hector, and Achilles each hold for their respective *phílos hetaîros*, "beloved companion"), as well as 15.439, 9.450, 16.460, 24.66ff.; compare also *Odyssey* 15.543 = 17.56, 14.83–84, 8.309, and 10.37.

³⁶ Agamemnon calls Achilles "this man" since he refuses to mention his name even in this speech of "apology" (see Edwards 1991, 245 on 19.83). See 142 n. 21, above. Note also Agamemnon's view of the exchangeability of one person for "many hosts of fighting men," a point of view that Achilles does not share (above, 102–8), even though the reference here is to him.

³⁷ For the social nature of words for emotions in epic, see above, 138.

Achilles cannot count the Achaeans' *timḗ* worth having until his own *philótēs* for them somehow supersedes the *philótēs* of Zeus. But the paradigm of Meleagros is all too fitting, in that the importuning of the hero's best friends is as yet inadequate to achieve such a goal. Even Phoenix's attempt to express and elicit Achilles' *philótēs* backfires. After he dismisses the value of the Achaeans' *timḗ*, Achilles takes him to task for showing favor to Agamemnon:

> μή μοι σύγχει θυμὸν ὀδυρόμενος καὶ ἀχεύων,
> Ἀτρεΐδῃ ἥρωϊ φέρων χάριν· οὐδέ τί σε χρὴ
> τὸν φιλέειν, ἵνα μή μοι ἀπέχθηαι φιλέοντι.
> καλόν τοι σὺν ἐμοὶ τὸν κήδειν ὅς κ' ἐμὲ κήδῃ·
> ἶσον ἐμοὶ βασίλευε καὶ ἥμισυ μείρεο τιμῆς.

> Don't confuse my heart with lamenting and grieving,
> showing favor to the warrior son of Atreus; you should not
> be his *phílos*, so that you will not become hateful to me, your *phílos*.
> It's good for you to aggrieve with me the person who aggrieves me;
> be king equally with me, and share half of the *timḗ*.
> (9.612–16)

In other words, Achilles sees Phoenix's advocacy of Agamemnon's agenda as a breach of solidarity between *phíloi* 'friends', and he offers Phoenix an equal share with him in the *timḗ* he has as king. Presumably, that is a *timḗ* worth having, unlike the *timḗ* of the Achaeans that Phoenix was holding out to Achilles as a reward; Achilles' *timḗ* is between (and presumably among) *phíloi*, that is, the Myrmidons only. Phoenix's goal was certainly not that Achilles enforce the ties of *philótēs* between the two of them to the exclusion of Agamemnon and the other Achaeans. While Phoenix has been trying to reintegrate Achilles among the Achaeans, Achilles has been trying to detach Phoenix from them, and he eventually succeeds (9.658–59).

Even so, at the end of his answer to Phoenix, Achilles retreats from the decision he had announced at the end of his answer to Odysseus. Instead of leaving for Phthia in the morning with or without Phoenix (9.427–29), Achilles says that he and Phoenix will decide in the morning whether they will leave or stay (9.618–19). At first, it may seem unlikely that this change is a result of *philótēs* for the Achaeans impinging upon *mênis* rather than Achilles' realization, just voiced, that the decree of Zeus requires him to stay beside the ships for the rest of his life (9.608–10). The basis of that realization is unstated, but it implies that he has abandoned the choice of a return home (410–16); on the other hand, it is plain that the claims of *philótēs* between Achilles and Phoenix, which are emphatically *not* ties between blood relatives, are important to Achilles. Their decision in the morning would be their first as equal kings, and there is no doubt as to where Phoenix will stand.

So Achilles is taking one small step away from *mênis*, and he is about to take another. What Ajax now says as the embassy is preparing to leave is as significant as the persons to whom he says it. He begins by telling Odysseus that it is time to go back and report their bad result, since they are not about to accomplish the μύθοιο τελευτή, "goal of their speech act" (625).[38] He places the blame for that failure squarely on Achilles, of whom he speaks in the third person even though he is present:

αὐτὰρ Ἀχιλλεὺς
ἄγριον ἐν στήθεσσι θέτο μεγαλήτορα θυμόν,
σχέτλιος, οὐδὲ μετατρέπεται φιλότητος ἑταίρων
τῆς ᾗ μιν παρὰ νηυσὶν <u>ἐτίομεν</u> ἔξοχον ἄλλων,
νηλής.

    for Achilles
has taken on a savage spirit in his chest, inflexible man,
and he pays no heed to the *philótēs* of his companions,
that we are <u>honoring</u> him with beyond all others beside the ships,
  pitiless.
                                                   (628–32)

Instead of talking about his own friendship for Achilles, as Phoenix had done, Ajax speaks plainly of the exceptional *philótēs* with which "we" as a group honor "him" but which he is too hard-hearted to recognize. Such an unrespected bond to the social group is a key theme of Phoenix's story of Meleagros, and Ajax speaks about it in Achilles' presence as though he were absent.[39] In fact, the third-person address is in itself a metaphor for the message, which is that Achilles is an *absent presence,* not an exile but a pariah who does not recognize his ties to the group of *phíloi* despite their

---

[38] For the translation of *múthos* as 'speech act', see Martin 1989, 14–42.
[39] On the connotations of third-person address for Achilles, see above, 108 n. 34, 137 n. 9, and 136–38.

efforts to the contrary. (Indeed, as soon as his *mênis* was legitimated, as we saw, Achilles became a third person even to himself!)[40] Then Ajax finds a legal analogy to Achilles' situation in that of a man whose brother or child has been killed:

> καί ῥ' ὁ μὲν ἐν δήμῳ μένει αὐτοῦ πόλλ' ἀποτείσας,
> τοῦ δέ τ' ἐρητύεται κραδίη καὶ θυμὸς ἀγήνωρ
> ποινὴν δεξαμένῳ·

> and the one (the killer) remains there after paying much in return,
> while the manly heart and spirit of the other is restrained
> and he accepts compensation.
>
> (633–35)

Just when he starts to explain the relevance of this analogy, Ajax makes a decisive change in the grammar of his speech. Suddenly, he addresses Achilles directly, in the second person:

> σοὶ δ' ἄλληκτόν τε κακόν τε
> θυμὸν ἐνὶ στήθεσσι θεοὶ θέσαν εἵνεκα κούρης
> οἴης· νῦν δέ τοι ἑπτὰ παρίσχομεν ἔξοχ' ἀρίστας,
> ἄλλα τε πόλλ' ἐπὶ τῇσι· σὺ δ' ἵλαον ἔνθεο θυμόν,
> αἴδεσσαι δὲ μέλαθρον· ὑπωρόφιοι δέ τοί εἰμεν
> πληθύος ἐκ Δαναῶν, μέμαμεν δέ τοι ἔξοχον ἄλλων
> κήδιστοί τ' ἔμεναι καὶ φίλτατοι, ὅσσοι Ἀχαιοί.

> but the gods have put
> an implacable, evil spirit in your chest because of only one
> girl, yet here we are offering you seven who are far the best,
> and many other things besides. So put on a kindly[41] spirit,
> and respect the roof over our heads, since from the mass of all the Danaans,
> we are your guests, and we are eager to be by far the most cherished
> and dearest to you of all the Achaeans.
>
> (636–42)

---

[40] See above, 137–38. The other, similar irony in Ajax's accusation, namely, that Achilles' withdrawal from the social group was actually in the name of its own abused prerogatives and standards of conduct that it was unable or unwilling to defend, goes unnoticed in this context because of the blanketing effect of Ajax's emotional appeal to the demands of friendship among warriors.

[41] For the semantic restriction of the word ἵλαος 'kindly' to persons with *mênis*, see above, 126 n. 69.

The grammatical shift from third- to second-person address is a conversion, an enactment through words of the change in the relationship between Achilles and the Achaeans that Ajax is exhorting him to effect, a metaphor for the "goal of the speech act." Ajax is arguing that society has effective rules for the compensation of death that permit a killer and the blood relatives of his victim to live on in the same social context. Accordingly, sevenfold payment for the loss of "only one girl," κούρης οἴης (637–38), should be more than adequate, especially since it comes from those who are best friends to Achilles. Instead of being an absent presence to the Achaeans, he should cease being a "he" and become one of them, a friend to be addressed as a "you." Given the assumption here again that friends are more valuable than blood relatives and that Achilles' nearest and dearest friends are making the offer, he should certainly be able to accept the more than adequate compensation being provided and restore his solidarity with his friends and even with Agamemnon.[42]

Ajax's is the most direct attack so far on Achilles' alienation. It wins his concurrence (9.645) and a message to report (649) which Achilles himself seems to present as a further concession. Citing his continuing *khólos* 'anger' at the way Agamemnon dishonored him, he stipulates that he will not fight until Hector comes to the huts and ships of the Myrmidons and sets fire to the ships (650–55). Does this negatively phrased minimal commitment nevertheless represent an incremental change in his response? Achilles is plainly adopting the model of Meleagros that Phoenix had offered as a negative example, and he is identifying Ajax's plea, if not the whole embassy, with the penultimate group of pleaders in the tale, the group of nearest and dearest friends who *fail to persuade* the hero (585–87). Ajax's speech contains an appeal to friendship that actively alienates and then integrates Achilles into the group of *phíloi,* and it also provides a new item of content, a legal analogy about acceptable compensation (*poiné* [633]) for the death of a family member. But the Shield of Achilles incorporates this same analogy and carries it one step farther. It depicts a figure in a le-

---

[42] In fact, the argument from analogy is also effective if Ajax is assuming that blood relatives are more important than friends, but that seems relatively unlikely in the context of the story of Meleagros, Phoenix's speech, and of the emphasis being placed in this passage on the importance of "friends" who are not blood relatives. On the other hand, a parallel passage in book 24 explicitly assumes that blood relatives are more *phílos* than friends (46–47). It may be difficult to imagine that any loss would be harder to compensate than the loss of a child, but variants on the Meleagros tale collected by Kakridis 1949, in which the hero's life energy is attached to a quenched firebrand that his mother tosses into the fireplace when she is angered at him, argue that another culture may view such matters otherwise. There is also the behavior of Meleagros's mother toward her son in the Homeric version of the tale. See above, 146 n. 32.

gal dispute who is violently refusing to accept the compensation (*poinē* [18.499]) offered for a slain relative, exactly as Achilles is refusing to accept Agamemnon's *ápoina* 'ransom' (9.120) at this very moment.[43] Refusing compensation in such a situation is a course of action that cannot easily be condemned or accepted, since the shield portrays a legal dispute with a prize of two gold talents for the person who offers the best solution to the judicial problem it represents; we still do not know the results of their deliberation. So in both cases, Ajax's legal analogy and Phoenix's epic story, Achilles is adopting the parallel proffered, but in the opposite sense from that intended. On the basis of the further parallelism between the legal analogy and the embassies to Meleagros, we are entitled to wonder whether Achilles' refusal of the prizes that Agamemnon offers really is harmful to his *timē*, as Phoenix claims (604–5). The essential point is that Achilles' behavior cannot be conveniently dismissed as wrong or praised as righteous. Instead, it is a type of dangerous and powerful action that distresses a society's classification system in such a way as to compel discussion, rethinking, and the redefinition of basic categories of behavior. At least, those seem to be its consequences within the world of Achilles' Shield and in certain real societies.[44] In this respect, it is utterly consistent with Achilles' persona as the hero with *mēnis*.

But the original question remains unanswered: in view of the parallelism it establishes with the *failed* embassy of friends to Meleagros, does Achilles' negatively phrased, minimal commitment to Ajax and the Achaeans to return and fight at the last possible moment represent an incremental, not to say decisive, change in his response? The answer is an unqualified yes, not least because it is recognizable as Achilles' choice between the two mutually exclusive destinies his mother had told him of, namely, *nóstos* 'return home' and *kléos* 'immortal glory in poetry' (9.410–16), and because it thereby entails an affirmation of the heroic assumptions that he had rejected with such force in his response to Odysseus. *Kléos* 'immortal glory' is by definition embodied and preserved in epic song. Moreover, the choice of *kléos* is also a choice of *philótēs*, in that it requires Achilles' subsequent acceptance of a future demand that he return, to be made by a nearer and dearer friend than Phoenix or Ajax. So Achilles is identifying himself *with and as* an epic hero in making known his grudging, deferred choice, in predicting the teleology of his *mēnis*.

---

[43] See Muellner 1976, 100–106, for the interpretation of the passage (18.497–508) and the argument that this figure represents Achilles himself. See also Westbrook 1992 for confirming Near Eastern parallels and precision on the details of the legal issues.

[44] I am referring to the conceptual framework of Mary Douglas (1966): see above, 26–28.

The *Mênis* of Achilles and Its Iliadic Teleology    155

What is there about Ajax's speech that has brought about this incremental change? It is the climax of a metonymic sequence of attempts to enforce the claims of *philótēs* 'friendship' on Achilles, each one incorporating the previous one and going one step beyond it. First there was Odysseus's reminder of Peleus's warning that Achilles should show *philophrosúnē* 'friendliness, solidarity' even if he still hated Agamemnon, which only alienated Achilles and contributed to his decision to return home to Phthia. Then came Phoenix's expression of his own *philótēs* and its general value in epic tradition, which reinforced Achilles' claim on Phoenix but also elicited a deferral of his decision to return home to Phthia. Lastly, there was Ajax's blunt statement of the prior claims of the *phíloi* in a speech that actively alienates and then integrates Achilles into the social group. It results in his abandonment of *nóstos* and in a minimal commitment to fight at the last possible moment. Furthermore, considering the way that Achilles in his answer to Odysseus defined *psukhḗ* 'life's breath' as an absolute value beyond exchange value (406–9), Ajax's advocacy of Agamemnon's compensation on the analogy of acceptable compensation for murder seems to rescue the notion of exchange value for someone's death. Yet the Shield figure's staunch refusal to accept any compensation leaves the issue unresolved (18.497–508). That is important, since "immortal" *kléos* is the alternative ultimate value for which a hero is supposed to exchange his life. The possibility that there is no way to compensate for the loss of life keeps alive the issue of the relative value of *kléos* and *psukhḗ* 'life's breath' in the world of Achilles' shield. Raising an issue about the relative value of epic poetry itself is what to expect from the figure of Achilles.

## *Mênis* versus *Philótēs*: Friendship and Death

Such are the first steps in the transformation of Achilles' *mênis* into *philótēs*.[45] The next step is, according to the example of Meleagros, Pa-

---

[45] It may or may not be significant that Odysseus reports (9.677–94) to Agamemnon only the alienated response that Achilles gave to him, omitting the concessions Achilles subsequently made to Phoenix and Ajax. The epic conventions for relaying messages constrain messengers to report the message addressed to them in complete or abbreviated form; perhaps the audience is to take Odysseus's report of the reply he received as a kind of acronym standing for all three replies. On the other hand, it is as though Odysseus did not even hear the interchanges between Phoenix and Ajax and Achilles. This "snub" may be a pendant to the "snub" by which Achilles addresses Phoenix and Ajax as his two dearest friends, ignoring Odysseus (on this issue, see Nagy 1992). In both cases, the *phíloi* receive treatment that separates them from Odysseus, and Odysseus has again snatched the initiative, this time as messenger, despite Achilles' specific instructions to Ajax

troklos's, not simply because he is Achilles' dearest friend but also because of his name, which is simply the reverse of the name of Meleagros's wife, Kleopatre.[46] The functional parallelism between these two figures goes hand in hand with the formal equivalence of their names. Both reside at the top of the "ascending scale of affection" for the respective heroes of their tales, and both intervene to remind the hero of his social obligations and to end his withdrawal from battle to save the community. There is also a relevant third example of the syntagma that makes up their names. In book 6, after Hector has finally found his wife, Andromache—in searching for her, he had encountered in succession his mother, his brother, and his sister-in-law—she describes to him the death of her seven brothers and her father at the hands of Achilles on a single day as well as the subsequent death of her mother. In a particularly intensified variation on the ascending scale of affection,[47] she tells him that, in the absence of all blood relatives, he, Hector, is her father, mother, and brother, as well as her spouse (6.429–31); then she tells him to stay with her on the tower and to set his army by the fig tree, in order "not to make his boy an orphan and his wife a widow" (432). In other words, the hero's wife is asking him to *withdraw* from the fighting because he is by far the most valuable person to her. But he refuses:

ἦ καὶ ἐμοὶ τάδε πάντα μέλει, γύναι· ἀλλὰ μάλ' αἰνῶς
αἰδέομαι Τρῶας καὶ Τρῳάδας ἑλκεσιπέπλους
αἴ κε κακὸς ὣς νόσφιν ἀλυσκάζω πολέμοιο·
οὐδέ με θυμὸς ἄνωγεν, ἐπεὶ μάθον ἔμμεναι ἐσθλὸς
αἰεὶ καὶ πρώτοισι μετὰ Τρώεσσι μάχεσθαι,
ἀρνύμενος <u>πατρός</u> τε μέγα <u>κλέος</u> ἠδ' ἐμὸν αὐτοῦ.

All these things are a care to me, my wife; but I would be terribly
ashamed before the Trojans, the men and the trailing-robed women,
if like a coward I were to shirk from battle;
nor does my heart bid me to, since I learned always to be true
and to fight in the front ranks of the Trojans,
striving to win great <u>kléos</u>, my <u>father's</u> and my own.[48]

(441–46)

---

concerning which message to relay (9.649; compare line 657, ἦρχε δ' Ὀδυσσεύς). See above, 139 with n. 14.

[46] Howald 1924, 1946; on the thematic dimensions of the correspondence, see Nagy 1979, 104–17.

[47] The passage—but not its relevance to Patroklos and Kleopatre—is featured by Kakridis (1949) in his discussion of the ascending scale of affection.

[48] I agree with Nagy (1979) who supposes (105 and 115) that an earlier semantics of the

Hector then goes on to describe the future that awaits his enslaved wife in terms that recall the summary of Kleopatre's predictions to Meleagros (9.591–94). It is no coincidence that this, the only example in the epic corpus of the words *kléos* and *patḗr* in the same phrase (not in a name), specifies the transcendent value in his life, beyond his wife, that will keep Hector fighting for Troy. For him, the nearest and dearest person and the goal of heroic glory lie along *divergent* paths because he is a hero in the center of his social group, not withdrawn from it. There is no question of Hector's withdrawing from obligations to the social group; his goal is to strive for glory and save his city, which in his case necessitates a painful separation from his wife. For Meleagros and Achilles, on the other hand, the epic tradition will vouchsafe them *kléos* if they heed the words of the person who is nearest and dearest to them and protect the social group whose needs and safety that person embodies and expresses. Patroklos and Kleopatre each represent epic glory and social solidarity rolled up into one, and the goal for heroes like Achilles or Meleagros is to settle their anger and reintegrate themselves into society. To put it another way, a most significant and fateful aspect of Hector's identity is that Andromache's name lacks the word *kléos*.

By contrast, the existence of a special companion named Patroklos in the story of Achilles implies that its hero will achieve the glory conveyed by the epic tradition when he heeds the aforementioned Patroklos's claims upon him, if his *mênis* gives way to *philótēs*. Indeed, the name of Patroklos and the function bound to it suggest that the acquisition of glory is in itself a gesture of friendship and a social benefaction. I have maintained that Achilles' substitution of Patroklos for himself when the paradigm of Meleagros and his own concession to Ajax in book 9 both call for Achilles himself to return to the fighting was a gesture of *philótēs*, of solidarity with the host of Achaeans. Achilles accedes to Patroklos's request that he set aside his *mênis* in these words:

ἀλλὰ τὰ μὲν προτετύχθαι ἐάσομεν· οὐδ' ἄρα πως ἦν
ἀσπερχὲς κεχολῶσθαι ἐνὶ φρεσίν· ἤτοι ἔφην γε
οὐ πρὶν μηνιθμὸν καταπαυσέμεν, ἀλλ' ὁπότ' ἄν δὴ

---

collocation of πατήρ and κλέος was 'the *kléos* of the ancestors', that is, the stories told about them, as in the phrase τῶν πρόσθεν ... κλέα ἀνδρῶν / ἡρώων, "the glorious deeds of the former men who were heroes" (9.524–25). (For πατέρες meaning 'ancestors', see, for example, *Iliad* 6.209.) Hector is using the phrase in a secondary context in which its meaning has been reinterpreted as "my father's *kléos*," on the assumption that Hector's achievements reflect on Priam as well as himself, just as a hero's identity consists in his own name and that of his father.

νῆας ἐμὰς ἀφίκηται ἀϋτή τε πτόλεμός τε.
τύνη δ' ὤμοιιν μὲν ἐμὰ κλυτὰ τεύχεα δῦθι,
ἄρχε δὲ Μυρμιδόνεσσι φιλοπτολέμοισι μάχεσθαι.

But let these things be past and forgotten; there was no way
to be ceaselessly angry in my heart; indeed, I said
that I would not cease my *mênis* except when
the shout and the battle reached my ships.
But you put my armor on your shoulders,
and lead the war-loving Myrmidons to fight.

(16.60–65)

This passage has been understood in two ways. It may mean that the moment has not come for Achilles to reenter the battle.[49] Then Achilles' substitution of Patroklos for himself is a sign of the hero's persisting unwillingness to give up his anger—he has been speaking of his residual bitter feelings toward Agamemnon just before this passage. Moreover, most commentators now consider the substitution a stubborn deferral of his own return for which he is punished by the terrible death of the substitute, a "tragic error" for which he is considered blameworthy to varying degrees.[50]

Another possible interpretation, which I prefer, is that the moment has in fact come to which Achilles referred in his concession to Ajax, but that he honors Patroklos's desire to don his armor and defend the Achaeans to signal a gesture of friendship, not to perpetuate his *mênis*. Achilles explicitly sends him out to ward off the devastation—using the words *loigòn amûnai* at 16.80 that Phoenix had of Achilles' saving the day, 9.495[51]—when Hector

---

[49] In support of this view, Lattimore translates line 61 ἤτοι ἔφην γε, "and yet I have said," as though the moment stipulated in Achilles' concession to Ajax had not actually arrived. But the particle ἤτοι serves to assert the truthfulness of a statement, not to introduce an objection to a previous one. See LSJ⁹ s.vv. ἤτοι and ἦ, and Denniston 1954, 553: on ἤτοι = ἦ τοι, "τοι serves to bring home a truth of which the certainty is expressed by ἦ: 'Verily, I tell you'." Along the same lines as Lattimore, Richard Janko (1992, 323) wishes to restore an etymological meaning of "furiously" to ἀσπερχές in line 61 as against "ceaselessly" (D scholia); but cf. Chantraine 1968–79, s.v., who views "ceaselessly" as a semantic development from "furiously." The historical semantics of the adverb αἰεί 'always, without stopping' are parallel; see Benveniste 1937. Scodel 1989 also vouches for Achilles' word here.

[50] To the paradoxical formulation of Whitman (1958, 137)—"Now he has paid the price of human loss for his godlike intransigence"—compare the views of Ruth Scodel (1989) or James Redfield (1975, 91–98). Janko (1992, 309–10) considers the situation "morally ambiguous" in that the death of Patroklos is a "punishment" but at the same time "the result of a set of misunderstandings." To me this account of the situation seems internally inconsistent; the narrative is not morally ambiguous.

[51] Note that the unequivocal implication of this language is that the fire set to the ships is actually a manifestation of *Achilles' mênis* that Patroklos is extinguishing, and in fact it *is* a direct

The *Mênis* of Achilles and Its Iliadic Teleology  159

sets fire to the ships (16.60–63, 114–29), which is one of the two conditions Achilles had specified at 9.650–53. The issue then becomes whether or not the fighting has yet come to Achilles' *own* ships. The text locates the fight at the end of book 15 around Protesilaos's ship and does not specify that battle's proximity to Achilles' ships,[52] but the parallelism between Patroklos's role/name and Kleopatre's suggests that the limit Achilles had in mind is reached when Patroklos asks Achilles to relent. Furthermore, when Zeus earlier predicted the death of Patroklos (15.53–67), he said that Achilles would rouse him to action when the Achaeans, routed, "fall among the ships of Achilles," ἐν νηυσὶ πολυκλήϊσι πέσωσι / Πηλεΐδεω Ἀχιλῆος (63–64). In the event, as I just mentioned, Achilles does so when Hector sets them afire. The "inconsistency" here, if it truly is one, bespeaks the nature of cross-reference in a tradition of performance. A poet in such circumstances does not conceive of cross-reference in the same way as writers who can flip pages forward or back and verify their terms. I would suggest that the two signals or limits, fighting at Achilles' ships and Trojan fire on the ship, are variants with equivalent narrative functions.[53] Finally, there is Achilles' explicit desire to win back the girl, get the gifts, and achieve *timé* (16.84–90): all these are symptomatic of a recommitment on Achilles' part to the human domain and to its rewards, rewards that he had abandoned in book 9 in favor of the *timé* from Zeus that validated his *mênis* and effectively exiled him from the society of the Achaeans. Phoenix had warned Achilles that he would lose such *timé* by returning to battle too late. Achilles is now attempting to retrieve what Meleagros had not been able to.

As it turns out, Patroklos's identification with Achilles, like Achilles' identification with him, is overdetermined. In his function as Achilles' *therápōn* 'sidekick', his death in Achilles' armor and Achilles' reaction to it (as well as Thetis's) are superimposed on the details of the death of Achil-

---

result of Achilles' "passive" *mênis*. On the relationship between *mênis* and *loigòn amûnai*, see Nagy 1979, 75 and n. 26 above. On fire as the typical expression of *mênis*, see above, 7, 18, and 101–2. See above, 135–36 n. 4, on the absence of literal value in Patroklos's "disguise" as Achilles.

[52] Compare 24.391–95, where the disguised Hermes claims to be a Myrmidon who, because of Achilles' anger at Agamemnon, passively witnessed Hector ἐπὶ νηυσὶν ἐλάσσας / Ἀργείους κτείνεσκε, "driving the Argives to the ships and killing them." Significantly, the ship of Protesilaos is located *next to* Achilles' ship (on the left side of it, toward the center of the ships, since Achilles' is at the extreme right): Cuillandre 1943, 32–34.

[53] For another interesting cross-reference, compare Thetis's recounting to Hephaistos of the embassy to Achilles in book 9: τὸν δὲ λίσσοντο γέροντες / Ἀργείων, καὶ πολλὰ περικλυτὰ δῶρ' ὀνόμαζον, "the elders [sic] of the Argives beseeched him, and named many very famous gifts" (18.449–50). The expression τὸν δὲ λίσσοντο γέροντες, "and the elders beseeched him," recurs only in Phoenix's description of the first group of ambassadors to *Meleagros*.

les and its aftermath in the *Aethiopis* tradition.⁵⁴ So the substitution of Patroklos for Achilles works only too well. In other words, Patroklos's death in Achilles' stead on behalf of the host of fighting men is an enactment of Aristotle's definition of friendship: he is a "he" who has become "another I." In this context, it bears mentioning that Patroklos is one of two heroes whom the otherwise rigidly third-person narrator of the *Iliad* actually addresses in the second-person singular, as a "you," right before the moment of his death (16.787). That is a grammatical symptom of the special sympathy and *philótēs* his character evokes and expresses. One could characterize Patroklos's substitution for Achilles as the combination of a character who embodies solidarity (a "you") with one who embodies remoteness (a "he") because each is the "other's I." What we expect in such a situation, and what the Meleagros story also leads us to expect, is that Achilles himself would take on the sympathetic aspect embodied by Patroklos and show his *philótēs* for the Achaeans by reentering the battle and saving the day. Instead Achilles has reversed the dramatis personae with exactly the same goal in mind, namely, to choose *philótēs* and end his *mênis*, a twist that is consistent with and expressive of Achilles' overdetermined identification with Patroklos.

Before sending him out, Achilles actually warns Patroklos not to get carried away and arouse the dangerous attention of Apollo (16.91–96). But Patroklos crosses over limits that Achilles warned him not to, and he first avoids but then incurs the *mênis* of Apollo in a moment of great glory that is the mirror image of Achilles' own death.⁵⁵ It is as though any putative limit on the identity between the two heroes cannot stand. Their friendship, the fusion of their identities, is an absolute. When Achilles hears of Patroklos's death, he responds literally and by allusion as though he himself had died. The identification of Patroklos with Achilles, whose bones will eventually be buried in one and the same *sêma* 'tomb', is almost indissoluble (*Odyssey* 24.76–77). Any notion that Achilles is "to blame" for Patroklos's death falls

⁵⁴ On the relationship between the death of Patroklos and the death of Achilles, see Pestalozzi 1945; Schadewaldt 1965, 155–202; and Kullmann 1960. The term *therápōn*, whose etymology was proposed by Nadia Van Brock (1959) and whose usage and significance in epic is studied in detail by Steven Lowenstam (1981), is a loan word from Hittite or Luvian that once meant 'ritual substitute for the king', a scapegoat who died in his stead. In other words, a role as the king's ritual substitute lingers on in the theme associated with the title *therápōn*, even if the older lexical meaning of the term has long since been lost.

⁵⁵ On the circumstances of the death of Patroklos, see above, 133–36, 145 n. 28 and Chapter 1, 13–17. The death of Patroklos as a victim of Apollo's *mênis* pertains to the ritual antagonism between Achilles and Apollo and the rule that heroes with *mênis* (except Achilles) are susceptible to incurring it. If such a formulation appears contradictory, that is only a consequence of the fusion of the two *phíloi*, see above, n. 28.

afoul of this persisting bond of affection and identity between him and his faithful companion; Achilles is only the literally surviving half of a symbolic whole. When he learns of Patroklos's death, he expresses not guilt for causing it but terrible grief at such a loss (18.22ff.), regret for not having been able to protect him and his other companions who were slain by Hector (18.98–99, 102–3),[56] and a desire to avenge his death (18.114–15) and so win *kléos* (18.121) at the expense of his own life.

No moral or epistemological failure is distilled from this event—Achilles' hopeless wish (18.108–10) that *éris* 'strife' and *khólos* 'anger' perish from humankind notwithstanding—nor any "tragic" error. It is not a terminological quibble to aver that this poem is no tragedy but an epic, with its own appropriate structures and ideas of poetic form and the human condition. Instead of reflecting *tragic* notions about human behavior or the hero's moral value, the death of Patroklos actually propels Achilles into "the realm of *kléos*,"[57] which is only an epic way of saying that the death of Patroklos is consistent with this poem's overall teleology and conventions. Insofar as possible, that teleology ought to be reconstructed in the epic's own terms. From the standpoint of the transformation of Achilles' *mênis* into *philótēs* that I have been mapping, the major differences between his speech sending out Patroklos in book 16 and his speech on learning of his death in book 18, when he commits himself to join the fighting, are twofold. First, Achilles now voices his decision to win *kléos* and his readiness to die after avenging Patroklos. These are facets of the same fundamental idea, for the *kléos* that epic can bestow on "the best of the Achaeans" is a compensation for his death. Consequently, Achilles cannot fully choose to win *kléos* without accepting the reality of his own death. On deciding to send out Patroklos, his goal (μύθου τέλος, "the goal of my speech act" [16.83]) had been different: to preserve and enhance his *timế* in "making a light" for the

---

[56] For some commentators, what I characterize as regret is instead "guilt." Guilty feelings are familiar to the modern reader, but appearances to the contrary notwithstanding, guilt is not a cultural universal, nor is it wise to retroject from our perspective the interior emotions of a poetic figure like Achilles who appears in a world in which feelings are so powerfully and effectively externalized. (That is not to say that the epic lacks a way of representing what it considers to be interior thoughts and feelings when it wishes to. I am referring to the convention of speaking to one's *thumós* as exemplified by Hector's monologue at 22.98ff.). The issue is important whatever one's view on the question of whether Achilles should feel he is to blame for Patroklos's death; but whether Achilles is or is not portrayed as "guilty" (in the emotional sense) cannot easily be separated from the question of whether or not he is guilty (in the moral sense). I suggest that he is not being portrayed as guilty in *either* sense, which is not to deny that he deeply regrets the death and wishes he had acted to prevent it.

[57] This is the formulation of Sinos 1980, 104; see also Nagy 1979, 102–3. The point is to highlight the relationship between Patroklos's name and his narrative function in this regard.

fighting Achaeans (16.84–96). *Timḗ* is of this world; *kléos*, a term that the epic uses for itself, belongs to the hereafter.

The second major difference lies in the scope of Achilles' *philótēs*. Whereas before, his gesture of *philótēs* had been a total identification with his best friend Patroklos, now his concern is to avenge that friend's death but also to redress his neglect of the social group. Here he says:

> νῦν δ' ἐπεὶ οὐ νέομαί γε φίλην ἐς πατρίδα γαῖαν
> οὐδέ τι Πατρόκλῳ γενόμην φάος οὐδ' ἑτάροισι
> τοῖς ἄλλοις, οἳ δὴ πολέες δάμεν Ἕκτορι δίῳ.

> but now since I am not returning to my beloved fatherland
> and I was not at all a light to Patroklos or to the companions,
> the other ones of whom many were subdued by godlike Hector.
> (18.101–3)

whereas before, on sending out Patroklos, Achilles had stressed his exclusive bond with him in an admitted fantasy[58] about the absence of *any* others fighting at Troy:

> ἀλλὰ πάλιν τρωπᾶσθαι, ἐπὴν φάος ἐν νήεσσι
> θήῃς, τοὺς δ' ἔτ' ἐᾶν πεδίον κάτα δηριάασθαι.
> αἲ γάρ, Ζεῦ τε πάτερ καὶ Ἀθηναίη καὶ Ἄπολλον,
> μήτε τις οὖν Τρώων θάνατον φύγοι, ὅσσοι ἔασι,
> μήτε τις Ἀργείων, νῶϊν δ' ἐκδῦμεν ὄλεθρον,
> ὄφρ' οἶοι Τροίης ἱερὰ κρήδεμνα λύωμεν.

> But turn back when you make a light among the ships,
> and leave them [= Argives and Trojans] to fight on the plain.
> In the name of father Zeus, Athena, and Apollo, I wish
> that no one of the Trojans would escape death, as many as they are,
> nor any of the Argives, but that we two alone would escape destruction
> in order to loosen the sacred headbands of Troy.
> (16.95–100)

The reason for these incremental changes in Achilles' stance is, I believe, transparent and consistent with the whole trajectory of *mênis* in the *Iliad*, not at odds with it. The death of the person whom Achilles valued above all

---

[58] For the convention of wishing by Zeus, Athena, and Apollo as an avowed impossibility, see above, 102 n. 21.

others is the most devastating of events, but it is also consistent with the expression of *philótēs* that caused Achilles to send him out in his stead in the first place. It has made all too clear his own mortality, the solidary bond that definitively ties him to Patroklos and the Achaeans and severs him from his mother and Zeus. Achilles actually makes explicit the connection between Patroklos's death and his now absolute awareness of the reality of his own death in a subsequent encounter with the Trojan Lykaon, a young man who had been fortunate enough to escape death from Achilles once before and now offers him a ransom (ἄποινα [21.99]) in exchange for his life:

> ἀλλά, φίλος, θάνε <u>καὶ σύ</u>· τίη ὀλοφύρεαι οὕτως;
> κάτθανε <u>καὶ Πάτροκλος</u>, ὅ περ σέο πολλὸν ἀμείνων.
> οὐχ ὁράᾳς οἷος καὶ ἐγὼ καλός τε μέγας τε;
> πατρὸς δ' εἴμ' ἀγαθοῖο, θεὰ δέ με γείνατο μήτηρ·
> ἀλλ' ἔπι τοι καὶ ἐμοὶ θάνατος καὶ μοῖρα κραταιή·
> ἔσσεται ἢ ἠὼς ἢ δείλη ἢ μέσον ἦμαρ,
> ὁππότε τις <u>καὶ ἐμεῖο</u> Ἄρη ἐκ θυμὸν ἕληται
> ἢ ὅ γε δουρὶ βαλὼν ἢ ἀπὸ νευρῆφιν ὀϊστῷ.

> No, my friend, die, <u>you, too</u>; why are you lamenting so?
> <u>Patroklos, too</u>, died, even though he was much better than you.
> Don't you see how big and fine I am?
> I am the son of a noble father, and a goddess mother gave me birth;
> but death and mighty destiny are upon you and me both.
> It will be either dawn or afternoon or noontime
> when someone in battle will pluck out <u>my spirit, too</u>,
> either hitting me with a spear or an arrow from a bowstring.
> (21.106–13)

Achilles' triple repetition of adverbial καί 'too' makes it unmistakably plain that he has won (and so is conveying) a fearsome clarity about his own death and others' through Patroklos's. Moreover, there is a word in epic diction for the solidary bond that arises from a death in the community, and it is featured significantly in the context of Achilles' progress toward *philótēs* and away from *mênis*. The word is *kêdos*, whose root meaning is thought to be 'care, concern', with two branching derivatives, 'grief, funeral rites' and 'marriage bond, kinship by marriage'. The missing link that escapes and therefore mystifies this purely lexical derivation is social and concrete: the solidarity reconstituted in the community by rituals for the dead and by marriage.[59] So when Kleopatre describes to Meleagros the *kḗdea* '(shared) woes' that befall people whose city is captured (9.592), she succeeds in awakening his social conscience; or when Ajax describes himself and the others asking Achilles to return to the fighting as *kḗdistoi . . . kaì phíltatoi hóssoi Akhaioí*, "most caring . . . and dearest among all the Achaeans," he is attempting to enforce the reciprocal obligations that bind them to Achilles and vice versa. So also when Achilles himself is offended by Phoenix's apparent support for Agamemnon in book 9, he tells him "you should not be *phílos* to him, so that you will not become hateful to me, your *phílos;* it is good to aggrieve with me [*kḗdein*] whoever aggrieves [*kḗdei*] me" (9.613–15). Here again it is a question of enforcing the solidarity between those who share grief. Finally, *kḗdea* is the cover term that both Achilles and Thetis use to denote the death of Patroklos when they first suspect it has occurred (18.8, 53). The basic point is simple: in the Homeric world, no one grieves alone, since death and the feelings it arouses are by definition social phenomena that bind people to each other like love itself.[60] Accordingly, Achilles' grief at the death of Patroklos automatically generates a potent bond to the world of mortal men and women whose lamentation he now leads (18.315–16, 354–55).

There are three aspects to this bond that tie it to the present moment in the unfolding story and so determine the function and form of subsequent episodes. The first needs to be specified only from the standpoint of the end of the sequence. Achilles is now focused on his *philótēs* with Patroklos and the Achaeans, on avenging Patroklos by slaying Hector (18.89–93, 114–26). He evinces no wider perspective on his bond to the mortal race; a gruesome index of its narrowness is his promise to decapitate twelve Trojans over Patroklos's grave (18.336–37). The second aspect is worth specifying in terms of previous episodes. The bond of *philótēs* and the formal reintegration of Achilles into Achaean society through the renunciation of his *mênis* and the public distribution to Achilles of the gifts from Agamemnon successfully terminate his alienation, and in a particularly poignant way.[61] Just as the inception of Achilles' withdrawal was punctuated by the

---

[59] For analysis of the convergence of marriage and lament rituals and formulas, see Alexiou 1974, 120.

[60] This extends to the expression of grief in γόος 'public lament', which in the traditional language of epic is the product of ἵμερος 'desire' (23.14, 108, 153, 24.507; cf. 24.227: γόου ἐξ ἔρον εἵην); ἵμερος is also sexual desire associated with Aphrodite and *philótēs* in its sexual sense (3.139, 14.198).

[61] On the way in which Agamemnon's compensation is awarded to Achilles by the group, see above, 141–42.

oath on the scepter, in which Achilles correctly imagined himself in the third person being absent and missed by the Achaeans—

ἦ ποτ' Ἀχιλλῆος ποθὴ ἵξεται υἷας Ἀχαιῶν
σύμπαντας.

truly a longing for Achilles will come over the sons of the Achaeans,
all of them together.

(1.240–41)

—so now Achilles imagines his presence in the front ranks, fighting with his spear, in the same third-person format:

ὥς κέ τις αὖτ' Ἀχιλῆα μετὰ πρώτοισιν ἴδηται
ἔγχεϊ χαλκείῳ Τρώων ὀλέκοντα φάλαγγας.

So some one of you would see Achilles in the front ranks once more
devastating the ranks of the Trojans with his bronze spear.

(19.151–52)

Achilles received his spear from his mortal father, Peleus, and did not give it to Patroklos when he went into battle; it contrasts with the immortal armor that Patroklos wore and the new armor Achilles is about to put on. So Achilles is imagining others perceiving his return to solidarity with the group, plying a weapon that in itself embodies the bond to mortality that his presence implies.[62] In this context, the third-person self-reference serves to bracket and highlight the group's perception of a change in the hero's relation to it. Achilles, who in his *mênis* was lost to the group and alienated even from his self—in short, a first person who was a third person, as in Rimbaud's "Je est un autre"—has now become a present third person, a third person who is a first person—in other words, a *phílos* (recall Aristotle's ἕτερος ἐγώ, "another I").[63] As such, his versatile language behavior contrasts with Agamemnon's inability, in this very same scene, to address Achilles directly as a "you," as a member of the same social group as he, despite Achilles' repeated success in doing so to him.[64]

The third aspect of Achilles' *philótēs* is that, while it binds him to hu-

---

[62] On the symbolic value attached to Achilles' spear, see 16.140–44; Shannon 1975, 31; and *Cypria* fr. 3 (Allen).
[63] See above, 136 with n. 5 for a grammatical analysis of Aristotle's definition of friendship.
[64] On Agamemnon's reluctance to present himself in this scene, see above, 142 n. 21.

mans, it also distances him from the world of the immortals and the *timḗ* of Zeus. In analyzing the social and cosmic aspects of the quarrel between Achilles and Agamemnon in book 1, I noted that Achilles gave up his ties to the Achaean community in the name of his ties to the divine one.[65] Now he is moving in the opposite direction, working toward a resolution of any latent competition with Zeus inherent in his *mênis* as well as of the overt competition with Apollo that implicitly threatens him with the god's *mênis*.[66] As Gregory Nagy has shown, Achilles' choice of *kléos* is predicated on his being the "best of the Achaeans." In the context of the Theogonic myth of succession and the latent potential competition of Achilles with Zeus, his achievement of such superiority along with the metaphoric immortality conferred by the poetic tradition—for although the hero perishes, the *kléos* does not—looks like a compensation for Achilles' lost chance to succeed Zeus.[67]

But that is not the only compensation that Achilles receives. There is also the armor made for him by Hephaistos to replace the armor Hector had stripped from Patroklos's corpse. As Achilles reminds Thetis, Peleus had received his now-lost set of armor as a gift from the gods on the day "that they threw you into the bed of a mortal man" (18.84–85; cf. 17.194–97). The wedding of Peleus and Thetis is an event that resonates with the Homeric *mênis* theme because of the inherent danger in the sexual encounter of a mortal man with a goddess, but Achilles' statement betrays the viewpoint of the goddess, for whom the encounter was a degradation in cosmic status.[68] It is as though the gift of the armor was a compensation intended to elevate the status of Peleus because it was immortal (ἄμβροτα τεύχεα [17.194, 202]). Actually, the usual epithet for objects crafted by Hephaistos, especially golden ones, is *áphthitos* 'imperishable', which is also the most archaic epithet of *kléos*.[69] So there are grounds to suggest the existence of an analogy between the armor given to Peleus, the armor given to Achilles, and the everlasting glory conferred upon Achilles by the epic tradition, *kléos áphthiton*. All these "immortal" compensations for death have a plausible Theogonic dimension as well, especially if we recall

---

[65] See above, 114–16.

[66] See above, 96–102.

[67] On the myth concerning Thetis's choice to marry Peleus, see above, 95–96, 121–23.

[68] See above, 18–28, for the dangerous dynamics of mortal men having sex with goddesses and its connection with the *mênis* theme.

[69] As in 14.238ff.; 2.46, 186; 18.369–70. For the applications and meaning of *áphthitos*, see the comprehensive survey in Nagy 1979, 178–89, esp. sec. 8 n. 1. Nagy points out that the V scholia to 14.238 claim that *everything* made by Hephaistos is *áphthitos* (πάντα τὰ Ἡφαιστότευκτα ἄφθιτα). Cf. Nagy's insight that things which are *áphthitos* have "compensatory" immortality (ibid., 189).

that Hephaistos himself, the fabricator of Achilles' panoplies, was born as the goddess Hera's answer to Zeus's "procreation" of Athena.[70] In the myth, Hera's ability to generate, without Zeus's participation, a male god with the ability to craft immortal, even "animated" objects for the conduct of war compensates for and competes with Zeus's ability to confirm his sovereignty over the world by giving birth to a single divine child, Athena, whose sphere also combines craft and force. Hera's competition is as much between herself and Zeus as between her son and Zeus, and Hephaistos himself reminds his mother of exactly such a predictably disastrous confrontation with his nonbiological father at the end of book 1. The idea seems to be that although Zeus's male procreative powers and the sovereignty that they eternally guarantee are unique, the power of the consummate artisan to create metaphorical immortal children with a masculine form of craft is plausible competition for them. In parallel fashion, instead of cosmic sovereignty or literal immortality, Achilles, a hero who once refused to accept any form of restitution, will now accept substitutes that serve to define the upper limits of the human condition in contradistinction to the divine: the metaphoric immortality of representation in epic, and a metaphoric possession of the world in the form of a shield that is an immortal artistic representation of the cosmos created by the most cunning of divine artisans. Perhaps it is not a coincidence after all that the description of the contents of the shield begins, like the *Theogony*'s cosmogony, with the making of earth and sky, Gaia and Ouranos.[71]

Indeed, Achilles' new readiness to accept such symbolic compensation is signaled dramatically in the text. Massive devastation by celestial fire is the prime expression of *mênis*, but in book 18, when Achilles must rescue the corpse of Patroklos from the Trojans and has no literal weapons with which to do so, he stands at the top of the ditch while Athena wreaths his head with a golden cloud from which a shining fire blazes up into the bright sky (18.205–6, 214, 225–27). This metaphoric fire burns no one, for Achilles must obey his mother and remain at a distance from the battle until he is

---

[70] For an analysis of the birth of Hephaistos in the *Theogony*, see above, 125–26. On the relationship between the name Hera and the noun ἥρως 'hero', see Pötscher 1961; and Householder and Nagy 1972, 770–71. See Nagy 1979, 187ff. for the additional analogical dimension of hero cult. Hera and Hephaistos help Achilles in his battle with the river Xanthos (21.324–82).

[71] *Pace* Edwards 1991, 211, who sees (that is, he states but provides no argument for his preference) these lines as an inventory of the contents of the whole shield rather than "an anthropomorphic Gaia, Ouranos, and Thalassa." The capitalization of nouns like Gaia and Ouranos begs the question: it remains to be seen that the distinction we posit between capitalized and uncapitalized forms of such words existed for the epic.

really armed (18.215–16), but along with the perspicuous shriek[72] from Achilles and Athena that accompanies it, the fire disturbs the Trojans and rouses the Achaeans just enough to enable them to save out the body of Patroklos. I suggest that this fire from Achilles' head is the fire of *mênis* converted into a symbolic instrument of the hero's *philótēs*. In the *aristeía* 'deeds of valor' of Achilles that ensues upon his acquisition of the new panoply from Hephaistos, *mênis* is actually invoked *in a simile* to describe the devastation the hero wreaks:

> αὐτὰρ Ἀχιλεὺς
> Τρῶας ὁμῶς αὐτούς τ' ὄλεκεν καὶ μώνυχας ἵππους.
> ὡς δ' ὅτε καπνὸς ἰὼν εἰς οὐρανὸν εὐρὺν ἵκηται
> ἄστεος αἰθομένοιο, θεῶν δέ ἑ <u>μῆνις</u> ἀνῆκε,
> πᾶσι δ' ἔθηκε πόνον, πολλοῖσι δὲ κήδε' ἐφῆκεν.
> ὡς Ἀχιλεὺς Τρώεσσι πόνον καὶ κήδε' ἔθηκεν.
>
> Meanwhile Achilles
> kept on killing the Trojans themselves and their horses alike.
> As when the smoke rises up into the broad heaven
> when a city is ablaze, and the <u>*mênis*</u> of the gods has sent it up,
> and it has made suffering for all and set grief upon many.
> So Achilles made suffering and grief for the Trojans.
>
> (21.520–25)

The hero with *mênis* has become a hero *like mênis*, as the grammatical and verbal parallelism of the last two lines in this passage seems to stress. The point is not that Achilles is somehow diminished or limited by comparison to the indiscriminate, fiery destruction of *mênis*, only that since he has chosen *philótēs*, his *mênis* has become metaphorical and so consistent with his metaphorical immortality and metaphorical sovereignty.

## The Teleology of *Mênis* in the *Iliad*

Achilles may appear to have shed his *mênis*, but he still situates himself with impunity in the powerful and dangerous place at or beyond the con-

---

[72] The shriek is described in visual terms ('perspicuous' ἀριζήλη [219 and 221]), I suggest, because it is analogous to the thunder of the thunderbolt. The adjective ἀρίζηλος is actually used of the thunderbolt in 13.244.

ventional limits of behavior, for that is a continuing, even an abiding aspect of his persona. In other words, the teleology of Achilles' *mênis* is metonymic. His *philótēs* has swallowed, not displaced it, in the same way that Zeus swallowed Metis herself. Achilles' station at the limits of behavior is certainly the principle behind his abusive treatment of the corpse of Hector, which includes threats to eat it raw as well as violent attempts to disfigure it.[73] We have already seen how violation of the proper ritual treatment of the dead is an offense to *thémis* that is worthy of *mênis*.[74] So for Hector's corpse, given the principle that *mênis* against Achilles himself has been suspended in the *Iliad*,[75] the gods are compelled to intervene. In book 23 (185–91), Aphrodite keeps dogs away from it day and night, and Apollo hides it with a cloud to prevent the sun from drying its sinews and limbs; again, in book 24 (18–21), Apollo hides it with a golden aegis to keep Hector's skin intact and so prevent the corpse from being disfigured even though Achilles has dragged it behind his chariot around Patroklos's tomb. In the meantime, nearly all the gods decide they should have Hermes steal Hector's corpse. Only Hera, Poseidon, and Athena disagree, the narrator tells us, and cling to their original hostility to Troy, Priam, and Paris because of Paris's insult to the other goddesses in choosing Aphrodite (24.25–30).[76] Apollo, who could share Poseidon's inveterate hatred for Troy but does not, inveighs against Achilles' intransigence and savagery:

ἀλλ' ὀλοῷ Ἀχιλῆϊ, θεοί, βούλεσθ' ἐπαρήγειν,
ᾧ οὔτ' ἄρ φρένες εἰσὶν ἐναίσιμοι οὔτε νόημα
γναμπτὸν ἐνὶ στήθεσσι, λέων δ' ὣς ἄγρια οἶδεν,
ὅς τ' ἐπεὶ ἄρ μεγάλῃ τε <u>βίῃ</u> καὶ ἀγήνορι θυμῷ
εἴξας εἶσ' ἐπὶ μῆλα βροτῶν, ἵνα δαῖτα λάβῃσιν·
ὣς Ἀχιλεὺς ἔλεον μὲν ἀπώλεσεν, οὐδέ οἱ αἰδὼς
γίγνεται, ἥ τ' ἄνδρας μέγα σίνεται ἠδ' ὀνίνησι.
μέλλει μέν πού τις καὶ <u>φίλτερον ἄλλον</u> ὀλέσσαι,

---

[73] On the mistreatment, see Segal 1971a; on proper treatment of the body of the dead person, see Vernant 1989; see also above, 144 n. 27, 145.

[74] See above, 32–33.

[75] Concerning this rule, see above, 131, 144–46.

[76] Contrast Aphrodite's care for Hector's body in book 23. The current passage does not relate Poseidon's hatred of the Trojans to the judgment of Paris, as supposed by the b and T scholia. The point being made is that all three divinities still retain their original hatred against the Trojans, including Paris, for his mistake: in stressing that mistake, the narrator specifically mentions the "goddesses" (24.29) he offended. Poseidon's hatred, however, is due to the treatment he and Apollo received from Laomedon, an episode retold to Apollo by Poseidon at 21.441–57. There Poseidon appeals to Apollo on the basis of their solidarity in suffering at Laomedon's hands and asks Apollo to retreat from conflict with Zeus (21.462–77) over the Trojans.

170   The Anger of Achilles

> ἠὲ κασίγνητον ὁμογάστριον ἠὲ καὶ υἱόν·
> ἀλλ' ἤτοι κλαύσας καὶ ὀδυράμενος μεθέηκε.
>
> but you gods want to help destructive Achilles,
> whose mind is not within limits, nor is the thought
> in his chest flexible, but he knows wild things like a lion
> when he gives in to his great *bíē* and proud spirit
> and attacks men's flocks, to get himself a meal:
> so Achilles has lost his pity, nor does he have
> respect, which greatly harms and helps men.
> A man may lose someone even more *phílos*,
> either a brother from the same womb or even a son;
> but he really weeps and laments and then lets go.
>
> (24.39–48)

The diction here echoes earlier lines concerning persons whose actions merit the ultimate sanction[77] as well as Odysseus's remarks about the Cyclops who devours his guests instead of feeding them: ἄγριον οὔτε δίκας εὖ εἰδότα οὔτε θέμιστας, "a wild thing who knows well neither acts of justice nor *thémistes*" (9.215).[78] Like Ajax in book 9 (632–36), Apollo calls Achilles pitiless and contrasts his reaction to the loss of a friend to the loss of "someone even more *phílos*," namely, a blood relative. So the current dispute about Hector's corpse, which opposes Hera, Poseidon, and Athena to Apollo and Aphrodite, once more evokes the specter of *mênis* against Achilles—and among the gods themselves. It is striking that the group of gods opposed to Apollo consists of the same three divinities who wished to bind Zeus in the Theogonic *mênis* story that Achilles told in book 1. Apollo's view that Achilles must release Hector's body is the one that Zeus adopts in order to resolve the dispute and the one opposed by the previously rebellious triad. So the conclusion of the story of Achilles' *mênis* is evoking the same cosmic tensions as the beginning and the same principles for their resolution, namely, the exceptional capacity of Zeus to impose cosmic order, to bring about what *thémis* requires.[79] In the story told by

---

[77] See above, 144–45, regarding Poseidon and Phoenix, with 144 n. 27 on the restriction of metaphorical forms of γναμπτ- to such contexts.

[78] Also similar are the disguised Odysseus's "lies" about the wanton acts he committed "giving in to his *bíē* and strength," βίῃ καὶ κάρτεϊ εἴκων (*Odyssey* 18.139), a man "completely without *thémis*," πάμπαν ἀνὴρ ἀθεμίστιος (18.141). The passage is suggestive for the hypothesis in Clay 1983 about the *mênis* of Athena against Odysseus himself, even if the "true" Odysseus is emphatically not a man of *bíē* but of cunning.

[79] A simple and powerful principle of closure, by which the origins of conflict in a tale rise to

## The Mênis of Achilles and Its Iliadic Teleology 171

Achilles in book 1, his mother, Thetis, was instrumental in averting *mênis* and protecting the divine order from violent disruption; here in book 24, Zeus chooses her for the same role, which she fulfills not by sustaining him with a threat of overwhelming force but by asking her son, Achilles, to change his mind.

In fact, the story of Achilles' abuse and subsequent ransom of Hector's body recapitulates the major themes of the embassy to Achilles in book 9, but with a different outcome. It looks as though Achilles will continue in his antisocial behavior and refuse to comply with what Apollo is demanding, namely, that having lost and mourned someone *phílos* (there Briseis, here Patroklos), he finally 'let go' μεθέηκε (24.48). But as soon as Thetis comes to him with word that Zeus is angry and wants him to ransom Hector's corpse (24.134–37), Achilles immediately acquiesces. The key to his agreement lies in what she says to him before relaying Zeus's message:

> τέκνον ἐμόν, τέο μέχρις ὀδυρόμενος καὶ ἀχεύων
> σὴν ἔδεαι κραδίην, μεμνημένος οὔτε τι σίτου
> οὔτ' εὐνῆς; ἀγαθὸν δὲ γυναικί περ ἐν φιλότητι
> μίσγεσθ'· οὐ γάρ μοι δηρὸν βέῃ, ἀλλά τοι ἤδη
> ἄγχι παρέστηκεν θάνατος καὶ μοῖρα κραταιή.

> My child, until what will you eat your heart out mourning
> and grieving, remembering neither food
> nor bed? It is good even to mingle with a woman in love [*philótēs*];
> for you will not live long, but already
> death stands beside you and mighty destiny.
>
> (24.128–32)

Thetis reminds him about food, sex, and death—three things that will help him to let go of Patroklos, to end his mourning and give back the body of Hector, for the simple reason that all three are central to his *philótēs*, his solidarity with his fellow humans. Each layer of the epic cosmos, after all, is

---

the surface of the narrative at the moment of its conclusion, has long been understood as an element of the structure of book 24. So the Judgment of Paris is first explicitly discussed in 24.29–30, and the Marriage of Peleus and Thetis is brought to mind by Hera shortly thereafter (24.62). There are many other correspondences between books 1 and 24. Also central to this issue is Cedric Whitman's fundamental insight that the *Iliad* recapitulates the whole of the Trojan War in terms of the tale of Achilles, which accounts for the place of the Catalog of Ships or the way in which Andromache's anagnorisis is a metaphorization of the Fall of Troy (Whitman 1958, Segal [1971c], etc.), as well as the talk of the war's beginning at the end of a poem about Achilles' *mênis*.

delimited in terms of food, mortality, and sexual partners, be they mortal, immortal, or, in Achilles' case, completely lacking.[80] In expressing the extreme grief he feels for his best friend by violently abusing Hector's corpse, Achilles has placed himself once again at the edges of humanity, and his mother does nothing but reset him in his place in the human world. In doing so, Thetis also sets the agenda for the rest of the *Iliad*. By way of food, sex, and consciousness of mortality, Achilles is to define and enact his place in the world as a whole, to make plain his solidarity not only with Patroklos, the Myrmidons, and the Achaeans, but with the human race. That is the last incremental step in the teleology of Achilles' *mênis* turned *philótēs*, and it has been prepared for by the whole trajectory of *mênis* in the poem up to this point.

The decision to return Hector's body is the first step in the fulfillment of Thetis's agenda. It signals the end of Achilles' mourning for Patroklos. Moreover, Achilles turns his decision to ransom Hector into a reconfirmation of his solidarity with Zeus:

τῇδ' εἴη· ἄποινα φέροι καὶ νέκρον ἄγοιτο,
εἰ δὴ πρόφρονι θυμῷ Ὀλύμπιος αὐτὸς ἀνώγει.

Let it be that way: whoever brings the ransom may also take the corpse,
if the Olympian himself wholeheartedly bids it.

(24.139–40)

In one gesture of acceptance, Achilles has ended both his latent conflict with Zeus and his overt conflict with Apollo. His language also affirms the rules of reciprocal exchange whose breach began the quarrel and *mênis* in book 1. As soon as Achilles accepts the idea of ransoming Hector, Zeus immediately acknowledges what it implies in terms of his *philótēs*:

αὐτὰρ ἐπὴν ἀγάγῃσιν ἔσω κλισίην Ἀχιλῆος,
οὔτ' αὐτὸς κτενέει ἀπό τ' ἄλλους πάντας ἐρύξει·
οὔτε γάρ ἐστ' ἄφρων οὔτ' ἄσκοπος οὔτ' ἀλιτήμων,
ἀλλὰ μάλ' ἐνδυκέως ἱκέτεω πεφιδήσεται ἀνδρός.

Now when he [Hermes] brings him [Priam] within the hut of Achilles,

---

[80] For Greek cosmic definitions in terms of food, see Detienne 1994, and Detienne and Vernant 1979 (English translation, 1989); in terms of sexual partners, above, 18–28, on the danger in sexual relations that cross cosmic boundaries.

he himself will not kill him and he will restrain all the others;
for he is neither senseless nor inconsiderate nor wicked,
but he will very properly[81] spare a man who is his visitor.[82]

(24.155–58)

The adverb ἐνδυκέως 'in proper ritual sequence' occurs eight times in the *Odyssey* modifying the verb *philéō* 'treat as *phílos*'.[83] It is also made clear in the *Odyssey* that visitors and guests are like *phíloi* in that their proper treatment is a matter of *thémis*.[84] So Zeus understands Achilles' simple assent to the exchange of Hector's body as a guarantee of *philótēs*, of ritually proper behavior as a restrained and gracious host to old Priam.

As simple, popular, and conventional as was the open exchange offered by Chryses but rejected by Agamemnon in book 1, so arduous and tension-filled and fragile is the hidden one that actually succeeds in book 24. For Priam to visit Achilles requires divine intervention by Hermes, given the concrete problem of passing unseen back and forth across enemy lines in a wagon with horses and mules. We are even told twice that it is crucial to escape the notice of Agamemnon, since his awareness of the transaction between Priam and Achilles would both delay it and make it much more costly (24.654–55, 686–88). Moreover, when Priam does arrive in Achilles' hut, he carries out an act that "no other human ever yet endured" (505): he actually kisses the hand—and the hand is a regular metonym of a warrior's destructive force, his *bíē*[85]—of the man who killed his children, Achilles. I have just spoken of the surprising readiness of Achilles to effect this exchange, but even that is almost compromised at one point, when Priam refuses Achilles' offer that he be seated and asks him to hand over the corpse τάχιστα 'most quickly' (553–58). A breach of etiquette, that impatience riles Achilles enough to threaten Priam with physical harm in his own hut and in violation of the behests of Zeus (569–70). When Achilles' companions are preparing Hector's body to turn it over to Priam, they have it washed and anointed out of sight of both men, concerned, we are told, lest the sight of his son might grieve and anger Priam so that Achilles would get upset and kill him (582–86).

---

[81] Nagy (1996, chap. 2), has argued that the meaning of the word ἐνδυκέως, heretofore blandly glossed "kindly," is "in proper ritual sequence."

[82] On the meaning of the term ἱκέτης 'he who comes, visitor' in Homer, see Muellner 1976, 87.

[83] *Odyssey* 7.256, 14.62, 15.305, 15.543, 17.56, 17.111, 19.195, and 24.272.

[84] See above, Chapter 2, 37–39.

[85] As in *Iliad* 3.431, 12.135; *Odyssey* 12.246, 21.315, 373.

In other words, Achilles is now operating at the boundaries of what is humanly possible,[86] but mainly because at this point he is testing the higher limits of the rules of exchange. When Priam arrives in his hut, he tries to win Achilles' pity and respect by bringing to mind Achilles' own father and imagining his loneliness but also the hope that Peleus has of seeing his son again (487-92). In contrast, he presents his own pitiable despair that has brought him to the extraordinary moment of actually supplicating the man who has slain so many of his own children (504-6). Priam's speech elicits a bout of weeping from both men, Priam for Hector, Achilles for his father and for Patroklos (509-12). So the emotional claim that Priam makes on Achilles' affection for his distant and lonely father is effective in turning each toward his own pain. But when they recover and Achilles begins to speak, he takes a step that appreciably extends the notion of *philótēs:* sympathetic identification with the father of his deepest enemy, the slayer of his best friend.[87] Twice Achilles sees their encounter through Priam's own eyes, first in remarking on the courage it took Priam to come alone before the eyes of the man who killed many of his brave sons (519-21), then in imagining how Priam feels to have been so prosperous and to have suffered such loss of wealth and family (543-47). Bridging the gap between himself and Priam pushes Achilles yet one step further, into a definition of the human condition, into a concrete specification of what Priam and Achilles have in common as members of the human race. According to Achilles, what distinguishes mortals from gods is not just death or its absence, but *kḗdea,* the 'griefs' that ritually bind a bereaved community.[88] The gods have no *kḗdea,* but for human beings, they are the limiting condition. Grief over Patroklos is what made Achilles' return to the human community absolute and irrevocable. Now, in the context of this almost impossible exchange, the bonds of *kḗdea* close the gap between Achaeans and Trojans, if only for the twelve days' truce that Achilles promises to enforce for Hector's funeral.

At the conclusion of Achilles' consolatory meditation, Priam actually refuses his invitation that he be seated, on the grounds that Hector is still *akēdḗs* 'ungrieved for'. Achilles takes offense at this refusal. He knows only too well that the gods have been instrumental in bringing about this ex-

---

[86] By using the word *humanly* I do not intend to retroject any cross-cultural or universal agenda; I mean *humanly* as the epic tradition finally defines it.

[87] Richard Martin points out to me that Achilles' extended definition, in action, of *philótēs* is strictly analogous to the traditional poet's creative effect upon diction and theme; for more on the metapoetic aspect of Achilles, see above, 138-39.

[88] On the meaning of this term, see above, 163-64. It is true that Thetis is a goddess with *kḗdea,* but that is exceptional—and precisely because of the two mortals to whom she is bound, Peleus and Achilles (18.429-41).

change, he says, but he is not reluctant to undo it even so (24.563–70). Apparently Priam is rushing Achilles to effect the exchange; Achilles' long perspective on human suffering is lost on Priam, just as the intensity of the old man's unfulfilled grief escapes the younger man.[89] Yet the bonds of sorrow hold while Achilles slowly enacts the proper gestures. Once the body is cleaned and anointed and covered, Achilles himself places it on the litter with a vow to Patroklos explaining the ransom and promising him his share of it. Achilles' touching participation in the ritual preparation of Hector's body is a drastic turnaround from his abuse of it, but it also makes plain that the funeral of Hector has become an integral part of Achilles' story, in that its *kḗdea* enact the humanness of both men. After Achilles finally partakes of food (621–27) and lies with a woman, Briseis (675–76), our version of the *Iliad* actually concludes with the funeral of Hector, because that funeral is in fact the teleology of Achilles' *mênis*. It has become a token of the *philótēs* that incorporates and restores as it also transcends the conventional boundaries between mortals. Instead of succeeding Zeus as a cosmic sovereign, Achilles bequeaths to us the self-perpetuating artistic representation of an idealistic, disturbing, and consoling definition of the human condition. We are human and *phíloi* insofar as we eat, sleep, and grieve together.

---

[89] For a similar refusal of an offer to sit and assume a distant perspective on the world, compare Hector's rejection of Helen's invitation that he ponder with her their fates which are "destined to become the subjects of song for generations to come" (6.354–58).

APPENDIX

# The Etymology of *Mênis*

After the in-depth contextual analysis of *mênis* provided above, it should be possible to resolve some of the lingering questions about its etymology. In this appendix, I propose to (1) point out the existence of a word ultimately related to *mênis* that is attested in the oldest surviving texts from ancient Iran, the Avestan *Gāthās*, and from ancient India, the hymns of the *Rig Veda*, and (2) determine which of the currently competing etymologies of *mênis* best concurs with its meaning.

## An Indo-Iranian Term Related to *Mênis*

All of the current etymologies actually do converge on one point, namely, that Greek *mênis* is ultimately a derivative of the Indo-European root *\*men-* 'activate the mind'.[1] The noun that I wish to bring into consideration is an archaic derivative of this same root in Vedic Sanskrit, *manyú-* 'zeal, desire, anger', an action noun exactly cognate with the Avestan word *mainiiu-* (*maniiu-*) '(good/bad) spirit'. The only archaic words parallel to it in form are *vāyu-* 'wind; the war god, Vāyu' in Vedic and its exact Avestan cognate *vaiiu-* 'air', both from a root *vā-* 'blow', IE *\*h₂ueh₁-* (attested in Greek ἄησι 'blows'); and Greek υἱύς 'son', Tokharian B *soy*, Tokharian A *se* 'son' from *\*suh_x-ɪu-*. In regard to *manyú-*, there is disagreement on the

---

[1] For the meaning of this root, see the monograph of Meillet 1897, 10: "one can easily discern that this root signifies that the mind is aroused . . . either for understanding or for desiring or for getting angry or for warning" [facile perspicias hac radice "mentem moueri" significatum esse . . . uel ad intellegendum uel ad cupiendum uel ad irascendum uel ad monendum].

point at which its stem ends and its suffix begins, but it is clear that, like *mênis*, it is an ancient derivative of the root *\*men-*.[2]

In the *Gāthās*, the Old Avestan hymns of Zarathustra (= Zoroaster), *mainiiu-* is the name for the twin conflicting spirits, one good and the other evil, who stand at the origin of the world:

aṱ tā mainiiū paouruiiē   yā yə̄mā x<sup>v</sup>afənā asruuātəm
manahicā vacahicā   šiiaoθanōi hī vahiiō akəmcā
åscā hudåŋhō   ərəš vīšiiātā nōiṱ duždåŋhō

aṱ cā hiiaṱ tā hə̄m mainiiū   jasaētəm paouruuīm dazdē
gaēmcā ajiiāitīmcā   yaθācā aŋhaṱ apə̄məm aŋhuš
acištō drəguuatąm   aṱ ašāunē vahištəm manō

Yes, there are two fundamental spirits, twins which are renowned to be in conflict. In thought and in word, in action, they are two: the good and the bad. And between these two, the beneficent have correctly chosen, not the maleficent.

Furthermore, when these two spirits first came together, they created life and death and how, at the end, the worst existence shall be for the deceitful but the best thinking for the truthful person.

(Yasna 30.3–4)[3]

In the sixth stanza of this same hymn, we learn that the *daēuua*, the traditional gods as opposed to the Ahura of Zoroastrianism, chose the deceptive, evil *mainiiu-*, and "they then rushed into fury with which they have afflicted the world and mankind." So at the beginning of Yasna 45, Zarathustra warns:

nōiṱ daibitīm   duš.sastiš ahūm mərą̄šiiāṱ
akā varanā   drəguuå hizuuā āuuərətō

---

[2] On the form and history of *manyú-*, see Mayrhofer 1963, II, and Mayrhofer 1986–, II. s.v. *manyúḥ*; Wackernagel and Debrunner 1954, 842, sec. 680; and Renou 1930, 1:232, sec. 185. Frisk (1946), working with a different definition of *mênis* than mine, found no cognates to it in Indo-European but considered the concept of righteous divine anger to be inherited; Considine (1966, 22 with n. 11) challenged Frisk's view of its ethical connotations, on which see n. 42 below. But *mênis* is not a word for divine anger—indeed, it actually requires an attribute such as "of Achilles," "of Zeus," or "of gods," which would be redundant and inconsequent if it were—but for an active emotion that includes the specific social and cosmic results that it inevitably entails; it is the sanction against tabu behavior.

[3] Text and translation: Insler 1975, 32–33.

Appendix: The Etymology of *Mênis*   179

May not the deceitful one of evil doctrine destroy the world for a second time, he who has turned hither with his tongue and his evil preference.

(Yasna 45.2)⁴

The world was first destroyed when the *daēuua* chose the evil *mainiiu-*. Now it is time for the correct choice. The hymn continues:

aṯ frauuaxšiiā  aŋhəuš *mainiiū* paouruiiē
yaiiā̊ *spaniiā̊*  ūitī mrauuaṯ yə̄m *angrəm*
nōiṯ nā manā̊  nōiṯ sə̄nghā nōiṯ xratauuō
naēdā varanā  nōiṯ uxδā naēdā šiiaoθanā
nōiṯ daēnā̊  nōiṯ uruuanō hacaintē

Yes, I shall speak of the two fundamental spirits of existence (*mainiiū*), of which the virtuous one (*spaniiā̊*) would have spoken thus to the evil one (*angrəm*): "Neither our thoughts nor teachings nor intentions, neither our preferences nor words, neither our actions nor conceptions nor souls are in accord."

(Yasna 45.2 [Insler])

The two *mainiiu-* represent a contrastive pair of initial beings such as we have seen in the context of Hesiodic cosmogony.⁵ According to some authorities, they are the Zoroastrian replacement for the inherited Indo-Iranian primordial god, Vāyu, a cosmic starting point whose name means 'air, wind'.⁶ As Malamoud points out, the word *mainiiu-* by itself is so lacking in intrinsic color that it is necessary to specify whether it is *spaniiā̊* 'good' or *angrəm* 'bad'.⁷ But the concept of a cosmogonic moral force represented by this word is not irrelevant to the study of Greek *mênis*, as I hope to demonstrate.

In the Vedic hymns, by contrast, the cognate of *mainiiu-*, *manyú-*, offers a range and richness of significations that borders on incoherence. Surveying its uses in the *Rig Veda*, in the more recent *Atharva Veda*, and in rituals described in subsequent texts, Charles Malamoud has attempted not to dismiss the multiplicity of its meanings but to discover their underlying

---

⁴ Text and translation: Insler 1975, 74–75.
⁵ See above, 57–59. For the semantic dualism of derivatives of the root *\*men-*, see also Meier-Brügger 1989, 43, who speaks of a primordial subject/object contrast within the root.
⁶ As mentioned above, the name Vāyu is exactly parallel in form to *mainiiu-*. On *mainiiu-* replacing Vāyu, see Dumézil 1947, 90–91; Duchesne-Guillemin 1962, 179, 182–83, 199; Malamoud 1968, 504 n. 2. On Vāyu in general, Wikander 1941.
⁷ Malamoud 1968, 504 n. 2.

180   The Anger of Achilles

core.⁸ His point of departure for integrating the whole history of meanings in this word is one of its latest attestations in the *Rig Veda,* Hymn 10.83, in which the noun *manyú-* has become a new, "abstract" divinity, abstract in that he lacks a biography and a developed mythology. For Malamoud, such late hymns represent not a new departure, but a recapitulation of the representation of *manyú-* in all the earlier parts of the *Rig Veda:* "for the most recent parts of the collection, the whole Veda is alluded to in each hymn."⁹ Hymn 10.83 and its shorter sequel, Hymn 10.84, were actually recited to foment the lust for battle in warriors, and they were also part of a divination ritual that preceded the battle itself. While murmuring these two hymns to Manyu, a diviner would stand between the two opposing armies and set fire (with a fire called *āṅgirasa* 'burning coal', a term associated with the fire god Agni) to a special bundle of branches. The side that drew the smoke from the burning bundle was declared the loser.¹⁰

These ritual uses of the hymns to Manyu make clear that the frame of reference for *manyú-* in them is the world of the warrior, but that is only one, albeit a fundamental, aspect of the term. In fact, Georges Dumézil has tried to show that Manyu in 10.83 is operative in all three spheres of the Indo-European ideology as he reconstructs it, namely, the priest's domain of sovereignty and magic, the warrior's domain of force, and the people's domain of fertility and well-being.¹¹ Here are the first four stanzas of the hymn whose content he analyzes in this way:

1. yás te manyo ávidhad vajra sāyaka    sáha ójaḥ puṣyati víśvam ānuṣák
sāhyā́ma dā́sam ā́riyaṃ tváyā yujā́    sáhaskṛtena sáhasā sáhasvatā
2. manyúr índro manyúr evā́sa devó    manyúr hótā váruṇo jātávedāḥ
manyúṃ víśa īḷate mā́nuṣīr yā́ḥ    pāhí no manyo tápasā sajóṣāḥ
3. abhī́hi manyo tavásas távīyān    tápasā yujā́ ví jahi śátrūn
amitrahā́ vṛtrahā́ dasyuhā́ ca    víśvā vásūnī́ bhárā tuvám naḥ
4. tuvám hí manyo abhíbhūtiyojā́ḥ    svayambhū́r bhā́mo abhimātiṣāháḥ
viśvā́carṣaṇiḥ sáhuriḥ sáhāvān    asmā́su ójaḥ pṛ́tanāsu dhehi

1. The man who served you, o Manyu, o thunderbolt, o arrow, he causes his

---

⁸ Malamoud 1968.
⁹ Malamoud 1968, 507: "pour les parties les plus récentes du recueil, le Veda tout entier est alludé dans chaque hymne."
¹⁰ Malamoud 1968, 493–94; although Malamoud does not mention it, a scenario like the one in the ritual is explicitly described in 7.25.1, where Indra is invoked to intervene in the confrontation between two armies *sámanyavo* 'with equal *manyú-*'!
¹¹ Dumézil 1948, 101–11.

superior force to flourish, his formidable force, complete in continuous fashion. May we force the Dāsa [enemies] and the Arya with you as our ally, with a superior force born from a superior force endowed with superior force.

2. Manyu (was) Indra, Manyu himself was (some) god, Manyu is also a *hotar* [sacrificer], he is Varuṇa, (he is Agni) the Jātavedas. The tribes of mankind invoke Manyu: protect us, Manyu, together with the burning fire (of your weapon)!

3. Attack, o Manyu, you who are stronger than the strong (itself)! Scatter and kill your enemies with the burning fire (of your weapon) as an ally! As killer of adversaries, killer of enemies, and killer of Dasy-u's, bring all the goods to us!

4. Yes, you, o Manyu, who has a formidable force (that constitutes) superiority, (you are) the outbreak (of anger), spontaneously generated, forcing (victory) on the aggressors. Common to all populations, dominator, endowed with superior force, grant us formidable force in battles!

(10.83.1–4)[12]

Dumézil points out that in the second strophe, Manyu is first identified with the warrior par excellence, Indra; then with Varuṇa, a sovereign and priestly god whom Dumézil considers to be here represented with the attributes of the fire god, Agni; and lastly, the hymn tells us that the tribes of humans praise Manyu. It is problematic to associate Varuṇa, as Dumézil wishes to, with the term *hotar* 'sacrificer' and the epithet Jātavedas, both of which belong to Agni, a divinity who can bypass trifunctional sequences since he fits all three of the functions.[13] I would suggest that Agni as fire god has been inserted into the three-part sequence with good reason, because of the overwhelming association of *manyú-* in this and other hymns (as also in the ritual noted above) with fire.[14] In the concluding line of this same strophe, that association is explicit: "protect us, Manyu, together with the burning fire!" But there are other trifunctional features in this hymn in which the tripartite sequence remains intact; they strengthen Dumézil's point. For instance, in the first and fourth strophes, there is a sequence of terms referring to the force gained by devotees of Manyu. In the first

---

[12] Vedic text provided here and elsewhere is from van Nooten and Holland 1994; translation here based on Renou 1966, 15:172; translations of *Rig Veda* elsewhere are my renderings of the German in Geldner 1951 unless indicated otherwise.

[13] On Agni's commonness to the three functions, see Nagy 1990a, 85–121, especially 99–110.

[14] For the specific association of Agni with Indra's *ójas-* 'force' and *vájra-* 'thunderbolt', see *Rig Veda* 10.52.5, 1.109.7, and Nagy 1990a, 109.

strophe mention is made of *sáhas*, which denotes force superior to that of another person, power over another; then *ójas*, a term for physical force that is part of the vocabulary of Indra; these two nouns are then followed by the adjective *víśvam* 'complete', a word related to and, according to Dumézil, playing upon the noun *víś* 'clan', regularly used for massed humans in references to the third function. Then, in the fourth strophe, the three terms recur: "Common to all populations (*víśvácarṣaṇiḥ*), dominator endowed with superior force (*sáhas*), grant us formidable force (*ójas*) in battles."[15]

Taking his cue from Dumézil's demonstration that Vedic *manyú-* is not simply a term restricted to the warrior sphere but functional in other contexts as well, Malamoud asserts that it is also not a term for a passing emotion like anger or rage. Instead it is the name of a permanent faculty in both humans and gods whose content varies in precise ways. As he states it, *manyú-* is a faculty "placed on the same plane as the essential forces of cosmic life."[16] Among humans, *manyú-* belongs to specific individuals who are typically hostile or wicked: strangers (1.104.2: *dása*; 7.60.11: *arí*), enemies (6.25.2, 10.152.5: *amítra*), malicious persons of one sort or another.[17] Also attested is a more generalized *manyú-* in groups of people that does not escape the attention or surpass the power of Indra (7.78.6), Varuṇa (7.61.1), and Agni (8.71.2). For Malamoud, all these instances of apparently negative *manyú-* are in fact self-affirmations by individuals or groups that put them into active conflict or competition with others, not proof that *manyú-* itself is inherently negative.[18] He cites the following lines as evidence that one person's negative *manyú-* can be counteracted by Indra's positive *manyú-*:

indro manyúm manyumíyo mimāya

Indra who thwarts the *manyú-* of him who wishes to thwart his *manyú-*

(7.18.16)

prá yó manyúṃ ríriksato mináti

---

[15] On the third function associations of the word *víś*, see Nagy 1990a 281–82. Dumézil notes other trifunctional sequences as well. For instance, in the second line of the third stanza, there is a sequence of three compounds all ending with the suffix *-há* '-slayer': *amitrahá*, literally slayer of adversaries, but with a play on Mitra, the sovereign god paired with Varuṇa; *vṛtrahá*, slayer of the Vṛtra, the serpent whom Indra slew; and *dasyuhá*, slayer of the Dasyu, the massed enemies of the Arya.

[16] Malamoud 1968, 499.

[17] Also 8.19.15: *dūdhí* 'malicious person'; 8.36.4: *rírikṣant* 'who seek to destroy'; 3.23.12: *śárdhant* 'insolent person'; 5.6.10 *adhṛj* 'competitor'.

[18] Malamoud 1968, 499–500.

(Indra) who thwarts the evil *manyú-* of those bent on harm

(7.36.4)

Among the gods—principally Indra and those associated with him, but also (Mitra-)Varuṇa, Brahmaṇaspati, and Agni—*manyú-* is "the élan that makes [the god] accomplish the deeds that affirm his divinity."[19] For instance, the *manyú-* of Mitra-Varuṇa correlates with their specific function as divinities:

yád dha tyán mitrāvaruṇāv ṛtád adhi     ādadā́the ánṛtaṃ svéna manyúnā
dákṣasya svéna manyúnā

You two, Mitra and Varuṇa, have placed disorder (ánṛtaṃ) apart from order (ṛtá́d) thanks to the proper *manyú-* of the Effective One, thanks to his *manyú-*.[20]

(1.139.2)

For Agni, his *manyú-* is explicitly reflexive—what suits his particular desire and expectation:

káyā te agne aṅgira     ū́rjo napād úpastutim
vārāya deva manyáve

How, o Agni, o Angiras, o son of the power-nourisher, (are we going to) present you with praise (so that it will be) according to your wish, o god, (conforming to your) *manyú-*?[21]

(8.84.4)

Finally, Indra's *manyú-*, the most commonly attested, was expressed when he slew the serpent Vṛtra with his thunderbolt as Sky and Earth trembled.[22] Here is a sample of passages:

---

[19] Malamoud 1968, 500. He points out, however, that the *manyú-* of Brahmaṇaspati is "paradoxically Indraic" (500 n. 7), as in 2.24.14.

[20] Translation after Renou 1966, 5:8. Interpretation after Geldner 1951, 1:193: "when you two, Mitra and Varuṇa, separated right from wrong with your *manyú-*, with the proper *manyú-* of your strength of mind."

[21] Translation after Renou 1966, 13:80. One can also compare 6.16.43: *ágne yukṣvā́ hí yé táv a / áśvāso devá sādhávaḥ / áraṃ váhanti manyáve* "harness your excellent steeds, Agni, who go according to your *manyu-*."

[22] For the mythology and the poetics of dragon slaying, see Watkins 1995.

ádha dyaúś cit te ápa sā́ nú vájrād    dvitā́namad bhiyásā svásya manyóḥ
áhiṃ yád índro abhí óhasānaṃ    ní cid viśvā́yuḥ śayáthe jaghā́na

Heaven itself gave way before your thunderbolt and especially in fear of your *manyú-* when Indra struck down for all time the boastful serpent in his lair.

(6.17.9)

imé cit táva manyáve    vépete bhiyásā mahī́
yád indra vajrin ójasā    vṛtrám marútvām̐ ávadhīr

From fear these two great ones (Sky and Earth) were trembling before your *manyú-*, when you, club-bearing Indra, in league with the Maruts, smote the Vṛtra with formidable force.

(1.80.11)

yád asya manyúr adhvanīd ví vṛtrám parvaśó rujan
apáḥ samudrám airayat

When his *manyú-* fumed, while he broke the Vṛtra to pieces limb by limb, then drove the waters to the sea.

(8.6.13)

táva tvíṣo jániman réjata dyaú    réjad bhū́mir bhiyásā svásya manyóḥ

The Sky trembled at your birth [from fear of] your fire, the Earth trembled from fear of your *manyú-*.

(4.17.2)

It should be clear by now that the personages with whom Manyu is identified in the second strophe of Hymn 10.83—Indra, Varuṇa, Agni, and the tribes of humans—are in fact those to whom the noun *manyú-* is attributed in the earlier hymns. But Malamoud pushes his analysis of the word's core meaning a step further to explicate the sense of two words attested as qualifiers of *manyú-*, a noun which rarely has any. One is the adjective *satyá*, the other the rare word *svayaṃbhū́* (attested only at 10.83.4 in the *Rig Veda*). Malamoud defines *satyá* to mean "destined for accomplishment, sure to be realized," such that *manyú-* so qualified is the "élan which makes someone bring to fulfillment their desires, translate their thoughts into deeds."[23] The

---

[23] Malamoud 1968, 502–53.

Appendix: The Etymology of *Mênis* 185

*manyú-* of Indra is *satyá* in 4.17.10 and causes universal fear; or the poet says at 10.112.8:

prá ta indra pūrvíyāṇi prá nūnáṃ    vīríyā vocam prathamā́ kṛtā́ni
satīnā́manyur

Now I will sing, Indra, of your earlier, your primordial exploits, you whose *manyú-* is *satīnā́*

where *satīnā́* means 'realized'. So in regard to the following assertion of the primacy of *manyú-* in Indra's exploits, which was deprecated by Louis Renou on the grounds that it was a "contamination" caused by a rhetorical "condensation of formulas":

śrát te dadhāmi prathamā́ya manyáve    áhan yád vṛtráṃ nā́riyaṃ vivér apáḥ

I put my confidence in your initial *manyú-*, when you struck down the Vṛtra, when you accomplished the heroic deed.

(10.147.1)

Malamoud counters that such a "condensation" could not have taken place unless *manyú-* actually was a primordial determinant of deeds at the origins of the world, like Old Avestan *mainiiu-*.[24] Such a quality in *manyú-* is confirmed by the second qualifier explicated by Malamoud, the neologism *svayaṃbhū́* 'spontaneously generated', a rare epithet elsewhere attested, for example, of the king in the *rājasūya* ritual, in which he "symbolically creates space and time, organizes the universe around him, and reproduces the cosmic process of creation and maturation."[25]

In sum, Vedic *manyú-* has the following semantic and thematic attributes:

—It denotes not a transient emotion, but a permanent, primordial, conflictive, and active cosmic force among gods and men.
—It operates in all three of the domains of Indo-European society as reconstructed by Dumézil.
—It is fundamentally characteristic of Indra, in whom it is expressed by the fear-inspiring thunderbolt and fire.

[24] Renou and Benveniste 1934, 108–9; Malamoud 1968, 504 and 504 n. 2.
[25] I refer the reader to Malamoud's detailed discussion (1968, 505–7) of this complex term.

Old Avestan *mainiiu-* shares in the first of these attributes, but not the others. Given the Zoroastrian function of *mainiiu-* at the zero point of the world, however, inherited features of the term may have been stripped from it. All three of these semantic and thematic attributes are present in Greek *mênis* and are especially strongly associated with Zeus.[26] In the Indic pantheon, however, Indra has taken over the functions of the inherited divinity represented in the Greek pantheon by Zeus, wielder of the thunderbolt and king of the gods. Accordingly, I would suggest that the semantics and thematics of *manyú-* listed above were associated in Indo-European with the root \**men-* and the lord of the pantheon. They were thence inherited, on the one hand, by Vedic *manyú-*, which is chiefly associated with Indra, and, on the other, by Greek *mênis*, which is chiefly associated in Greek epic with Zeus, his thunderbolt, and its destructive fire. Homeric *mênis* is also actively associated with the root noun of \**men-*, Greek *ménos*,[27] to which it is ultimately related.

### Three Etymologies of *Mênis*

The details of the connection between the root \**men-* and the word *mênis* are the subject of confusion and dispute. In order to clarify the issues, I first offer a summary of the three currently competing views on the formation of *mênis*. Then I will explain and justify my preference among them.

In 1931, Eduard Schwyzer proposed that the word was derived from the root \**mnā-* attested in the verbs *mi-mnê-skō* 'remind' and *mnáomai* 'be mindful of'.[28] With the addition of a noun suffix *-ni-*, Common Greek \**mnā-nis* became *mânis* (*mênis* in Attic-Ionic) when the first nasal consonant disappeared as a consequence of its dissimilation from the second one. Schwyzer found formal support for this hypothesis in the poetic expression *mnámōn Mênis teknópoinos* 'mindful (from the verb *mnáomai*) child-avenging *Mênis*' attested in the opening choral ode of Aeschylus's *Agamemnon* (155). But he subsequently lost confidence in the etymology, apparently because there is no parallel in Greek for the dissimilation of the nasal consonants.[29]

---

[26] See above, 26–27, for details on the three functions of *mênis*; for an additional example of *mênis* preserving the sovereignty of Zeus, see 119–20.
[27] As noted by Watkins 1977, 198–99.
[28] Schwyzer 1931, 213–17.
[29] Schwyzer 1968, 1:260; 1:495 n. 8; as Watkins 1977, 188, points out, no dissimilation occurs in words such as *mnâma* or *mnâmōn* where the nasal consonant is -m- instead of -n-. The Hesychian gloss μvανόοι may be an error for μvακόοι.

In 1977, however, Calvert Watkins revived the etymology that Schwyzer had himself withdrawn. Watkins tried to demonstrate that *mênis* is not only dangerous to provoke but also a dangerous word to utter. On his view, it is unthinkable that a speaking subject, god or Achilles, use the word to speak of his or her own *mênis*. Every time the occasion presents itself, persons speaking of their own *mênis* use a substitute, such as the words *khólos* or *mēnithmós* or *ménos*.[30] At the same time, Watkins asserted, *mênis* is only used once by any mortal subject; the one example, it turns out, occurs at a moment in the *Iliad* that requires an absence of reticence, when Phoenix asks Achilles to return to battle.[31] The usage restriction that Watkins noticed is significant for the etymology of the word, because if *mênis* is a tabu word, then, like other tabu words and phrases, it could have undergone unpredictable phonological deformation (as opposed to an otherwise unattested regular phonological change). The problem of the unparalleled loss of the nasal consonant in Schwyzer's etymology is solved.

In addition, Watkins found more contextual evidence (like the Aeschylean phrase cited above) to confirm Schwyzer's etymology. He showed that the word *ópis* is a near synonym of *mênis* with a straightforward etymology: it is a derivative of the root *\*op-*, which, like the root of *mnáomai* 'remember, keep in mind', denotes a form of sense perception. One can compare its verbal derivative *opízomai* 'look at, pay attention to', a word which is actually attested in epic with the noun *mênis* as its direct object.[32] As *mênis* is to *ópis*, so *mnáomai* is to *opízomai*. Watkins pointed to passages in epic or lyric poetry where *mênis* is associated with or even defined by forms of the verb *mémnēmai* 'remember'. Since the root *\*mnā* (< *\*mneh$_2$-*) is a "Theme II" enlargement of the root *\*men-* (attested in Greek *ménos*, etc.), it must have been generated in Indo-European rather than independently in Greek and Sanskrit, even though the Theme II root is only attested in Greek and late Vedic Sanskrit. In support of this part of his hypothesis, Schwyzer had already found parallels to the suffix *-ni-* in Armenian and Old Church Slavonic, where it is attached to roots whose form is comparable to *\*mnā-*. Watkins concludes that, along with the formation of its root, the suffixation of *mênis* is of Indo-European date.[33]

In 1985, Patrick Considine, in disagreement with Watkins and Schwyzer, revived a different neglected hypothesis on the etymology of *mênis*. It

---

[30] Watkins 1977, 187–209, esp. 193–94.
[31] *Iliad* 9.517. But Watkins's statement that this is the only occasion on which a mortal utters the root noun (194: "le mot *mênis* n'apparaît qu'une seule fois dans le discours d'un mortel") is incorrect. See below, p. 193, for a list of persons who do so and the consequences for his argument.
[32] See also n. 35 below for the Luvian evidence supporting this semantic typology.
[33] Watkins 1977, 204–5.

was first suggested in 1949 by Carl Darling Buck,[34] and it is most easily expressed as an analogy: *baínō* 'go': *bā-*, *bē-* :: *maínomai* 'rage' : *mā-*, *mē-*, whence Common Greek \**mā-nis*, Attic-Ionic *mênis*. The advantage of this hypothesis over Schwyzer's is clear: the form of *mênis* can be explained in positive terms, in parallel to an attested phonological process, rather than by way of a unique dissimilation or a tabu deformation.[35] But the Buck-Considine etymology is certainly speculative. It explains one enigma by comparing another, since the alternation between *baínō* 'go' / *bā-* and *bē-* (\**gʷem-* / \**gʷeh₂-*), which can only be a morphophonemic phenomenon, is an isolated occurrence among the Indo-European languages. Considine tries to prove that *phaínō* 'show' / *phā-*, *phē-* is a parallel to it, suggesting that Vedic *bhánati* 'speaks' presupposes a root \**bhen-* whose alternation with \**bhā-* would be the same as \**gʷem-* / \**gʷeh₂-*.[36] For *phā-* in contrast to *phan-* the only attested form is *pephḗsetai* (future of the verb *phaínō*), a *hápax legómenon* that has been explained as analogous to *bḗsetai* 'he will go'![37] But

---

[34] Buck 1949, II 34. Considine wrote a dissertation on divine anger (1969) and three articles on the etymology and meaning of *mênis* (1966, 1985, and 1986). The 1985 article gives the fullest exposition of his hypothesis on the etymology. My thanks go to Brent Vine for his generous and expert analysis of the linguistic problems raised by Considine's papers.

[35] However, Considine 1985, 145–46, considers the value of the etymology to be semantic rather than phonological. For him, the problem with Watkins's views is that *in Greek* (not, for example, in Latin, where *memini* 'remember' derives from \**men-*) derivatives of the root \**mnā-* always mean 'think, remember' while those derived from the root \**men-* mean 'to be enraged'. But in my view the distinction is, if not false, at least exaggerated: Greek *ménos*, for example, has a range of meaning from 'heightened state of mind' to 'fury,' and it is directly associated with the verb *mémnēmai* in epic diction: cp. the description of the actions performed by Athena/*Men*-tes (*sic*) on Telemachus as explained in Nagy 1974b, 266–68; τῷ δ᾽ ἐνὶ θυμῷ / θῆκε μένος καὶ θάρσος, ὑπέμνησεν δέ ἑ πατρός (*Odyssey* 1.320–21) 'in his spirit she put *ménos* and courage and reminded him [verb *hupémnēsen* from the root \**mnā-*] of his father'. Moreover, as the semantic typology for the parallel word *ópis* cited above shows, the meaning 'rage, fury' can be either an old or a new development from the meaning 'aroused thought, perception'. Watkins 1986 offers even stronger evidence in regard to that semantic typology. In an inscription (Starke 1980, 142–44), the cognate of the root \**mnā-* (\**mneh₂-*) in Luvian actually means 'see', exactly like the meaning of the Greek root \**op-* whose derivative *ópis* is a synonym of *mênis*. Antoine Meillet fully understood and accounted for this range of meanings in the root \**men-*; see his definition cited in n. 1 above.

[36] The forms cited are Considine's, sometimes with and sometimes without laryngeals. See Mayrhofer 1963, 469–70 s.v. *bhánati* for other possibilities (that Considine considers less convincing).

[37] So Frisk 1970, s.v. φαίνω. In the formulaic system of epic, in fact, the form πεφήσεται 'will appear' varies with τετεύξεται 'will happen', and both have the same metrical value: compare ‖τετεύξεται αἰπὺς ὄλεθρος# 'sheer destruction will occur' (*Iliad* 12.345, 358) with ‖πεφήσεται αἰπὺς ὄλεθρος# 'sheer destruction will appear' (*Iliad* 17.155); compare also ἀναφαίνεται αἰπὺς ὄλεθρος# in the same context (17.244) but also elsewhere (11.174) and even a conjugated, demetaphorized form of the same expression: ὄρος αἰπὺς πέφαντο# (*Hymn to Apollo* 428). Forms of φαίνομαι are more systematically attested in these formulae than forms of τευχ-. In fact, τετεύξεται may well be a more recent form replacing πεφήσεται. According to Chantraine 1958, 448, πεφήσεται from φαίνω was the model for πεφήσεται the future of θείνω 'slay, smite' (\**gʷhen-*);

an isolated form should not be the basis for analogical formations. Reduplicated future middles like *memnḗsomai* provide a better model, as Chantraine pointed out.³⁸ Considine's whole argument is neither more nor less than a possibility.³⁹

## Mênis as a Tabu Deformation

In terms of the phonological criteria of historical linguistics, it is clear, Watkins's etymology is the strongest of the three. But the validity of his revival of Schwyzer's etymology depends on the notion that *mênis* was a tabu word. Watkins supports that idea not by discussing the meaning of the word, but by citing a usage constraint on the root noun *mênis* in Epic diction: a speaking subject cannot utter the word in referring to his or her own *mênis*. But the value of this usage constraint as evidence of a language tabu has been seriously challenged. Jean-Claude Turpin has pointed out that tabu words are deformed *so that they can be uttered*.⁴⁰ Apparently, the deformation of *mênis* was a failure! Turpin also maintains that a tabu on the first-person usage of a word is unexampled and inconsistent with the structure of the relationship between the persons of the verb in general terms. In his view, if a first-person usage was forbidden, so should a second-person usage.⁴¹ So Turpin willingly embraces Schwyzer's original hypothesis despite its unresolved phonological difficulties.⁴²

---

but it is at least possible that the latter is also an old form and represents another example of the morphophonemic alternation (here *$g^when$- / *$g^whā$-). See below on the relationship in Indo-European between the -ɟe/o- suffixed presents based on the degree zero of the root and an old athematic present; the form in question for this root is attested in Old Church Slavonic *žinjǫ* 'cut, harvest'. However, both examples of πεφήσεται are more simply understood as analogous to futures such as μεμνήσομαι, etc.

³⁸ Chantraine 1968–79, s.v. θείνω.

³⁹ Considine probably goes too far in suggesting that μαίνομαι itself is derived from a degree-zero *$mh_2$- followed by a "nasal extension" (therefore *$mh_2n$-), which is a form that cannot be motivated in Indo-European; alternatively, he suggests that it is a secondary derivative of an unattested verb *μάω or *μάομαι which became μαίνομαι within Greek itself, like δράω, δραίνω, etc. The traditional explanation derives μαίνομαι from *$mn$-ɟe-toi, a form that has an exact cognate in Vedic *mányate*, Old Avestan *mainiietē*, Cuneiform Luvian *maliti* 'thinks', Old Irish *muinethar*, etc.

⁴⁰ Turpin 1988, 247–60.

⁴¹ Turpin is referring to Benveniste 1966c, 225–36, on the structure of the relationship between the verbal persons; but the existence of a structural contrast between the first and second persons of the verb as against the third person does not eliminate the distinction between the first and the second persons!

⁴² Considine 1985, 162–63 n. 7, and 1986, 58, also denies that *mênis* is a tabu word. He admits that the word "expresses a response of awe" and that it is "too solemn except in a religious use,"

190    The Anger of Achilles

For my part, I propose to answer Turpin's objections to Watkins's hypothesis and to provide additional support for the notion that *mênis* was a tabu: its attested meaning. First, with regard to the contradiction in maintaining that a word is at the same time tabu and deformed, since the purpose of deforming a word is to make it possible to utter it: the loss of one consonant, the second nasal of *\*mnā-nis*, barely qualifies as a deformation, but the only way to salvage Watkins's hypothesis is to suppose that the word, once deformed, has become tabu again. That seems doubtful at best. Yet I do know of one parallel: the English word *pee* was originally a children's euphemistic form, like French *pipi*, for the vulgar word *piss*, but it is no longer perceived as a euphemism and has become mildly obscene.[43] If there is one example of such a phenomenon, there may well be others. It is plausible, it seems to me, that a deformed word can again become tabu if, for one reason or another, the word in question loses its oppositional relationship to the tabu word from which it was originally deformed. If the tabu word has disappeared completely, or if the derivational relationship between the two words is lost completely for other reasons, the original word's functions can be taken on by the new, deformed word, which will then also acquire the same prohibitions as the old one, provided that the social conditions that motivated the deformation in the first place continue to flourish. Such a process is just a special case of the lexical renewal rule specified in Kuryłowicz's Fourth Morphological Typology, and, as Claude

which for him accounts for the fact that one does not speak of one's own *mênis*. But if the word is solemn and if it expresses "a response of awe" and if that is why people do not utter it, then it is tabu. The parallel that Considine offers, namely, that in English one cannot speak of one's wrath (Considine 1985, 163 n. 7) has nothing in common with the prohibition on the usage of *mênis*. English wrath is a word of epic style that no one uses in everyday speech, whereas the prohibition on *mênis* that Watkins has described is of an epic word within epic diction.

There is also a logical inconsequence in Considine's earlier (1966, 22 n.11) contention that *mênis* has no moral value since words signifying "divine wrath" are certain to be used in connection with the transgression of a moral precept. But if it had no moral connotations, why would the word mean "divine wrath" in the first place? In effect, Considine's point denies the value of contextual restrictions and associations in recovering the meaning of words. Moreover, he contends that Frisk failed to show that *mênis* was an ethical term because he did not show that it was used more often than other words for wrath in cases of moral transgression. Since *mênis* is *only* used for cases of moral transgression, his objection is ill-taken and easily countered by the first use of the words *khólos* 'anger' and *kótos* 'rancor' at *Iliad* 1.81 and 82. They do not refer to a transgression but to Agamemnon's angry reaction to the bad news that Kalkhas is about to convey to him. But Considine does not provide what his point requires and what he cannot provide, namely, evidence that *mênis* is used in contexts *other* than those concerning the transgression of moral rules. As explained in Chapters 1 and 2 above, the word *mênis* is the name of the sanction for fundamental transgressions of the cosmic order, not "divine wrath"; see also n. 2 above.

[43] Morris et al. 1969, s.v. pee². My thanks to Leslie Kurke for this example.

Sandoz has made clear, tabu words can and do disappear.[44] In the case that concerns us, it behooves us to suppose that the prohibition on the undeformed form of *mênis* was so strong and effective that this form has disappeared, while the reasons to prohibit the utterance of the word remained.

It is worth stressing, however, that even if such a semantic process and its consequence, phonological deformation, did *not* take place in the case of *mênis,* the word may still be tabu. The usage and semantic content of a word in its proper social context determine whether or not it is tabu, not its deformation, and for *mênis,* there are other plausible explanations of its form. Turpin realizes that the constraint Watkins has noticed—the absence of subjects speaking of their own *mênis*—requires an explanation. He has even added to Watkins's dossier by pointing out that derived forms such as the verb *mēníō* are not attested in the first person.[45] According to Turpin, however, these usage restrictions can be explained by "the very nature of the idea." *Mênis* is not "the anger of the gods," but it is in itself a divine object; consequently, it is never said to reside in the mental equipment of Homeric persons as do other words meaning "anger." The epic even takes the trouble to make explicit the emotional consequences of *mênis* as though they were not in fact part of its meaning, as though *mênis* were a "numinous object" independent of human feeling. That is why one cannot speak of *one's own mênis.*[46]

Turpin's observations on the independence of *mênis* are pertinent. Yet if it is not possible to attribute *mênis* to oneself, then why on his explanation is it possible, as he admits it is, to attribute *mênis* to "you" or "him" or "her"? Furthermore, his description of certain states of mind as external objects in the epic world is questionable. The strict separation between mind and

---

[44] Kuryłowicz 1966, 121–38: "When, as the result of a morphological transformation, a form undergoes differentiation, the new form corresponds to the primary (founding) function, while the old form is reserved for the secondary function" (my translation). It frequently happens that the "old form" disappears, as with *mênis.* Sandoz 1984, 144, who speaks of the disappearance of a word as the strictest and simplest form of linguistic tabu.

[45] Turpin 1988, 252 n.23, 256; although there is an expressive exception in Athenian tragedy, Euripides *Hippolytus* 146 *mēníō theoîsin* "I have *mênis* against the gods," which is actually a *double* inversion of the word's usage rules. It is the only example of the verb in the first person, and there is no other instance of mortals with *mênis* against the gods (as opposed to the reverse, which is common).

[46] For a similar explanation of the avoidance of first person usage, see Redfield 1979, 97 n. 5. Redfield views *mênis* as an "anger that is dangerous to someone," as anger seen from without. This is the distinction between subject and object in another guise, on which see the following paragraph; on the systematic danger that his *mênis* constitutes to Achilles himself, see above, Chapter 5.

body that is second nature to us cannot be projected upon the Homeric world, since the physical and external aspect of mental states that we consider immaterial and interior is a constantly recurring feature of epic language and thought. In this respect, *mênis* does not seem to me different from a term such as *átē* 'moral blindness', also a divine and numinous force: Agamemnon wishes to represent his *átē* as something distinct from himself, but in a context where he intends to dissociate himself from it and deflect blame for what he has done.[47] *Mênis* is independent and "almost a hypostasis," as Turpin does well to point out, but these qualities do not require that epic personages cannot consider it to be theirs.

The last problem that Turpin raises is the credibility of a tabu on the first grammatical person that does not also fall upon the second (and for that matter, also the third). In fact, Greek epic contains at least one exact parallel to such a tabu. When epic characters are asked their identity, they do not respond with their name, only with their patronymic and place of birth; but in the second and third persons, people often refer to each other by name with or without a patronymic.[48] The prohibition against speaking one's own name can, however, be violated in special circumstances, such as the moment when Odysseus finally identifies himself to the Phaeacians by his name and his patronymic, or when a goddess reveals herself to mortals. For Sandoz, who describes a whole range of language tabus from "systematic avoidance" to "simple reticence," such flexibility in the rules of speech is predictable and commonplace.[49] For an example of an exclusion of the first person in contrast with the two others that is closer in context to *mênis*, I cite Walter Burkert's dictum on Greek funerary customs and beliefs: "Ritual and belief are almost exclusively concerned with the death of others; one's own death remains hidden."[50] In this perspective, the prohibition against using the word *mênis* by a subject who is speaking of his own *mênis* can be motivated by reasons and feelings comparable to those evinced by one's own death. With respect to the horror surrounding *mênis*, it suffices to consider the complete list of verbs of which it is the direct object in epic diction: *hupodeídein* 'be afraid of', *aporrhíptein* 'hurl away', *aleúesthai* 'shun', *opízesthai* 'watch out for', *apoeipeîn* 'renounce'.[51]

---

[47] See his excuses to Achilles and the Achaeans at *Iliad* 19.86–144; Dodds 1951, 2–4, shows how Agamemnon cannot avoid his responsibility to compensate Achilles for the mistake he has made.

[48] For the rule and its expressive exceptions, see Muellner 1976, 74–75 n. 9.

[49] Sandoz 1984, n. 17.

[50] "Ritual und Glaube haben es fast ausschließlich mit dem Tod der anderen zu tun; der eigene Tod bleibt im Dunkel": Burkert 1977, 293.

[51] As noted by Watkins 1977, 193.

Appendix: The Etymology of *Mênis* 193

So it is possible to salvage from Turpin's critique the hypothesis that *mênis* is a tabu deformation. Even so, the extent to which *mênis* is tabu needs to be qualified. According to Watkins, epic persons behave as if forbidden to speak of their own *mênis*. Instead of uttering it, they employ a substitute word, such as *ménos, khólos, mēnithmós,* or *ópis*. But in fact this speech tabu is not very stringent. On two occasions, Achilles speaks of his own *mênis* with a verbal derivative of the root noun, ('while I have / had *mênis'—emeũ apomēnísantos: Iliad* 9.426, 19.62), and on two other occasions he uses the secondary suffixed form, *mēni-thmós* (16.62, 202). A gross offense to convention does not seem intended. The relaxation of a speech tabu for secondary forms of a tabu word is possible but not automatic. If the derivational link is apparent to native speakers, and the denotation of the founded form is unchanged from the founding form, it is almost difficult to credit. To cite an example of the relaxation of the tabu for a founded form, a word like "Christian" has no tabu attached to it although "Christ" is tabu in many contexts (as in 'taking the Lord's name in vain'), because the semantic reference and usage of the tabu term and its derivative are not the same. On the other hand, French *emmerder* in its transitive form is as vulgar as its founding form *merde*, because the semantic and the derivational links are transparent and in force; but the reflexive form of the same verb, *s'emmerder*, is not vulgar. When Achilles says *emeũ apomēnísantos* in *Iliad* 9.426, he is patently referring to the theme of the poem expressed in its first line with a verb overtly derived from the noun. The same is true of the other instances cited just above where he uses a *mênis* derivative. Moreover, Watkins mistook the overall rarity of *mênis* in spoken discourse.[52] Epic mortals (Kalkhas, *Iliad* 1.75; Aeneas, 5.178; Phoenix, 9.517; Menelaos, 13.624; Telemachus, *Odyssey* 2.66; Nestor, 3.135; Aithon/Odysseus, 14.283) utter the root noun as frequently as the poetic narrator (six times) and more often than the gods (Hermes, *Odyssey* 5.146; Athena, *Iliad* 5.34; Thetis, 19.35; Aphrodite, *Hymn to Aphrodite* 290). Nor is the distribution of *mênis* derivatives meaningfully different from that of the root noun. It is spoken by mortal speakers eleven times, by the narrator seven times, and by gods once. On each occasion the derivative either refers to an otherwise identifiable instance of a nonderived form of *mênis*, or it occurs in a context comparable to one in which the root noun is also used.[53]

On balance, then, and with the qualifications stated as to the nature and

---

[52] See above, 187 and n. 31.
[53] To mention what first appears to be the most difficult example, see the discussion above in Chapter 2, 37–39, of the plausible *mênis* of a beggar.

strength of the speech tabu, Watkins's revival of Schwyzer's etymology appears to be the most consistent with the word's meaning and usage. In fact, the absence of a stringent speech tabu against *mênis* supports Watkins's overall argument better than its presence. It seems plausible to argue that what *once was* a tabu word has been deformed and is therefore relatively utterable. Reticence is by no means ruled out by the semantic or the phonological evidence, and reticence is in fact a diminished form of speech tabu.[54] This discussion inevitably raises a further question about the semantic content of *mênis* that no one has yet addressed. To put it simply, *why* should this word be tabu? Whence the horror surrounding it? The hypothesis that *mênis* is a tabu word may be sustainable on the basis of its usage and despite Turpin's pointed objections, but it is still not clear why a word that means "solemn anger," as Watkins defines it, should be dangerous to speak (and possibly still dangerous even after deformation). The answer to this question, however, imposes itself after a systematic review of the usage of the word in context like the one undertaken above in Chapters 1 and 2. *Mênis* is an emotion that acts to change the world. It is not a word for "solemn anger" but the sacred name of the ultimate sanction against tabu behavior, and epic personages invoke it to forestall people from breaking fundamental cosmic rules. So it would not be surprising if the word *mênis* were endowed with the same dread as the behavior that can bring it down upon a whole community. It is also economical if a language tabu explains both the usage and the form of *mênis*.

[54] See again Sandoz 1984, 144. In an earlier study of the etymology and semantics of *mênis*, I supported Watkins's position on the speech tabu (Muellner 1991); that position now seems to me too rigidly formulated, which is not to deny the fundamental value of Watkins's study in other respects.

# References

Alexiou, Margaret. 1974. *The Ritual Lament in Greek Tradition*. Cambridge.
Ameis, Carl, and Carl Hentze. 1906, repr. 1965. *Ilias für den Schulgebrauch*. II Bd. 4 Hft. Gesang XXII–XXIV. Leipzig.
Auerbach, Erich. 1953. *Mimesis*. Translated by Willard R. Trask. Princeton, N.J.
Austin, Norman. 1966. The Function of Digressions in the *Iliad*. *Greek Roman and Byzantine Studies* 7:295–312.
Benveniste, Emile. 1935, repr. 1948. *Origines de la formation des noms en indo-européen*. Paris.
———. 1937. Expressions indo-européennes de l'éternité. *Bulletin de la Société de Linguistique de Paris* 38:103–12.
———. 1966a. Don et échange dans le vocabulaire indo-européen. In *Problèmes de linguistique générale*. 315–35. Paris.
———. 1966b. La phrase nominale. In *Problèmes de linguistique générale*. 151–86. Paris.
———. 1966c. Structure des relations de personne dans le verbe. In *Problèmes de linguistique générale*. 225–36. Paris.
———. 1966d. Problèmes sémantiques de la réconstruction. In *Problèmes de linguistique générale*. 289–307. Paris.
———. 1969. *Le vocabulaire des institutions indo-européennes*. Vols. 1 and 2. Paris.
Bremmer, Jan. 1988. La plasticité du mythe: Méléagre dans la poésie homérique. In *Métamorphoses du mythe en Grèce antique*, edited by Claude Calame, 37–56. Geneva.
Broccia, G. 1967. *La forma poetica dell' "Iliade" e la genesi dell'epos omerico*. Messina.
Buck, C. D. 1949. *A Dictionary of Selected Synonyms in the Indo-European Languages*. Chicago.
Burkert, Walter. 1977. *Griechische Religion der archaischen und klassischen Epoche*. Die Religionen der Menschheit. Stuttgart.
———. 1985. *Greek Religion*. Translated by John Raffan. Cambridge, Mass.
Buse, H. 1937. *Quaestiones Hesiodeae et Orphicae*. Halle.
Bussanich, J. 1983. A Theoretical Interpretation of Hesiod's Chaos. *Classical Philology* 92:212–19.

Cassirer, Ernst. 1955–57. *The Philosophy of Symbolic Forms*. Translated by R. Manheim. New Haven, Conn.
Chantraine, Pierre. 1954. Le divin et les dieux chez Homère. *Entretiens de la Fondation Hardt* 1:47–94.
———. 1958. *Grammaire homérique I: Phonétique et morphologie*. Paris.
———. 1963. *Grammaire homérique II: Syntaxe*. Paris.
———. 1968–79. *Dictionnaire étymologique de la langue grecque: Histoire des mots*. Paris.
Chirassi Colombo, I. 1977. Heros Achilleus Theos Apollo. In *Il mito greco*, edited by B. Gentili and A. Paioni, 231–69. Atti del Convegno Internazionale, Urbino, 7–12 May 1973. Rome.
Clader, L. L. 1976. *Helen: The Evolution from Divine to Heroic in Greek Epic Tradition*. Leiden.
Clay, Jenny Strauss. 1983. *The Wrath of Athena: Gods and Men in the Odyssey*. Princeton, N.J.
———. 1989. *The Politics of Olympus: Form and Meaning in the Major Homeric Hymns*. Princeton, N.J.
Considine, Patrick. 1966. Some Homeric Terms for Anger. *Acta Classica* 9:15–25.
———. 1969. The Theme of Divine Wrath in Ancient East Mediterranean Literature. *Studi Micenei ed Egeo-Anatolici* 8:85–189.
———. 1985. The Indo-European Origin of Greek ΜΗΝΙΣ. *Transactions of the Philological Society* 144–70.
———. 1986. The Etymology of Μῆνις. In *Studies in Honor of T. B. L. Webster*, ed. J. H. Betts, J. T. Hooker and J. R. Green. Bristol.
Cuillandre, Joseph. 1943. *La droite et la gauche dans les poèmes homériques, en concordance avec la doctrine pythagoricienne et la tradition celtique*. Rennes.
Denniston, J. D. 1954, repr. 1959. *The Greek Particles*. 2d ed. Oxford.
Detienne, Marcel. 1973. *Les maîtres de vérité dans la Grèce archaïque*. 2d ed. Paris.
———. 1979. *Dionysos Slain*. Translated by Mireille Muellner and Leonard Muellner. Baltimore.
———. 1994. *The Gardens of Adonis: Spices in Greek Mythology*. 2d ed. Translated by J. Lloyd. Princeton, N.J.
Detienne, Marcel, and Jesper Svenbro. 1969. Les loups au festin, ou La cité impossible. In *La cuisine du sacrifice en pays grec*, edited by M. Detienne and J.-P. Vernant. 215–37. Paris.
Detienne, Marcel, and Jean-Pierre Vernant. 1974. *Les ruses de l'intelligence: La mètis des Grecs*. Paris.
———. 1978. *Cunning Intelligence in Greek Culture and Society*. Trans. J. Lloyd. Hassocks (U.K.).
———, eds. 1979. *La cuisine du sacrifice en pays grec*. Paris.
———, eds. 1989. *The Cuisine of Sacrifice among the Greeks*. Translated by P. Wissing. Chicago.
Dodds, E. R. 1951. *The Greeks and the Irrational*. Berkeley, Calif.
Douglas, Mary. 1966, repr. 1979. *Purity and Danger: An Analysis of Concepts of Pollution and Taboo*. London.
Duchesne-Guillemin, Jacques. 1962. *La Religion de l'Iran*. Paris.
Dumézil, Georges. 1943. *Servius et la Fortune: Essai sur la fonction sociale de louange et de blâme et sur les éléments indo-européens du cens romain*. Paris.
———. 1947. *Tarpeia: Essais de philologie comparative indo-européenne*. Mythes Romains 3. Paris.
———. 1948. *Jupiter Mars Quirinus IV: Explications de textes indiens et latins*. Paris.
———. 1958. *L'idéologie tripartie des Indo-Européens*. Paris.

———. 1968. *Mythe et épopée, I: L'idéologie des trois fonctions dans les épopées des peuples indo-européens.* Paris.
———. 1971. *Mythe et épopée, II: Types épiques indo-européens: un héros, un sorcier, un roi.* Paris.
Ebeling, H. 1885, repr. 1963. *Lexicon Homericum.* Vols. 1 and 2. Leipzig, repr. Hildesheim.
Edwards, Mark W. 1991. *The Iliad: A Commentary,* vol. 5: *Books 17–20.* Cambridge.
Ernout, Alfred, and Antoine Meillet. 1959. *Dictionnaire étymologique de la langue latine: Histoire des mots.* 4th ed. Paris.
Evans-Pritchard, E. E. 1940, repr. 1960, 1969. *The Nuer: A Description of the Modes of Livelihood and Political Institutions of a Nilotic People.* New York.
Fenik, Bernard. 1968. *Typical Battle Scenes in the Iliad: Studies in the Narrative Techniques of Homeric Battle Description.* Hermes Einzelschriften. Wiesbaden.
Finley, M. I. 1977. *The World of Odysseus.* 2d ed. London.
Foley, John Miles. 1991. *Immanent Art. From Structure to Meaning in Traditional Oral Epic.* Bloomington, Ind.
Frame, Douglas. 1978. *The Myth of Return in Early Greek Epic.* New Haven.
Friedländer, Paul. 1913. ὑποθῆκαι. *Hermes* 48:558–616.
Frisk, Hjalmar. 1946. ΜΗΝΙΣ: Zur Geschichte eines Begriffes. *Eranos* 44:28–40.
———. 1970. *Griechisches etymologisches Wörterbuch.* Heidelberg.
Geldner, K., trans. 1954. *Der Rig-Veda aus dem Sanskrit ins Deutsche Übersetzt.* Harvard Oriental Series, vol. 34. 3 vols. Cambridge, Mass.
Gennep, Arnold van. 1909, repr. 1981. *Les rites de passage: Etude systématique des rites de la porte et du seuil, de l'hospitalité, de l'adoption, de la grossesse et de l'accouchement, de la naissance, de l'enfance, de la puberté, de l'initiation, de l'ordination, du couronnement des fiancailles et du mariage, des funérailles, des saisons, etc.* Paris.
Gentili, B., and A. Paioni, eds. 1977. *Il mito greco:* Atti del Convegno Internazionale (Urbino 7–12 May 1973). Rome.
Gnoli, Gherardo, and Vernant, Jean-Pierre. 1982. *La mort, les morts dans les sociétés anciennes.* Paris.
Grégoire, H. 1949. Asklepios, Apollon Smintheus, et Rudra: Etudes sur le dieu à la taupe et le dieu au rat dans la Grèce et dans l'Inde. With R. Goossens and M. Mathieu. *Académie royale de Belgique, Classe des lettres et des sciences morales et politiques: Mémoires.* 2d ser., 45:1.
Hainsworth, Bryan. 1993. *The Iliad: A Commentary,* vol. 3: *Books 9–12.* Cambridge.
Hamilton, Richard. 1989. *The Architecture of Hesiodic Poetry.* Baltimore.
Holway, Richard. 1989. Poetry and Political Thought in Archaic Greece: The *Iliad,* the *Theogony,* and Political Life. Ph.D. diss., University of California–Berkeley.
Householder, F. W., and Gregory Nagy. 1972. Greek. *Current Trends in Linguistics* 9:735–816.
Howald, E. 1924. Meleager und Achill. *Rheinisches Museum* 73:402–25.
———. 1946. *Der Dichter der Ilias.* Zürich.
Insler, S. 1975. *The Gāthās of Zarathustra. Acta Iranica* 8. Troisième série, textes et mémoires. I. Teheran.
Irmscher, Johannes. 1950. *Götterzorn bei Homer.* Berlin.
Jacopin, P.-Y. 1987. *La parole génerative: La mythologie des indiens Yukuna.* Diss., Université de Neuchâtel.

———. 1988. On the Syntactic Structure of Myth, or The Yukuna Invention of Speech. *Cultural Anthropology* 3:131–59.

Jakobson, Roman. 1939. Signe zéro. In *Mélanges de linguistique offerts à Charles Bally*, 143–52. Geneva.

———. 1957. *Shifters, Verbal Categories, and the Russian Verb*. Cambridge, Mass.

———. 1968. The Poetry of Grammar and the Grammar of Poetry. *Lingua* 21:597–609.

Janko, Richard. 1992. *The Iliad: A Commentary, Volume IV, books 13–16*. Cambridge.

Kakridis, Johannes. 1949. *Homeric Researches*. Lund.

Katz, Marylin. 1991. *Penelope's Renown: Meaning and Indeterminacy in the Odyssey*. Princeton, N.J.

Kirk, G. S. 1985. *The Iliad: A Commentary, Volume 1, Books 1–4*. Cambridge.

———. 1990. *The Iliad: A Commentary, Volume 2, Books 5–8*. Cambridge.

Koller, H. 1956. Das kitharodische Prooimion: Eine formgeschichtliche Untersuchung. *Philologus* 100:159–206.

Krischer, Tilman. 1971. *Formale Konventionen der homerischen Epik*. Munich.

Kullmann, W. 1960. *Die Quellen der "Ilias."* Wiesbaden.

Kuryłowicz, Jerzy. 1966. La nature des procès dits "analogiques." In *Readings in Linguistics*, edited by E. Hamp, F. Householder, and R. Austerlitz, 158–74. Chicago.

Lakoff, George. 1987. *Women, Fire, and Dangerous Things: What Categories Reveal about the Mind*. Chicago.

Lakoff, George, and Mark Johnson. 1980. *Metaphors We Live By*. Chicago.

Lakoff, George, and Zoltán Kövecses. 1987. The Cognitive Model of Anger Inherent in American English. In *Cultural Models in Language and Thought*, edited by D. Holland and N. Quinn, 195–221. Cambridge.

Lang, M. L. 1983. Reverberation and Mythology in the *Iliad*. In *Approaches to Homer*, edited by C. A. Rubino and C. W. Shelmerdine. 140–64. Austin.

Latacz, Joachim. 1966. *Zum Wortfeld "Freude" in der Sprache Homers*. Heidelberg.

Lawson, J. C. 1910. *Modern Greek Folklore and Ancient Greek Religion*. Cambridge.

Lévi-Strauss, Claude. 1970. *The Raw and the Cooked: Introduction to a Science of Mythology*. Translated by John Weightman and Doreen Weightman. Evanston, Ill.

———. 1976. *Structural Anthropology*. Translated by Monique Layton. Chicago.

Lloyd-Jones, Hugh. 1983. *The Justice of Zeus*. 2d ed. Berkeley, Calif.

Lohmann, Dieter. 1970. *Die Komposition der Reden in der Ilias*. Berlin.

Loraux, Nicole. 1978. Sur la race des femmes et quelques-unes de ses tribus. *Arethusa* 11:43–87.

———. 1986. Le deuil du rossignol. *Nouvelle Revue de Psychanalyse* 34:253–7.

———. 1987. Le lien de la division. *Le Cahier du Collège International de Philosophie* 4:101–24.

Lord, Albert Bates. 1960. *The Singer of Tales*. Cambridge, Mass.

———. 1991. *Epic Singers and Oral Tradition*. Ithaca, N.Y.

Lord, Albert Bates, and Milman Parry. 1954. *Serbocroatian Heroic Songs I: Novi Pazar: English Translations*. Cambridge.

Lord, M. L. 1967. Withdrawal and Return: An Epic Story Pattern in the Homeric *Hymn to Demeter* and in the Homeric Poems. *Classical Journal* 62:241–48.

Lowenstam, Steven. 1981. *The Death of Patroklos: A Study in Typology.* Königstein.
———. 1993. *The Scepter and the Spear: Studies on Forms of Repetition in the Homeric Poems.* Lanham, Md.
Lynn-George, Michael. 1988. *Epos: Word, Narrative, and the Iliad.* Basingstoke, U.K.
Malamoud, Charles. 1968. Manyúh Svayambhúh. In *Mélanges d'indianisme à la mémoire de Louis Renou,* 493–507. Paris.
Martin, Richard P. 1983. *Healing, Sacrifice, and Battle: Amēchania and Related Concepts in Early Greek Poetry.* Innsbruck.
———. 1989. *The Language of Heroes: Speech and Performance in the Iliad.* Ithaca, N.Y.
Mauss, Marcel. 1925. Essai sur le don, forme archaïque d'échange. *Année sociologique* n.s. 1:40–186.
———. 1967. *The Gift: Forms and Functions of Exchange in Archaic Societies.* Translated by Ian Cunnison. New York.
———. 1990. *The Gift: The Form and Reason for Exchange in Archaic Societies.* Translated by W. D. Halls. London.
Mayrhofer, Manfred. 1963. *Kurzgefasstes etymologisches Wörterbuch des Altindischen.* Heidelberg.
———. 1986–. *Etymologisches Wörterbuch des Altindoarischen.* Heidelberg.
Meier-Brügger, Michael. 1989. Zu griechisch μάτη 'Unbesonnenheit' und Sippe. *Glotta* 67:42–44.
———. 1993. A propos de la partie étymologique du dictionnaire de Chantraine. In *La langue et les textes en grec ancien: Actes du Colloque Pierre Chantraine,* edited by Françoise Létoublon, 267–68. Amsterdam.
Meillet, A. 1897. *De Indo-Europaea radice \*men- "mente agitare."* Paris.
———. 1923. *Les origines indo-européennes des mètres grecs.* Paris.
Mondi, Robert. 1989. ΧΑΟΣ and the Hesiodic Cosmogony. *Harvard Studies in Classical Philology* 92:1–41.
Morris, W., et al., eds. 1969. *The American Heritage Dictionary of the English Language.* New York.
Motto, A L., and J. R. Clark. 1969. ΙΣΗ ΔΑΙΣ: The Honor of Achilles. *Arethusa* 2:109–25.
Muellner, Leonard. 1976. *The Meaning of Homeric εὔχομαι Through its Formulas.* Innsbruck.
———. 1990. The Simile of the Cranes and Pygmies: A Study of Homeric Metaphor. *Harvard Studies in Classical Philology* 93:59–101.
———. 1992. Etymologie et sémantique de μῆνις. In *La langue et les textes en grec ancien: Actes du Colloque Pierre Chantraine,* edited by Françoise Létoublon, 121–35.
———. (forthcoming). μελιηδής.
Nagler, Michael. 1967. Towards a Generative View of the Oral Formula. *Transactions of the American Philological Association* 98:269–311.
———. 1974. *Spontaneity and tradition: A study in the oral art of Homer.* Berkeley, Calif.
———. 1990. The Proem to the *Odyssey. Classical Antiquity* 9:335–56.
Nagy, Gregory. 1974a. Perkūnas and Perunŭ. In *Antiquitates Indogermanicae: Gedenkschrift für Hermann Güntert,* edited by M. Mayrhofer, B. Schlerath, R. Schmitt, 113–31. Innsbruck.
———. 1974b. *Comparative Studies in Greek and Indic Meter.* Cambridge.

———. 1976. The Name of Achilles: Etymology and Epic. In *Studies in Greek, Italic, and Indo-European Linguistics Offered to L. R. Palmer*, edited by A. M. Davies and Wolfgang Meid, 209–37. Innsbruck.
———. 1979. *The Best of the Achaeans. Concepts of the Hero in Archaic Greek Poetry*. Baltimore.
———. 1982. Hesiod. In *Ancient Writers*, edited by T. J. Luce, 43–73. New York.
———. 1990a. *Greek Mythology and Poetics*. Ithaca, N.Y.
———. 1990b. *Pindar's Homer: The Lyric Possession of an Epic Past*. Baltimore.
———. 1992. Mythological Exemplum in Homer. In *Innovations of Antiquity*, edited by R. Hexter and D. Selden, 311–31. London.
———. 1994. The Name of Apollo: Etymology and Essence. In *Apollo: Origins and Influences*, edited by Jon Solomon, 3–7, 135–6. Tucson, Ariz.
———. 1996. *Poetry as Performance: Homer and Beyond*. Cambridge.
Nilsson, M. P. 1968. *Geschichte der griechischen Religion*. 3d ed. Munich.
Parker, Robert. 1983. *Miasma: Pollution and Purification in Early Greek Religion*. Oxford.
Parry, Adam, ed. 1971. *The Making of Homeric Verse: The Collected Papers of Milman Parry*. Oxford.
Pestalozzi, H. 1945. *Die Achilleis als Quelle der Ilias*. Zurich.
Petegorsky, Dan. 1982. Context and Evocation: Studies in Early Greek and Sanskrit Poetry. Diss., University of California–Berkeley.
Pötscher, W. 1961. Hera und Heros. *Rheinisches Museum* 104:302–55.
Rabel, R. J. 1990. Apollo as a Model for Achilles in the *Iliad*. *American Journal of Philology* 111:429–40.
Redfield, James. 1975. *Nature and Culture in the Iliad*. Chicago.
———. 1979. The Proem to the *Iliad*. *Classical Philology* 74:95–110.
Renou, Louis. 1930. *Grammaire sanscrite*. Vol. 1. Paris.
———. 1966. *Études Védiques et Pāṇinéennes*. Vols. V, XIII, XV Paris.
Renou, Louis, and Emile Benveniste. 1934. *Vṛtra et Vṛθragna: Étude de mythologie indo-iranienne*. Paris.
Richardson, N.J., ed. and comm. 1974. *The Homeric Hymn to Demeter*. Oxford.
Rijksbaron, Albert. 1984. *The Syntax and Semantics of the Verb in Classical Greek*. Amsterdam.
Risch, Ernst. 1944. Betrachtungen zu den indogermanischen Verwandschaftsnamen. *Museum Helveticum* 1:115–122.
Rosner, J. A. 1976. The Speech of Phoenix: *Iliad* 9.434–605. *Phoenix* 30:314–27.
Sahlins, Marshall. 1972. *Stone Age Economics*. Chicago.
Sandoz, Claude. 1984. Le tabou linguistique comme facteur de processus dérivationnels [à la lumière de faits i.e.]. In *E. Benveniste aujourd'hui*. Vol. 2.143–50. Paris.
Schadewaldt, Wolfgang. 1965. *Von Homers Welt und Werk*. 4th ed. Stuttgart.
———. 1966, repr. 1987. *Iliasstudien*. 3d ed. Berlin, repr. Darmstadt.
Schmidt, J. H. Heinrich. 1879, repr. 1969. *Synonymik der griechischen Sprache*. Leipzig, repr. Amsterdam.
Schmitt, Rüdiger. 1967. *Dichtung und Dichtersprache in indogermanischer Zeit*. Wiesbaden.
———, ed. 1968. *Indogermanische Dichtersprache*. Darmstadt.
Schwabl, Hans. 1966. Hesiods *Theogonie*: Eine unitarische Analyse. *Sitzungsberichte der Österreichische Akademie der Wissenschaften, Philosophisch-Historische Klasse*, 250: 5. Vienna.

———. 1970. Hesiod. In *Paulys Real-Encyclopädie der classischen Altertumswissenschaft; neue Bearbeitung . . .*, edited by A. F. Pauly, G. Wissowa, and W. Kroll, cols. 434–86. Stuttgart.
Schwartz, M. 1982. The Indo-European Vocabulary of Exchange, Hospitality, and Intimacy. *Proceedings of the Berkeley Linguistics Society* 8:188–204.
Schwyzer, Eduard. 1931. Drei griechische Wörter. *Rheinisches Museum* 80:213–17.
———. 1968. *Griechische Grammatik*. Munich.
Scodel, Ruth. 1989. The Word of Achilles. *Classical Philology* 84:91–99.
Seaford, Richard. 1994. *Reciprocity and Ritual: Homer and Tragedy in the Developing City-State*. Oxford.
Segal, Charles. 1968. The Embassy and the Duals of *Iliad* 9.182–98. *Greek Roman and Byzantine Studies* 9:101–14.
———. 1971a. *The Theme of the Mutilation of the Corpse in the Iliad*. Leiden.
———. 1971b. Nestor and the Honor of Achilles. *Studi Micenei ed Egeo-Anatolici* 13:90–105.
———. 1971c. Andromache's Anagnorisis. *Harvard Studies in Classical Philology* 75:33–57.
———. 1974. The Raw and the Cooked in Greek Literature: Structure, Values, Metaphor. *Classical Journal* 69:289–308.
———. 1994. *Singers, Heroes, and Gods in the Odyssey*. Ithaca.
Severyns, A. 1944–48. *Homère*. Vols. 1, 2, 3. Brussels.
Shannon, Richard. 1975. *The Arms of Achilles and Homeric Compositional Technique*. Leiden.
Sinos, Dale S. 1980. *Achilles, Patroklos, and the Meaning of Philos*. Innsbruck.
Slatkin, Laura M. 1986. The Wrath of Thetis. *Transactions of the American Philological Association* 116:1–24.
———. 1987. Genre and Generation in the Odyssey. ΜΗΤΙΣ 2.2:259–68.
———. 1988. Les amis mortels: A propos des insultes dans les combats de l'*Iliade*. *L 'Ecrit du Temps* 19: *Négations*. 119–32.
———. 1991. *The Power of Thetis: Allusion and Interpretation in the Iliad*. Berkeley, Calif.
Snell, B., and M. Meier-Brügger, eds. 1955–. *Lexicon des frühgriechischen epos*. Göttingen.
Solomon, Jon, ed. 1994. *Apollo: Origins and Influences*. Tucson, Ariz.
Starke, F. 1980. Keilschriftluwisch *mana-*⁽ⁱⁱ⁾ 'sehen', *mammanna-*ⁱ 'schauen'. *Kadmos* 19:142–48.
Svenbro, Jesper. 1988. *Phrasikleia: Anthropologie de la lecture en Grèce ancienne*. Paris.
Turpin, Jean-Claude. 1988. Un prétendu tabou linguistique de la langue épique: ΜΗΝΙΣ. In ΗΔΙΣΤΟΝ ΛΟΓΟΔΕΙΠΝΟΝ. *Logopédies: Mélanges de philologie et de linguistique grecques offerts à Jean Taillardat*, 247–60. Paris.
Usener, Hermann. 1903, repr. 1966. *Dreiheit: Ein Versuch mythologischer Zahlenlehre*. Hildesheim.
Van Brock, Nadia. 1959. Substitution rituelle. *Revue Hittite et Asianique* 65:117–46.
Van Nooten, Barend, and Gary B. Holland, eds. 1994. *Rig Veda. A Metrically Restored Text*. Cambridge, Mass.
Vernant, J.-P. 1963. *Annuaire de l'Ecole Pratique des Hautes Etudes*, 6th section, 142ff.
———. 1974. Le mythe prométhéen chez Hésiode. In *Mythe et société en Grèce ancienne*, 177–94. Paris.
———. 1985a. *Mythe et pensée chez les grecs: Études de psychologie historique*. 2d ed. Paris.

———. 1985b. Le mythe hésiodique des races: Essai d'analyse structurale. In *Mythe et pensée chez les Grecs*, 48–85. Paris.
———. 1989. La belle mort et le cadavre outragé. In *L'individu, la mort, l'amour: Soi-même et l'autre en Grèce ancienne*, 41–79. Paris.
Vidal-Naquet, Pierre. 1981. *Le chasseur noir: Formes de pensée et formes de société dans le monde grec*. Paris.
Wackernagel, Jacob. 1910. Indoiranica 9: Zum Dualdvandva. *Kuhns Zeitschrift* 43:295–98.
———. 1950. *Vorlesungen über Syntax mit besonderer Berücksichtigung von Griechisch, Lateinisch, und Deutsch*. 2d ed. Basel.
Wackernagel, Jacob, and Albert Debrunner. 1954. *Altindische Grammatik*. Vol. 2.2 Die Nominalsuffixe. Göttingen.
Walsh, Thomas. 1989. Kótos and Khólos: Studies in the Semantics of Anger in Homeric Poetry. Ph.D. diss., University of California–Berkeley. (forthcoming as a book).
Warden, J. 1971. ΨΥΧΗ in Homeric Death Descriptions. *Phoenix* 25:95–103.
Watkins, Calvert. 1977a. A propos de ΜΗΝΙΣ. *Bulletin de la Société de Linguistique de Paris* 72:187–209. Reprinted in *Selected Writings*, ed. L. Oliver. 1994. 556–87. Innsbruck.
———. 1977b. On Μῆνις. *Indo-European Studies* 3:686–722.
———. 1986. How to Kill a Dragon in Indo-European. In *Studies in Memory of Warren Cowgill (1929–1985)*, 270–99. Berlin.
———. 1986. The Name of Meleager. In *O-O-PE-RO-SI: Festschrift für E. Risch zum 75. Geburtstag*, edited by A. Etter, 320–28. Berlin.
———. 1995. *How to Kill a Dragon: Aspects of Indo-European Poetics*. Oxford.
Waugh, L. R. 1982. Marked and Unmarked: A Choice between Unequals in Semiotic Structure. *Semiotica* 38:299–318.
West, M. L., ed. 1966. *Hesiod. Theogony*. Oxford.
———, ed. with prolegomena and commentary. 1978. *Hesiod: Works & Days*. Oxford.
Westbrook, Raymond. 1992. The Trial Scene in the *Iliad*. *Harvard Studies in Classical Philology* 94:53–76.
Whitman, Cedric. 1958. *Homer and the Heroic Tradition*. Cambridge, Mass.
———. 1970. Hera's Anvils. *Harvard Studies in Classical Philology* 74:37–42.
Whitman, Cedric, and R. Scodel. Sequence and Simultaneity in *Iliad* N, Ξ, and O. *Harvard Studies in Classical Philology* 85:1–15.
Wikander, Stig. 1941. *Vayu: Texte und Untersuchungen zur indoiranischen Religionsgeschichte I*. Uppsala.
Zieliński, Thaddaeus. 1899–1901. Die Behandlung gleichzeitiger Ereignisse im antiken Epos. *Philologus Supplementband* 8:405–49.

# Index of Sources

Aeschylus
  *Prometheus Bound*
    235, 77; 755–81, 95; 907–27, 95
  *Agamemnon* 155, 186
Alcaeus
  fr. B6.7 (L-P), 84
Apollodorus 1.1.4, 65; 1.1.5, 76; 1.2.1, 73, 76; 1.20.3, 69
Apollonius of Rhodes
  *Argonautica* 4.800ff., 95
Archilochus
  fr. 129 (West), 138
Aristophanes
  *Birds*
    685–702, 91; 1633, 91
  *Clouds* 388, 69
  *Knights* 693, 69
  *Lysistrata* 974, 89
Aristotle
  *Magna Moralia*
    1213a11–13, 136
  *Rhetoric*
    1401b18–19, 34

Diogenes Laertius 7.23, 136

Euripides
  *Cyclops* 219, 69
  *Hippolytus* 146, 191; 1290, 57
Eustathius, *Commentary on Homer's Iliad*
    1. 13.10, 2

*Gāthās*
  Yasna 30.3–4, 178
  Yasna 45.2, 179

Herodotus
  1.140, 100
Hesiod
  fr. 30 (M-W), 37
  fr. 43a.36–57 (M-W), 84
  fr. 43a.58 (M-W), 84
  fr. 280.11 (M-W), 59
  fr. 287 (M-W), 62
  fr. 343.6 (M-W), 84
  fr. 343.8 (M-W), 83
  *Shield of Herakles*
    479, 97
  *Theogony*
    11–20, 55
    11–21, 54
    25, 54
    35, 56
    44, 95
    45–51, 54
    53, 56
    55, 42
    73–74, 28
    73, 74
    104, 56
    105, 95
    106–13, 60
    108–10, 60
    111, 28
    114, 97
    116, 55, 58
    117–22, 57
    124, 66
    125, 66
    132, 58
    137, 62

Hesiod, *Theogony* (cont.)
138, 60, 61
139–46, 76
154–210, 60–66
154–55, 60
154, 60
155, 61
156, 61
157, 61
158, 61
159–160, 61
164–65, 67
164–66, 62
165, 71
166, 61, 63, 74
174, 62
175, 62
176, 63
177–78, 63
178, 65
180–81, 63
180, 64, 74
183, 60
185, 67
190–200, 66
190–91, 64
205–6, 67
207–11, 66
208, 66
209, 65
210, 65, 67
211–12, 66
211, 65
217, 67
220–22, 67
220, 67
358, 71
421, 106
425–27, 106
426, 106
453–506, 22
459, 67–69
460, 69
462, 68
463, 70
466, 70
467, 69, 71
470, 70
472–73, 71
473, 69
474–97, 72–80
477–80, 73–74
481–86, 73
487, 69
488–91, 73

Hesiod, *Theogony* (cont.)
490, 74
492–97, 73
494, 74
496, 74
497, 69, 74
501–6, 76, 83
505, 79
507, 82
511–20, 82
513, 85
517, 82
520, 82
521–34, 82
521, 83–84
529, 83
534, 83–84, 87
535–36, 86
535, 6
541, 86
551, 85
552, 86
556, 87
563, 85, 87
566, 85
567, 85
570, 83, 85
571–72, 83
579–84, 83
585–615, 83
585, 83, 86
589, 83, 86
590–612, 83
599, 86
600–12, 79
600 ff., 71
613–15, 83
615–16, 82–84
617, 84
617 ff., 76
625–26, 77
626, 88
687, 90
708, 101
726–31, 77
807, 57
814, 55
820–68, 22
833–35, 89
845, 89
853, 90
869, 89
882, 86
885, 28
886–900, 22

Index of Sources    207

Hesiod, *Theogony* (cont.)
   890, 92
   900, 92
   921, 125
   924–29, 125
   927, 58
  *Works and Days*
   35, 6
   48, 85
   57, 83, 85
   81–82, 85
   85, 85
   128, 62
   240–47, 37
Homer
  *Cypria*
   fr. 3 (Allen), 165
  *Hymn to Aphrodite*
   36, 25
   48–52, 22
   48, 21
   55, 19
   126–27, 19
   151–54, 19
   151ff., 23
   286–90, 20
   286, 21
   288, 20
   290, 8, 20, 36, 193
  *Hymn to Apollo*
   428, 188
  *Hymn to Demeter*
   49–50, 23
   129, 23
   204, 127
   273, 127
   274, 127
   292, 127
   303–4, 23
   307, 23
   310–13, 24
   322, 24
   326, 24
   330, 24
   348–55, 24
   350, 8, 30
   367–68, 25
   368, 127
   410, 8, 30
  *Hymn to Hermes*
   13, 84
   253, 97
   439, 84
  *Iliad*
   1.1 (var.), 97

Homer, *Iliad* (cont.)
   1.1, 50
   1.2–4, 48
   1.3–4, 99
   1.3, 92
   1.4–5, 131
   1.5, 129
   1.9–11, 84
   1.11, 50, 97
   1.15, 98
   1.16, 98
   1.17–21, 98
   1.22–23, 50, 98
   1.24, 98
   1.42, 99
   1.50–53, 101
   1.51, 99
   1.52, 101
   1.55–56, 106
   1.55, 136
   1.64–65, 49
   1.75, 8, 50, 193
   1.76–83, 116
   1.81–2, 190
   1.91, 107
   1.98, 24
   1.100, 126
   1.102–20, 116
   1.112, 98
   1.113, 98
   1.118–20, 50
   1.119–20, 50
   1.122–29, 104
   1.125, 30
   1.126, 104
   1.134, 105
   1.135–36, 105
   1.144–47, 105
   1.146, 104
   1.147, 126
   1.150–51, 106
   1.155, 142
   1.156–57, 106
   1.159, 106, 142
   1.161, 106
   1.162, 98, 107
   1.163, 106
   1.166–67, 50
   1.166, 30, 33, 106
   1.167, 106
   1.171, 50, 106
   1.175, 50, 108, 149
   1.177, 108
   1.178, 108
   1.179–80, 110

Homer, *Iliad* (cont.)
   1.182–84, 108
   1.182–87, 109
   1.185–86, 50
   1.186–87, 30
   1.186, 29
   1.192, 112
   1.197, 97
   1.207, 112
   1.208–9, 106
   1.218, 112
   1.229–31, 107
   1.233–44, 41
   1.237–39, 35
   1.238–39, 36, 107
   1.240–41, 137, 165
   1.240–44, 107
   1.240, 138
   1.244, 134
   1.247, 8, 30, 50, 106
   1.258, 110
   1.259–60, 111
   1.275, 24
   1.276, 98
   1.280–81, 108, 110
   1.280, 111
   1.282–84, 111
   1.292, 113
   1.293–303, 30
   1.294, 114
   1.296, 115
   1.297–303, 113
   1.299, 98
   1.304, 112
   1.305, 116
   1.307, 116
   1.327, 116
   1.331–32, 116
   1.333, 116
   1.335, 116
   1.337, 24
   1.340–44, 117
   1.343, 46, 110
   1.348, 24
   1.366, 139
   1.367–69, 98
   1.386, 126
   1.391–92, 50
   1.393, 118
   1.396–407, 119
   1.397–405, 81
   1.398, 120
   1.408–10, 37
   1.408–12, 119
   1.412, 145

Homer, *Iliad* (cont.)
   1.421–22, 122
   1.422, 106
   1.444, 126
   1.454, 100
   1.471–74, 128
   1.472–74, 139
   1.472, 126
   1.488–92, 123, 138
   1.488, 30, 106
   1.492, 138
   1.505–6, 123
   1.509–10, 124
   1.511–12, 124
   1.516, 124
   1.518, 124
   1.524–30, 124
   1.540–43, 124
   1.547–50, 124
   1.558–59, 124
   1.565–67, 124
   1.569, 144
   1.580–83, 126
   1.588–89, 127
   1.603–4, 128, 139
   2.46, 166
   2.123–28, 58
   2.185–86, 108
   2.197, 149
   2.371–72, 102
   2.484, 97
   2.550, 126, 132
   3.20, 112
   3.98, 6
   3.102, 6
   3.139, 164
   3.360, 13
   3.431, 173
   4.23, 97
   4.409, 44
   4.422–39, 10
   5.31, 10, 15, 16
   5.34, 8, 30, 193
   5.35, 10
   5.113, 145
   5.121–32, 10
   5.127–28, 13
   5.130–32, 13
   5.174–78, 49
   5.177, 50
   5.178, 8, 193
   5.311–18, 11
   5.325–326, 149
   5.356, 10
   5.385ff., 77

Index of Sources    209

Homer, *Iliad* (cont.)
   5.431ff., 13
   5.438, 12
   5.440–44, 13
   5.441, 15
   5.444, 8, 30
   5.455, 11, 15–16
   5.456, 11
   5.457, 13
   5.459, 13
   5.757–66, 11
   5.761, 11, 35, 46
   5.762–63, 12
   5.762, 11
   5.844, 16
   5.884, 12
   6.209, 157
   6.354–58, 175
   6.380, 126
   6.385, 126
   6.407ff., 90
   6.429–31, 156
   6.432, 156
   6.441–46, 156
   7.75, 137
   7.132–35, 102
   7.153, 62
   7.254, 13
   8.5, 5
   8.10–18, 137
   8.17, 6
   8.22, 137
   8.27, 137
   8.217, 101
   8.235, 101
   8.281, 92
   8.460, 97
   8.470, 137
   9.18, 145
   9.61, 158
   9.69–74, 110
   9.93, 143
   9.97–99, 36
   9.97, 35, 110
   9.110, 110
   9.115–16, 145
   9.116–18, 149
   9.120, 154
   9.158–61, 141
   9.160–61, 111
   9.161, 29
   9.168–70, 139
   9.179–81, 143
   9.186–90, 138
   9.196, 139

Homer, *Iliad* (cont.)
   9.197, 139
   9.198, 139
   9.204, 139
   9.214, 139
   9.251, 139
   9.256–58, 139
   9.300–303, 140
   9.301–3, 148
   9.308–429, 142
   9.312–13, 143
   9.317–20, 142
   9.325–27, 142
   9.328–35, 142
   9.339–40, 142
   9.341–42, 142
   9.343, 144
   9.359–61, 142
   9.364–65, 141
   9.372–73, 142
   9.378, 142
   9.393–400, 141
   9.401, 34
   9.406–9, 34, 155
   9.408–9, 142
   9.410–16, 151, 154
   9.415, 142
   9.423–25, 143
   9.426, 193
   9.427–29, 143, 150
   9.430–32, 139
   9.450, 149
   9.451, 147
   9.481, 144
   9.486, 144
   9.494–95, 144
   9.495, 158
   9.497–501, 144
   9.514, 144
   9.515–22, 146
   9.517, 146, 187, 193
   9.524–25, 157
   9.524–26, 146
   9.528, 146
   9.548, 147
   9.555, 148
   9.556–57, 147
   9.566–72, 147
   9.567, 147
   9.574–85, 147
   9.574, 147
   9.581, 147
   9.585–87, 153
   9.585, 147
   9.586, 147

Homer, *Iliad* (cont.)
9.591–94, 157
9.591, 147
9.592–94, 147
9.592, 164
9.597–605, 148
9.604–5, 154
9.607–10, 149
9.608–10, 150
9.612–16, 150
9.613–15, 164
9.618–19, 150
9.625, 151
9.628–32, 151
9.632–36, 170
9.633–35, 152
9.633, 153
9.635, 126
9.636–42, 152
9.637–38, 153
9.645, 153
9.649, 153, 156
9.650–53, 159
9.650–55, 135, 153
9.657, 156
9.658–59, 150
9.677–94, 155
11.55, 92
11.174, 188
11.218, 97
11.295, 12
11.297, 12
11.406, 12
11.746, 12
11.799–801, 135
12.40, 12
12.130, 12
12.135, 173
12.280, 101
12.345, 188
12.358, 188
13.244, 168
13.434–37, 77
13.624, 8, 49, 193
13.624ff., 37, 47
13.802, 12
14.95, 35
14.198, 164
14.238ff., 166
14.308, 64
14.508, 97
15.22–24, 5
15.53–67, 159
15.63–64, 159
15.87–103, 35

Homer, *Iliad* (cont.)
15.94, 6
15.117, 6
15.122, 97
15.123, 6
15.127, 126
15.129, 46
15.137–38, 7
15.161, 29
15.163–66, 29
15.163–67, 109
15.164, 110
15.166, 111
15.167, 29
15.177, 29
15.179–84, 29
15.183, 29
15.186–93, 29
15.186, 29, 114
15.189, 29, 30
15.195, 110
15.197–99, 29
15.198–99, 104
15.198, 112
15.203, 144
15.209–11, 114
15.209, 30
15.211–19, 115
15.217, 30, 115
15.218, 30
15.349, 149
15.385–87, 35
15.744, 101
16.52, 30
16.53, 30
16.60–63, 159
16.60–65, 158
16.61–63, 135
16.62, 193
16.63, 135
16.83, 161
16.84–90, 159
16.84–96, 14
16.91–96, 160
16.95–100, 162
16.97, 102
16.112, 97
16.114–29, 159
16.119–26, 135
16.121–29, 135
16.140–44, 165
16.202, 193
16.240–48, 14
16.242–43, 135
16.269–74, 134

Homer, *Iliad* (cont.)
    16.270, 134
    16.271–72, 134
    16.274, 145
    16.278–83, 135
    16.385–92, 36–37
    16.387–88, 35
    16.423, 136
    16.460, 149
    16.461, 142
    16.543, 136
    16.685, 14, 145
    16.698–704, 14
    16.705–11, 14
    16.705, 12
    16.711, 8, 30
    16.784–87, 16
    16.786, 12
    16.787, 160
    16.791, 16
    16.796–99, 17
    16.805, 145
    16.816, 16
    17.57, 149
    17.155, 188
    17.194–97, 166
    17.194, 166
    17.202, 166
    17.244, 188
    18.8, 164
    18.22ff., 161
    18.53, 164
    18.81ff., 149
    18.84–85, 166
    18.84–96, 162
    18.89–93, 164
    18.98–99, 161
    18.98–126, 145
    18.101–3, 162
    18.102–3, 161
    18.108–10, 161
    18.114–15, 161
    18.114–26, 164
    18.114, 92
    18.121, 161
    18.205–6, 167
    18.214, 167
    18.215–16, 168
    18.219, 168
    18.221, 168
    18.225–27, 167
    18.315–16, 164
    18.322, 97
    18.336–37, 164
    18.346, 101

Homer, *Iliad* (cont.)
    18.354–55, 164
    18.369–70, 166
    18.372–77, 126
    18.429–41, 174
    18.446, 138
    18.449–50, 159
    18.453, 15
    18.497–508, 154–55
    18.499, 154
    19.35, 193
    19.47–52, 142
    19.51–52, 142
    19.55, 142
    19.62, 193
    19.78–144, 142
    19.83–84, 142
    19.83, 149
    19.86–144, 192
    19.88, 145
    19.89, 142
    19.146, 142
    19.151–52, 165
    19.173–74, 141
    19.178, 126
    19.188, 142
    19.199, 142
    19.249, 141
    19.278–79, 141
    20.46, 12
    20.50, 12
    20.248, 145
    20.281, 13
    20.447, 12
    20.493, 12
    21.18, 12
    21.31, 145
    21.99, 163
    21.106–13, 163
    21.178, 144
    21.227, 12
    21.324–82, 167
    21.367, 126
    21.402, 16
    21.441–57, 169
    21.462–77, 169
    21.520–25, 168
    21.521–25, 48
    22.98ff., 161
    22.104, 44
    22.132, 12
    22.193–201, 89
    22.285, 13
    22.355ff., 33
    22.358, 8

## Index of Sources

Homer, *Iliad (cont.)*
  22.374, 101
  22.512, 101
  23.14, 164
  23.71ff., 32
  23.108, 164
  23.133, 100
  23.153, 164
  23.160, 97
  23.185–91, 169
  24.18–21, 169
  24.25–30, 169
  24.29, 169
  24.29–30, 171
  24.39–48, 170
  24.40–41, 145
  24.46–47, 153
  24.48, 171
  24.62, 171
  24.66ff., 149
  24.128–32, 171
  24.134–37, 171
  24.139–40, 172
  24.155–58, 172–73
  24.227, 164
  24.391–95, 159
  24.487–92, 174
  24.504–6, 174
  24.505, 173
  24.507, 164
  24.509–12, 174
  24.519–21, 174
  24.543–47, 174
  24.553–58, 173
  24.563–70, 175
  24.569–70, 173
  24.582–86, 173
  24.621–27, 175
  24.645–55, 173
  24.675–76, 175
  24.686–88, 173
  24.856, 142
*Odyssey*
  1.1, 84
  1.7, 41, 43
  1.58, 84
  1.197, 47
  1.235, 61
  1.242, 61
  1.320–21, 188
  1.320–22, 47
  1.587, 127
  2.64–69, 40
  2.66, 8, 193
  2.68–69, 35

Homer, *Odyssey (cont.)*
  3.89–91, 45
  3.132–36, 46–47
  3.135, 39, 41, 45, 193
  3.136, 45
  3.137–45, 46
  3.145, 41
  3.161, 45
  3.267–68, 99
  3.270–1, 99
  3.419, 127
  4.225–26, 42
  4.227, 73
  5.99, 20
  5.104–5, 21
  5.118, 20
  5.119–20, 18
  5.119, 20
  5.124, 18
  5.127–28, 21
  5.128, 18
  5.137–39, 21
  5.145–46, 18
  5.146, 8, 19, 193
  7.256, 173
  8.309, 149
  8.76, 34
  9.215, 170
  9.220, 86
  10.30, 84
  10.37, 149
  10.70, 126
  10.437, 4
  11.73, 8, 32
  11.489ff., 32
  12.246, 173
  13.254ff., 143
  14.56–58, 38
  14.62, 173
  14.82, 40
  14.83–84, 149
  14.156–64, 40
  14.283–84, 40
  14.283, 8, 36, 193
  15.305, 173
  15.543, 149, 173
  16.378, 40
  17.10–15, 39
  17.14, 8
  17.56, 149, 173
  17.111, 173
  17.455, 139
  18.139, 170
  18.141, 170
  18.346–404, 39

Homer, *Odyssey* (cont.)
    19.195, 173
    20.98, 64
    20.215, 40
    21.315, 173
    21.373, 173
    22.171–77, 43
    22.310–29, 43
    22.330–60, 43
    22.441–73, 43
    22.474–77, 43
    22.481, 41
    24.76–77, 160
    24.199–202, 99
    24.272, 173
    24.393, 126
    24.458, 41
    24.470–71, 41
    24.478–80, 42
    24.482, 42
    24.485, 42
    24.528, 42
    24.544, 42
    24.545, 43
Hyginus
    *Fabulae*
        94, 22

Ovid
    *Fasti* 3.796–808, 80

Pindar
    *Isthmian* 8.27–55, 95
    *Nemean* 2.1–3, 52
    *Pythian* 1.12, 97; 1.27, 77
Plato
    *Euthyphro* 6a2, 69
    *Ion* 531a, 52
Proclus
    *Chrestomathia* 2, 15; 104.21–24, 34

*Rig Veda*
    1.80.11, 184

*Rig Veda* (cont.)
    1.104.2, 182
    1.109.7, 181
    1.139.2, 183
    2.24.14, 183
    3.23.12, 182
    4.17.2, 184
    4.17.10, 185
    5.6.10, 182
    6.16.43, 184
    6.17.9, 184
    6.25.2, 182
    7.18.16, 182
    7.25.1, 180
    7.36.4, 183
    7.60.11, 182
    7.61.1, 182
    7.78.6, 182
    8.6.13, 184
    8.19.15, 182
    8.36.4, 182
    8.71.2, 182
    8.84.4, 183
    10.52.5, 181
    10.83.1–4, 180–81
    10.83.4, 184
    10.83, 180, 184
    10.84, 180
    10.112.8, 185
    10.147.1, 185
    10.152.5, 182

Sappho
    fr. 16.18 (L-P), 90; fr. 44 (L-P), 43
Servius
    On *Aeneid* 1.617, 22
    On *Aeneid* 2.649, 22
Sophocles
    fr. 373, 22
Strabo 13, p. 604, 99

Theognis 680, 69

# Index of Subjects

Achilles
  his alienation, 39, 123, 136–38, 142, 152–53, 164
  vs. Apollo (see ritual antagonism of god and hero)
  his death, 163
  his fusion with Patroklos, 160
  and the human condition, 174–175
  like *mênis*, 48
  vs. Odysseus, 130, 139, 143
  his panoplies, 166
  vs. Poseidon, 116
  and the rules of exchange, 106
  his social conscience, 116, 118, 140
  his social status, 104,107,112–14,142,163,171
  his solidarity with gods, 114
  and third person address, 151, 165
  and value (see value)
acronym, 139
Aeneas, 19, 49
*aéptous* (or *aáptous*), 124
*Aethiopis*, 160
aetiology, 87
Agamemnon
  his apology, 142
  his *mênis* vs. Achilles', 102–129
  his social status, 104–6, 111, 120
  his solidarity, 98, 103, 140, 149
  his sovereignty, 110
  and third person address, 165
*aganós*, 18
Agni, 180–81, 183
Ajax, 175
*akēdḗs*, 174

Alexiou, M., 70
alienation, 24, 39, 123, 137
Ameis, C., 33
Anchises and Aphrodite
  sexual transgression, 19–22
Andromache, 90, 156
  meaning of her name, 157
anthropology of emotions, 1, 4
Aphrodite
  birth of, 64
  See also Athena; Hephaistos
*áphthitos*, 166
Apollo
  and cosmic boundaries, 13–14, 23, 146
  his *mênis* and the *mênis* of Zeus, 96, 102
  Smintheus, 99–100
appeasement of *mênis*
  by poetry, 128, 132, 138, 139
Archilochus, 138
Ares, incurring *mênis*, 7–8, 10
Aristarchus, 2, 43
*aristeía*, 12
Aristoxenus, his prologue to the *Iliad*, 97
arrows, 20
  See also *kḗla*; thunderbolt
ascending scale of affection, 147, 156
Askalaphos, 10
*atasthalíai*, 41–44, 67
Athena
  vs. Aphrodite, 92–93
  her *mênis*, 39, 41, 45–47
  her virginity, 92
Auerbach, E., 81, 118
Austin, N., 81, 118

Index of Subjects 215

Basileía, 91
Beck, W., 3
beggars, 37–38
Benveniste, E., 35, 51, 82–83, 89, 108, 134, 137, 158, 184–85, 189
best of the Achaeans, 107–8, 121, 134, 161, 166
bíē, 121, 123, 129, 130, 173
binding, 7, 23, 77, 78, 82–84, 120
blood ties
  vs. ties of friendship, 147–48, 151, 153
book divisions, Homeric, 128
Bremmer, J., 146
Briseis, 30, 108, 109, 111, 114, 116, 138–39, 141–42
Buck, C. D., 188
Burkert, W., 27, 131, 192
Buse, H., 76
Bussanich, J., 55

Caesar, Julius, 137
castration of Ouranos/Sky
  as cosmic event, 68, 78
  metonymic logic of, 64–65, 78
catalog, as narrative, 56, 59
Chantraine, P., 16, 37, 62, 82, 84, 101–2, 124, 158, 188
Chaos, 55, 57, 68
Chirassi Colombo, I., 103
Clark, J. R., 34
Clay, J. S., 13, 47, 94, 131, 170
Clytemnestra, 99
conflict
  between generations, 61
  within generations, 71, 119
Considine, P., 3, 178, 187–89
corporate kin structure, 27
cosmic boundaries, 17, 19
cosmic hierarchy, enforced by *ménis*, 5–31
cosmic sanction, 39, 129, 145
counting (without zero), 55
craft
  *See* cunning
creation, of procreation, 58
cross-reference, in epic, 159
Cuillandre, J., 159
cunning, 70
  as creation, 61, 62
  and force, 73, 75–76, 81, 91, 93, 110, 121, 129–30, 167
  and mortal women, 86
  not a group trait, 87
  and the rule of metonymy, 93
Cyclopes, 76–79, 88, 92
  Thegonic vs. Odyssean, 79

daímonitsos, 12–16, 22
Dares, 10
dasmós, 30, 33, 106, 142
death, 172
  as demotion in cosmic hierarchy, 32
  and hiding, 61
  of immortals, 61, 77, 120, 127
Debrunner, A., 178
dédastai, 29, 30
Delphic Theoxenia, 34
Demeter, 23–24, 28, 39, 123, 127, 136
Denniston, J. D., 158
Detienne, M., 7, 33, 62, 65, 67, 70, 73, 76–78, 83, 88, 92, 139, 141, 171
diakridón, 6, 86
díkaios, 46
divine anger/wrath, 190
division
  cosmic, 29, 30, 33–34
  sacrificial, 33–34
  *See also* dasmós
Dodds, E. R., 192
Douglas, M., 26, 27, 32, 44, 131, 154
Duchesne-Guillemin, J., 179
Dumézil, G., 26, 95, 104, 130, 179, 180–82

Earth, 56, 57
Ebeling, H., 2
Edwards, M., 167
Eetion, 139
ekpaglós, 104, 112
Ēlúsion pedíon, 132
émēse, 63–64, 74–75
emotions
  guilt, 161
  social terms for, 149, 164
  universality of, 1, 133, 161
endukéōs, 173
epignámptō, 144
episode, definition of, 54
Erechtheus, 126–127, 131–132
erīnús, 71
Eros, 56–58
Evans-Pritchard, E. E., 27
exchange rules, 36–37, 40, 47, 49–51, 98, 112–13, 141–42, 174
  negative gifts, 85
  returning a gift to its giver, 114–15
  and value of wife, 99
  *See also* value
exémēse, 74, 75

Fenik, B., 10, 12
Foley, J. M., 54

## Index of Subjects

food, 23
  salted, 139
  sex, and death, 171
Frame, D., 43, 117, 143
Friedländer, P., 62
Frisk, H., 62, 101–2, 178, 188
funeral ritual, and *mênis*, 32–33, 145

Gaia, 56
Geldner, H., 181
*géras*, 33, 103–6, 108, 124
goods
  movable vs. immovable, 51
  two-footed and four-footed, 100
grief
  *See kêdea; kêdos*
guilt, 145, 161

Hamilton, R., 54, 60
Hector, 90, 156, 171, 173
Helen, 175
Helen, abduction of, 37, 49
Hentze, C., 33
Hephaistos, 127
  vs. Athena, 125–26, 167
  his birth, 125
  his metaphorical children, 126
Herakles, 130
Hermes, 84
heroes with *mênis*, incurring it, 121, 127, 131, 145
hiding, 61–62, 69
*hikétēs*, 173
*hílaos*, 126–27, 152
*hilássō*, 126–27
Holland, G., 181
Holway, R., 46, 122
*hoplótatos*, 60
hospitality rules
  *See* exchange rules
Householder, F., 167
Howald, E., 156
Hundred-Handers, 76–78, 88, 92

*Iliad*
  vs. *Odyssey*, 41, 47, 130
  sequel to *Theogony*, 95–131, 121, 124
  vs. *Theogony*, 26
impossible wish, 162
indiscriminate punishment, 5, 7, 107, 124, 137
Indo-European society
  tripartite ideology, 26, 120, 180–81
Indra, 181
initiate, instruction of, 62, 74
Insler, S., 178–79

*íps*, 100
Ithaca, etymology of, 84
Ithas-Ithax/Prometheus, 84

Jacopin, P.-Y., 27, 53, 55
Jakobson, R., 75
Janko, R., 158

Kakridis, J., 146, 148, 153, 156
*karnós*, 99
*karterós* (= *kraterós*), 109–10, 112
*katalégō*, 59
*katapínō*, 69
*katháptō*, 126
Katz, M., 99
*kêdea*, 147, 164, 174, 175
*kêdein*, 164
*kêdistos*, 164
*kêdos*, 163
*kêla*, 101
*kephalê*, 92
Ker, 66
Keres, 67
*khólos*, 7, 30, 41, 83–84, 111–12, 115, 146, 153, 186, 190, 192
kingship
  of Kronos, 68, 82
  of Ouranos/Sky, 68, 82
  of Zeus, 81–82
*kléa andrôn*, 95, 146
Kleopatre, 147, 164
  meaning of her name, 156–57
  vs. Patroklos, 156
*kléos*, 130, 154–55, 161
  vs. *tīmê*, 162
Koller, H., 52
*kótos*, 2, 190
Kövecses, Z., 1
*krínomai*, 86
Krischer, T., 12, 78
Kronos, 60, 62–63, 65, 69–71, 80
  vs. Rhea, 69
Kullmann, W., 160
*kunôpa*, 142
Kuryłowicz, J., 191

Lakoff, G., 1
lameness, 22, 127
Lang, M., 26
Latacz, J., 1
Lattimore, R., 158
Lawson, J. C., 56
Leonteus, 12
Lévi-Strauss, C., 53
Litai, 147

## Index of Subjects

Lloyd-Jones, H., 35
logic, metonymic
    *See* syntax of myth, metonymy of episodes
Lohmann, D., 104
*loígia érga*, 124
*loigós*, 103, 117, 119, 126, 144, 158
Loraux, N., 23–25, 33
Lord, A., 3, 8–9, 133, 139
Lowenstam, S., 6, 9, 15, 17, 30, 60, 108, 134, 160
Lynn-George, M., 81

*mainiiu-* (Avestan), 177–79, 185
    cosmogonic, 178
    twin conflicting spirits, 178
Malamoud, C., 179–85
Manyu, 180, 181
*manyú-* (Vedic), 177–86
    and Agni, 182
    and cosmogony, 184–85
    and fire, 181
    and humans, 182
    and Indo-European three functions, 181
    and Indra, 182–83
    and *ménis*, 185
Martin, R., 9, 64, 104, 112, 129, 151, 174
Mauss, M., 35, 37, 51, 98, 141
Mayrhofer, M., 178, 188
*médea*, 63
Meier-Brügger, M., 3, 18, 179
Meillet, A., 177, 188
Mekone, 6, 85–86
Meleagros, 146–54, 159, 164
*\*men-*, root, 177, 185
*ménis*
    definition, 8, 26, 50, 129, 138
    etymology of, 177–94
*mēnithmós*, 175, 186, 192
*ménos*, 111–112, 127, 186, 192
*mḗsato*, 63–64, 74–75
metaphor
    Achilles' shield, 167
    of fire from Achilles' head, 167
    immortal armor as, 166
    immortality, 166
    *ménis* as, 166, 168
method
    analysis of themes (*see* theme)
    Homeric textual variants, 97
    myth analysis (*see* syntax of myth)
    relation of epic world to real world, 51, 59, 61
Metis, 91–92, 125, 130
*mḗtis*, 62, 71, 80, 91, 125, 129–30, 143
    and *nóos*, 117, 143
metonymy, 60, 173

and aetiology, 87
and learning, 79, 91
of mythical episodes (*see* syntax of myth, metonymy of episodes)
of Prometheus, 83
verbal, 64, 74, 90
*miaiphóne*, 11, 16
middle, deposit of gifts in, 141
Moirai, 67
Mondi, R., 55
morality
    vs. world maintenance, 34, 44–45
Moros, 66
Morris, W., 190
mortal men
    vs. mortal women, 86
    vs. Zeus, 79, 85–87
Motto, A. L., 34
Muellner, L., 33, 40, 55, 108, 111, 118, 136, 139, 148, 154, 173, 192, 194
multiformity, 9, 22, 31, 97, 120, 146
    *See also* theme
*mûthos*, 151, 161
myth
    and reality, 51
    syntax of (*see* syntax of myth)

Nagler, M., 3, 41, 60
Nagy, G., 3, 9, 12, 22–23, 26, 33–34, 36, 43, 45, 47, 48, 52, 54–55, 58, 70, 75, 84–87, 89–90, 95, 98, 99–100, 102–4, 108, 117–18, 127, 129–32, 134, 138–39, 143–45, 155–56, 159, 161, 166–67, 173, 181–82, 188
Napoleon, 137
narrative
    genealogy of, 66
*nēdús*, 69–70, 75, 92
Nestor, 110–113, 175
Nilsson, M., 99, 100
nominalism, metonymic, 66–68, 71, 74, 80, 94–95
*nóos*
    of Zeus, 20, 25
    *See also* *mêtis*
*nóstos*, 43, 46, 130, 148, 154

oak and rock, 55
offenses, that incur *ménis*, 8, 129
Oineus, 147
ontogeny of epic, 95, 122
*ópis*, 36, 40, 67, 186, 192
*opízomai*, 187
*hoplótatos*, 60

Parker, R., 26
*párnops*, 99

## Index of Subjects

Parry, M. 3, 60
Patroklos
  as Achilles' stand-in, 16, 134, 136, 158, 159, 175
  approaching the wall, 15
  meaning of his death, 17, 131, 134, 145
  meaning of his name, 156–57
  his *philótēs*, 160
Peleus and Thetis, marriage of, 95–96, 121–22, 132, 166, 171
*pénthos álaston*, 70–71
performance
  of *Iliad*, 132
  of *Theogony*, 52
Persephone, 127
Pestalozzi, H., 160
Pestina, 100
Petegorsky, D., 9
*phérteros*, 109–10, 112
*phíloi*, 134, 139, 148
*philokteanótate*, 104
*philophrosúnē*, 139–40, 144, 155
*phílos*, 63
  definition, 136
  vs. *ekhthrós*, 61, 63, 140
*philótēs*, 41, 139–40, 144, 151, 154, 157, 162, 171, 173
  vs. *ekhthrḗ*, 61, 63, 140
  vs. Eros, 58
  extended definition of, 174
  vs. *mēnis*, 135–75
  vs. *tīmḗ*, 149–50
*phíltatoi*, 146
Phoenix, 143–44, 146, 148, 150, 153, 158
Phthia, 142
*phûla theôn*, 24, 29, 39
*phûlon hómoion*, 23
\**pleg*-, root, 11–12, 16–17, 29, 104
*poinḗ*, 152–53
  vs. *ápoina*, 154
Poseidon, 5, 6, 27–31, 33, 35, 50, 71, 109–11, 113–16, 169
potlatch, 141
Pötscher, W., 167
Priam, 173
procreation, creation of, 58
Prometheus, 120
  as herald, 84
*prooímion*, 52, 54, 65, 95, 96
Protesilaos, 159
*psūkhḗ*, 34, 155

Rabel, R. J., 103
reciprocity
  *See* exchange rules
Redfield, J., 3, 9, 158, 191

Renou, L., 89, 178, 181, 183–85
Rhea, 73
Richardson, N., 25
Rimbaud, A., 108, 137
Risch, E., 82
ritual antagonism of god and hero
  Apollo and Achilles, 96, 103, 107, 117, 146, 160, 169–70
  Apollo and Patroklos, 16
  Ares and Diomedes, 12, 18
  Athena and Odysseus, 131
  Zeus and Achilles (latent), 46, 96, 120, 166, 171, 175

Sahlins, M., 35, 103
Salmoneus, 37
salt, 139
Sandoz, C., 190, 192–93
Sarpedon, 136
Schadewaldt, W., 6, 160
Schmidt, J. J., 2
Schmitt, R., 100
Schwabl, H., 60
Schwartz, M., 134
Schwyzer, E., 186–87
Scodel, R., 158
sea, as sterile, 64
Seaford, R., 51
Segal, C., 19, 110, 145, 169, 171
sequence in performance, 53–54
  explicit attention to, 59
  from one myth to next, 45, 52, 94
sex, 172, 175
sexual difference, 64–65, 70, 75, 79, 83, 86–87
sexual transgression, 18, 25, 166
Shannon, R., 165
Shield of Achilles, 153–54
Sinos, D., 15, 134, 161
Sky, 64
Slatkin, L., 45, 46, 52, 66, 95, 119, 121–22, 140
*smínthos*, 99
Snell, B., 3
snub, of Achilles and Odysseus, 155
social status, 50
solidarity, 7, 17, 20, 25, 27, 36–37, 42, 65, 71, 136
  *Iliad* vs. *Odyssey*, 43–45
Starke, F., 36, 188
Stewart, C., 1
*streptós*, 144
structure
  of *Iliad* 1, 128
  of *Theogony*, 60
Svenbro, J., 33
syntax of myth, 53
  beginning, 56, 66, 118

Index of Subjects    219

and digressions, 81
from one myth to next, 55, 94, 121, 133
irreversibility, 87
like a train, 78
metonymy of episodes, 54, 57–59, 63, 65–67, 70, 73, 79, 87–88, 92, 143, 155, 169
and problem solving, 78
recapitulation, 73–74, 118, 143
teleology, 54–56, 66–67, 73, 78, 81, 86, 91, 93, 132–33, 136, 154, 161, 171, 175

tabu, 8, 31, 47, 49, 124, 129, 145, 174, 188–194
  deformation, 189–90
  derivatives of tabu words, 192
  vs. morality, 27–28
  power and danger of violation, 26, 32, 131, 154, 169, 172
  and reticence, 193–94
Tartarus, 56
*teikhesiplḗta*, 11, 15–16
Telemachus, 39–42, 47
teleology, 41, 54, 56, 66–67, 73, 78, 81, 86, 91, 93, 132
  of *ménis*, 136
  of *Theogony*, 55
theme, 3, 8, 31, 60, 71, 133, 146–47
  implied associations, 15
  lost associations, 160
Themis, 7, 11, 40, 53
*thémis*, 11, 17, 35–39, 46, 106, 169, 170, 173
*thémistes*, 35, 50–51, 106–8, 170
*Theogony*
  vs. *Iliad*, 94, 121, 170
  sequels to, 119, 121, 170
  structure of, 60
*theōn génos*, 95
*therápōn*, 15, 134, 160
Thetis, 119–25, 128, 132, 171
  and *kḗdea*, 174
third person, 136, 191
  address, 151, 152
  and Agamemnon, 142
  and *philótēs*, 138
  vs. second person address, 153, 160
  self-reference, 108, 137, 165
three (group counting), 13, 16
thunderbolt, 6–7, 18, 20, 22–23, 28, 37, 79, 82–83, 88, 123, 127, 129, 132, 168, 185
  arrow analogue, 20, 101–2
  of Indra, 183
  and sulfur, 41
  sword analogue, 35
*tīmḗ*, 28–29, 38, 50, 68, 97, 108, 123, 148, 159, 161
  vs. *kléos*, 162
  vs. *philótēs*, 149–50
*tísis*, 65

Titans, 65, 77–78, 88, 120
total social phenomenon, 36, 98
tragic error, 158, 161
transgression, social function of, 27
tripartite
  *See* Indo-European society
Turpin, J.-C., 3, 38, 189–91
Typhoeus, 120
  as Anti-Zeus, 89

value, 51
  exchange value, 34, 98, 155
  of life's breath, 34
Van Brock, N., 17, 160
van Nooten, B., 181
Vāyu, 12, 177, 179
Vernant, J.-P., 7, 35, 55–56, 62, 65–67, 70, 73, 76–78, 82–83, 88, 92, 169, 171
Vidal-Naquet, P., 62
Vine, B., 188

Wackernagel, J., 35, 100, 178
Walsh, T., 3, 7, 45, 111
Watkins, C., 3, 9, 36, 38, 40, 129, 135, 146, 183, 186–87, 192–93
Waugh, L. R., 75
West, M. L., 37, 55–56, 58, 62, 65, 73–74, 76–78, 89, 102
Westbrook, R., 154
Whitman, C., 33, 136, 140, 158, 171
Wikander, S., 179

Xenophon, 137
*xénos*, 38–40

Zarathustra, 178
zero, concept of, 56–57, 68, 77
Zeus
  vs. Achilles, 46
  his androgyny, 87, 92–93
  and Athena, 46
  vs. great heroes, 130
  vs. Hephaistos, 126–27
  instability of his authority, 80, 94
  vs. Kronos, 73
  vs. mortals, 83
  his *ménos*, 90
  vs. Poseidon, 29, 115
  post-Theogonic challenges to his authority, 80, 91
  vs. Prometheus, 82
  his successor, 91
  vs. Titans, 87
  vs. Typhoeus, 88–91
  Xenios, 37, 47–48
Zieliński's law, 78

# MYTH AND POETICS

A series edited by

GREGORY NAGY

*Helen of Troy and Her Shameless Phantom*
by Norman Austin
*The Craft of Poetic Speech in Ancient Greece*
by Claude Calame
translated by Janice Orion
*Masks of Dionysus*
edited by Thomas W. Carpenter and Christopher A. Faraone
*The Odyssey in Athens: Myths of Cultural Origins*
by Erwin F. Cook
*The Poetics of Supplication: Homer's* Iliad *and* Odyssey
by Kevin Crotty
*Poet and Hero in the Persian Book of Kings*
by Olga M. Davidson
*Play of Genres: A Folk Poetics of Middle India*
by Joyce Flueckiger
*The Ravenous Hyenas and the Wounded Sun: Myth and Ritual in Ancient India*
by Stephanie W. Jamison
*Poetry and Prophecy: The Beginnings of a Literary Tradition*
edited by James Kugel
*The Traffic in Praise: Pindar and the Poetics of Social Economy*
by Leslie Kurke
*Topographies of Hellenism: Mapping the Homeland*
by Artemis Leontis
*Epic Singers and Oral Tradition*
by Albert Bates Lord
*The Singer Resumes the Tale*
by Albert Bates Lord, edited by Mary Louise Lord
*The Language of Heroes: Speech and Performance in the* Iliad
by Richard P. Martin
*Heroic Sagas and Ballads*
by Stephen A. Mitchell
*The Anger of Achilles: Mênis in Greek Epic*
by Leonard Muellner

*Greek Mythology and Poetics*
by Gregory Nagy
*Myth and the Polis*
edited by Dora C. Pozzi and John M. Wickersham
*Knowing Words: Wisdom and Cunning in the Classical Traditions of China and Greece*
by Lisa Raphals
*Heroic Poets, Poetic Heroes: The Ethnography of Performance in an Arabic Oral Epic Tradition*
by Dwight Fletcher Reynolds
*Homer and the Sacred City*
by Stephen Scully
*Singers, Heroes, and Gods in the* Odyssey
by Charles Segal
*The Mute Immortals Speak: Pre-Islamic Poetry and the Poetics of Ritual*
by Suzanne Pinckney Stetkevych
*Phrasikleia: An Anthropology of Reading in Ancient Greece*
by Jesper Svenbro
translated by Janet E. Lloyd
*The Jewish Novel in the Ancient World*
by Lawrence M. Wills